## National Parks & Scenic Drives

Reader's Digest

New York / Montreal

A READER'S DIGEST BOOK

Copyright © 2022 RDA Enthusiast Brands, LLC
1610 N. 2nd St., Suite 102
Milwaukee, WI 53212-3906

All rights reserved. Unauthorized reproduction, in any manner, is prohibited.

Previously published as *Great American Road Trips: National Parks* and *Great American Road Trips: Scenic Drives*.
No additional changes were made.

Reader's Digest is a registered trademark of Trusted Media Brands, Inc.

ISBN 978-1-62145-823-4

We are committed to both the quality of our products and the service we provide to our customers.
We value your comments, so please feel free to contact us at TMBBookTeam@TrustedMediaBrands.com.

For more Reader's Digest products and information, visit our website:
www.rd.com (in the United States)
www.readersdigest.ca (in Canada)

Printed in China
1 3 5 7 9 10 8 6 4 2

Text, photography and illustrations for *Great American Road Trips: National Parks
& Scenic Drives* are based on articles previously published in *Country* magazine.

**PICTURED ON FRONT COVER:** Grand Tetons National Park, Wyoming,
Getty Images: YinYang; Christopher Kimmel; Yves Marcoux

**ILLUSTRATIONS** Anna Simmons

**IMAGE CREDITS FOR *GREAT AMERICAN ROAD TRIPS: NATIONAL PARKS***
Pages 8-9: 1916: Library of Congress/Getty Images; 1927: Trigger Image/Alamy Stock Photo;
1933: Everett Collection Inc/Alamy Stock Photo; 1935: Charles Johnson/Getty Images;
1958: John Springer Collection/Getty Images; 1968 (Shoshone Falls, Idaho): muddymari/Getty Images;
1968 (Glacier Point, Yosemite): Smith Collection/Getty Images; 1994: benedek/Getty Images;
1995: Thanks! Steve McKinzie/Getty Images; 2015: Arterra/Getty Images; 2016: Robert Alexander/Getty Images
Page 10: Cathedral Spires, Yosemite National Park, California, by Tim Fitzharris
Page 94: Balanced Rock, Big Bend National Park, Texas, by Tim Fitzharris
Page 118: Petit Portal arch, Pictured Rocks National Lakeshore, Michigan, by John McCormick
Page 152: Bass Harbor Head Light Station, Acadia National Park, Maine, by Ultima_Gaina/Getty Images

**ADDITIONAL PHOTO INFORMATION FOR *GREAT AMERICAN ROAD TRIPS: SCENIC DRIVES***
Page 6: Bandon Beach, Oregon
Page 56: Monument Valley Navajo Tribal Park, Arizona
Page 78: Eagle Harbor Lighthouse, Michigan
Page 110: Linn Cove Viaduct, North Carolina
Page 144: Cape Cod, Massachusetts

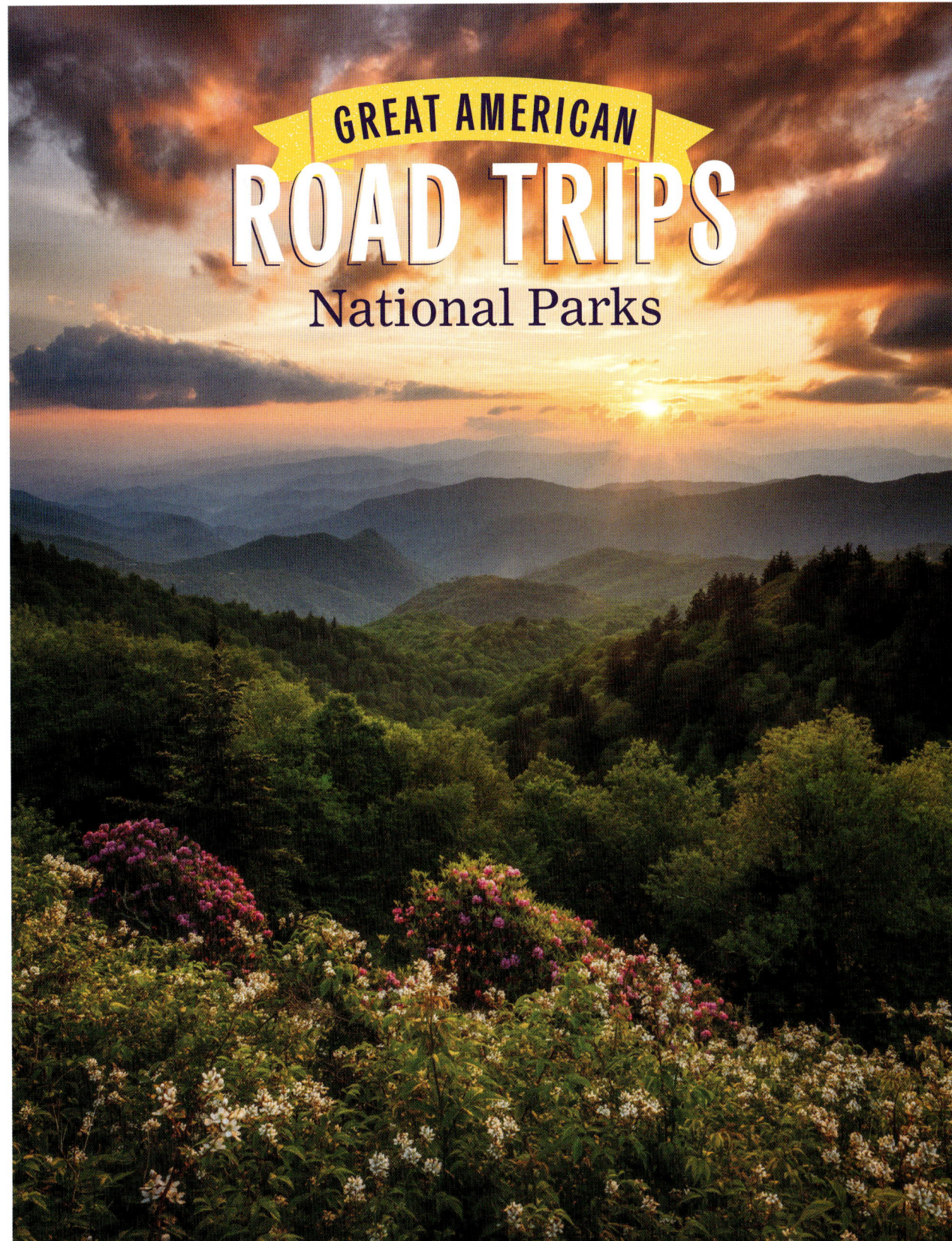

*Great Smoky Mountains National Park and its spring rhododendron and blackberry blooms.*

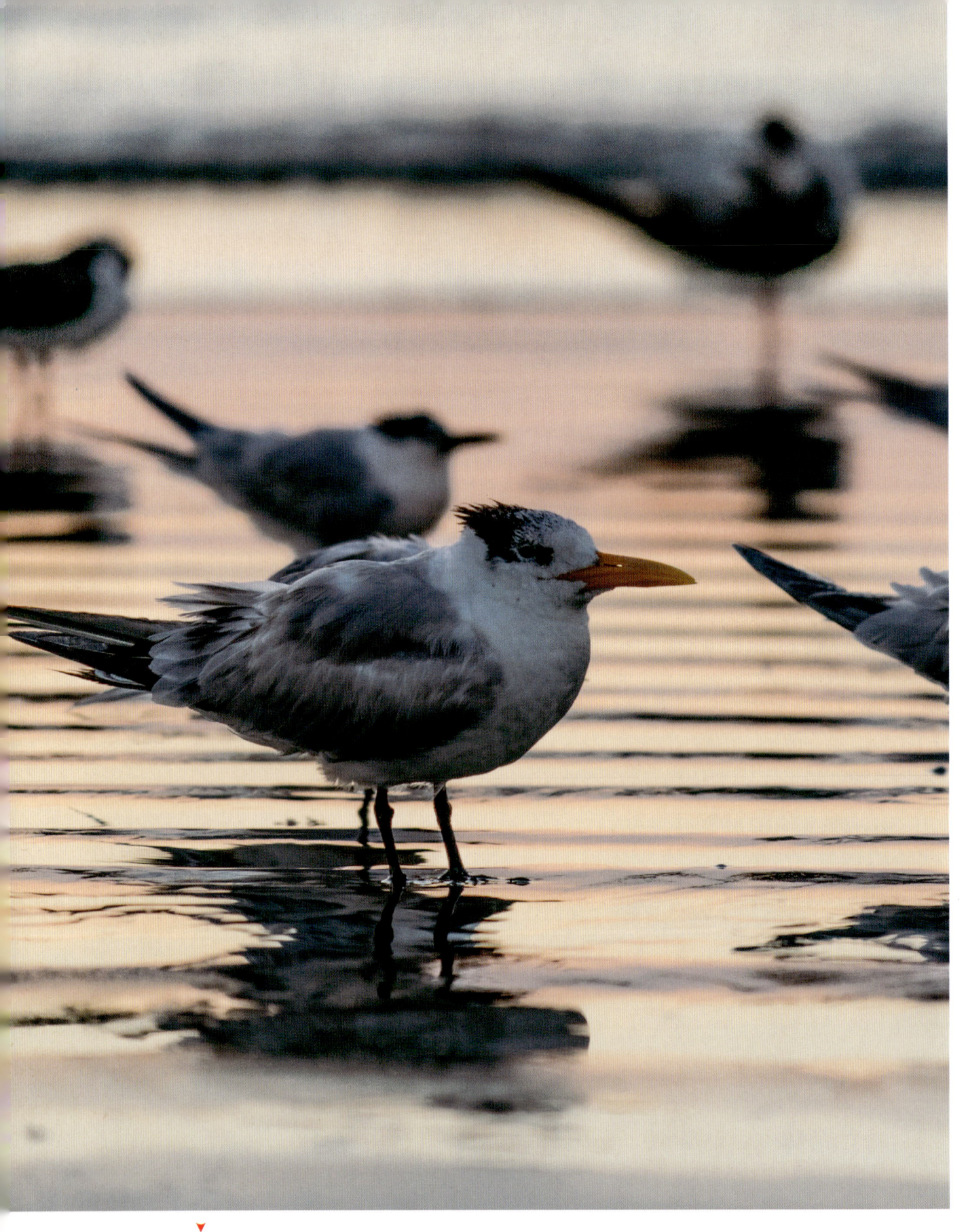

▼
*Birds on the beach in Cape Canaveral.*

# CONTENTS

## WEST
**DENALI** Alaska • 12
**JOSHUA TREE** California • 16
**LASSEN VOLCANIC** California • 18
**PINNACLES** California • 20
**REDWOOD** California • 24
**SEQUOIA & KINGS CANYON** California • 28
**YOSEMITE** California • 32
**BLACK CANYON OF THE GUNNISON** Colorado • 36
**GREAT SAND DUNES** Colorado • 38
**MESA VERDE** Colorado • 40
**ROCKY MOUNTAIN** Colorado • 44
Photo Gallery • 48
**HAWAII VOLCANOES** Hawaii • 54
**GLACIER** Montana • 58
**GREAT BASIN** Nevada • 62
**CRATER LAKE** Oregon • 64
**CANYONLANDS** Utah • 70
**ZION** Utah • 74
**MOUNT RAINIER** Washington • 78
**NORTH CASCADES** Washington • 80
**OLYMPIC** Washington • 82
**GRAND TETON** Wyoming • 86
**YELLOWSTONE** Wyoming • 88

## SOUTHWEST
**GRAND CANYON** Arizona • 96
**SAGUARO** Arizona • 102
Photo Gallery • 106
**BIG BEND** Texas • 110
**GUADALUPE MOUNTAINS** Texas • 112

## MIDWEST
**INDIANA DUNES** Indiana • 120
**ISLE ROYALE** Michigan • 124
**PICTURED ROCKS** Michigan • 128
**SLEEPING BEAR DUNES** Michigan • 130
Photo Gallery • 136
**THEODORE ROOSEVELT** North Dakota • 142
**BADLANDS** South Dakota • 146
**APOSTLE ISLANDS** Wisconsin • 148

## EAST
**ACADIA** Maine • 154
**SHENANDOAH** Virginia • 158
**CONGAREE** South Carolina • 164
**MAMMOTH CAVE** Kentucky • 166
Photo Gallery • 168
**HOT SPRINGS** Arkansas • 174
**GREAT SMOKY MOUNTAINS** Tennessee • 178
**CANAVERAL** Florida • 184
**EVERGLADES** Florida • 186
**VIRGIN ISLANDS** U.S. Virgin Islands • 188

*Joshua Tree National Park is an incredible place to watch golden sunsets.*

# MAJESTY PRESERVED

**THE NEXT TIME** you gaze into a stunning canyon stretching to the horizon, think of our personal freedoms. When you stare incredulously at a towering mountain range, consider the rich benefits of our democratic republic, and know that conserving land for the public's enrichment was a uniquely American idea at the start. The terrific momentum generated by Theodore and Franklin Delano Roosevelt to expand parklands in the early decades of the 20th century was unprecedented.

With minimal presidential power for such conservationist action at the time, only four national parks existed when Theodore became president in 1901—but landmark action was just over the horizon. By the time he left office in 1909, Americans enjoyed four more national parks, 18 national monuments, 51 federal bird sanctuaries, four national game preserves and 150 national forests, totaling 230 million acres of additional land set aside for public use.

Following his cousin's trailblazing, FDR improved parks while easing unemployment when he was president. As part of his New Deal relief program, FDR authorized the formation of the military-style Civilian Conservation Corps. Enrollees based in state and national parks advanced the conservation cause by reforesting land, fighting forest fires, creating or improving hiking trails, constructing fire lookout towers, building or restoring park lodges and more. In addition, FDR's Works Progress Administration employed artists from 1938 to 1941 to create eye-catching promotional posters for the parks. FDR not only added Olympic and Kings Canyon to the national parks list but also put many national monuments and all historic military sites under the umbrella of the National Park Service.

Other figures in American history helped maintain, grow and preserve the parks as well. John Muir is often called "father of the National Park System"

*Posters created in the 1930s by the Works Progress Administration to promote the parks.*

because of his advocacy for nature and his impassioned writings, which played an essential role in the establishment of Yosemite National Park, as well as the lands that would one day become Grand Canyon, Sequoia, Mount Rainier and Petrified Forest national parks.

Stephen T. Mather played an integral role in a key component of our parks: the National Park Service. Mather convinced Congress of the need for a National Park Service, and, in 1917, he became its first director. During his 12-year tenure, Shenandoah, Great Smoky Mountains and Mammoth Cave were added to the list of America's glorious protected lands.

New parks were added throughout the 20th century, with the aim of preserving nature, the land it calls home and the history contained within it. Michigan's Pictured Rocks became the country's first national lakeshore in 1966; California's Redwood, which houses the tallest trees on Earth, earned its national park designation two years later. And the number climbs still. With the addition of New River Gorge National Park in January 2021, awe-inspiring lands continue to be set aside for the appreciation and inspiration of future generations.

Our parks have proven instrumental in the protection of endangered and threatened species as well. Yellowstone played a key role in bolstering the populations of the American bison and gray wolf. Both species faced extreme challenges to their survival, but protection efforts at Yellowstone have allowed these animals a safe place to roam. Today, our parks are home to more than a thousand endangered or otherwise at-risk plants and animals, and they provide them a haven free from unlimited human interference.

Our national parks attracted more than 300 million visitors in 2019. Altogether, these travelers spent more than 1 billion hours hiking, biking, canoeing, sightseeing and more.

▶ *Top: Conservationist John Muir, right, with President Theodore Roosevelt at Glacier Point, Yosemite National Park, in 1906. Bottom: President Franklin D. Roosevelt visits a Civilian Conservation Corps camp.*

With this book, our wish is to provide a unique guide to these freedom-filled lands and emphasize why they're so special. Nature has risen recently on the list of popular American pastimes, but whether you're planning a trip or vacationing in your armchair, you'll enjoy fascinating stories and photos submitted by *Country* readers that speak to the majesty of these lands and their continued appeal.

We're excited that you're venturing into the glorious American wilderness with us, and we hope this book inspires you to treasure and explore these wondrous places in our country.

—EDITORS OF *COUNTRY*

# THE PARKS THROUGH THE YEARS

**1872**
Yellowstone becomes the first national park in the U.S. and the world.

**1890**
SEQUOIA
CALIFORNIA

YOSEMITE
CALIFORNIA

**1899**
MOUNT RAINIER
WASHINGTON

**1902**
CRATER LAKE
OREGON

**1906**
MESA VERDE
COLORADO

**1910**
GLACIER
MONTANA

**1913**
Walter Harper, Harry Karstens, Hudson Stuck and Robert Tatum reach the summit of Denali in Alaska.

**1915**
ROCKY MOUNTAIN
COLORADO

**1916**
National Park Service is created to protect the parks. Stephen Mather becomes the first director in 1917.

**1916**
HAWAII VOLCANOES
HAWAII

LASSEN VOLCANIC
CALIFORNIA

**1920**
The number of total annual park visits exceeds 1 million.

**1917**
MOUNT McKINLEY (DENALI)
ALASKA

**1968**
President Lyndon Johnson signs the Wild and Scenic Rivers Act to preserve certain rivers throughout the United States.

**1966**
Michigan's Pictured Rocks becomes the first national lakeshore.

**1968**
NORTH CASCADES
WASHINGTON

REDWOOD
CALIFORNIA

**1960**
Yellowstone starts a strict bear management program.

**1964**
CANYONLANDS
UTAH

**1958**
Alfred Hitchcock and the cast of *North by Northwest* arrive to film scenes at Mount Rushmore. When the park service revokes their permit, they shoot the chase scene using a replica.

**1968**
The manmade Firefall events, during which burning embers were dropped from the top of Glacier Point in Yosemite, are stopped.

**1970**
APOSTLE ISLANDS
WISCONSIN

SLEEPING BEAR DUNES
MICHIGAN

**1972**
GUADALUPE MOUNTAINS
TEXAS

**1973**
President Richard Nixon signs the Endangered Species Act.

**1975**
CANAVERAL
FLORIDA

**1978**
BADLANDS
SOUTH DAKOTA

THEODORE ROOSEVELT
NORTH DAKOTA

**1986**
GREAT BASIN
NEVADA

**1994**
JOSHUA TREE
CALIFORNIA

**1994**
SAGUARO
ARIZONA

**1919**
ACADIA
MAINE

GRAND CANYON
ARIZONA

ZION
UTAH

**1921**
HOT SPRINGS
ARKANSAS

**1926**
Congress authorizes the creation of Great Smoky Mountains National Park.

**1927**
Ansel Adams' photograph "Monolith Face of Half Dome" receives critical acclaim. His black-and-white prints of Yosemite make him and the park famous.

**1928**
Newlyweds Bessie and Glen Hyde disappear while rafting the Colorado River in Grand Canyon National Park. Their fate is a mystery to this day.

**1929**
GRAND TETON
WYOMING

**1933**
FDR creates the Civilian Conservation Corps, which built important infrastructure in the parks, including campsites, trails and roads.

**1933**
Historic sites come under jurisdiction of the National Parks Service.

**1944**
BIG BEND
TEXAS

**1947**
EVERGLADES
FLORIDA

**1956**
VIRGIN ISLANDS
ST. JOHN

**1941**
MAMMOTH CAVE
KENTUCKY

**1942**
WWII reduces the number of visitors by 11.5 million.

**1938**
OLYMPIC
WASHINGTON

**1940**
ISLE ROYALE
MICHIGAN

KINGS CANYON
CALIFORNIA

**1941**
Ansel Adams is hired to photograph the national parks.

**1935**
SHENANDOAH
VIRGINIA

**1995**
Gray wolves from Western Canada are relocated to Yellowstone.

**1999**
BLACK CANYON OF THE GUNNISON
COLORADO

**2003**
CONGAREE
SOUTH CAROLINA

**2004**
GREAT SAND DUNES
COLORADO

**2013**
PINNACLES
CALIFORNIA

**2015**
Alaska's Mount McKinley is renamed Denali.

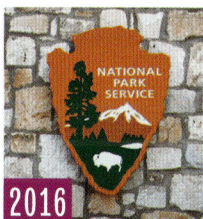

**2016**
100th anniversary of the National Park Service.

**2019**
INDIANA DUNES
INDIANA

NATIONAL PARKS 9

▼
*Quaking aspens welcome visitors to the Riley Creek Campground.*

WEST

STORY AND PHOTOS BY
**MICHAEL QUINTON**

# DENALI

SEE NATURE IN THE RAW ON THE ONLY ROAD THROUGH ALASKA'S FIRST NATIONAL PARK.

**WHETHER YOU'RE NEGOTIATING** the sharp switchbacks on Polychrome Pass or eagerly anticipating what surprises might lurk just around the bend, the Denali Park Road will keep you on the edge of your seat.

The 92-mile road is the only one through Alaska's Denali National Park and Preserve. It winds through diverse landscapes of spruce forests, braided riverbeds, alpine tundra and some of North America's most spectacular mountain vistas, including the country's highest peak. The 20,310-foot-high Denali (which means "the high one" in one of the Athabascan languages) is a hiker's and backpacker's paradise—but don't forget your bear spray.

The first 16 miles, to Savage River, are paved. After that, the road becomes well-maintained gravel.

Generally, the road is open to travelers between mid-May and September and to dogsled teams in the winter. There are six campgrounds along the way. Three of them, Sanctuary River, Igloo Creek and Wonder Lake, are reserved for tent camping.

Visitors must walk, bike or take a bus tour beyond the Savage River Bridge unless they have a private vehicle road permit. As a professional wildlife photographer, I was one of the lucky few able to enter a public lottery for one of these coveted permits.

Road construction began in 1923, when crews blasted rock and moved gravel to create it. The road stretches from the park entrance to Kantishna Roadhouse, a back country lodge, and was finished in 1938. In the 1960s, plans were made to widen and pave

NATIONAL PARKS 13

## WEST

**FUN FACTS**
Until 2015, the country's highest peak and the park's main attraction was officially called Mount McKinley, in honor of the President William McKinley, who was assassinated in 1901. In 2015, the mountain's name was reverted to its original Koyukon name, Denali, after a decades-long debate.

**SIDE TRIP**
After possibly returning from the Eielson Visitor Center (an 8-hour round-trip bus ride) or Wonder Lake (11 hours round-trip), resume the drive behind the wheel of your own vehicle. Grip it tight, though, because the next 65-mile stretch, which meets the scenic gorge of the Nenana River, is riddled with sharp turns, windy passes, canyon crossings and frost heaves. About 20 miles north of Nenana, the route reaches Skyline Drive, running along the ridgetops with spectacular views.

▼
*A candid moment between a grizzly bear sow and her cub.*

the road, but park officials opted to keep it and its surroundings as pristine as possible.

The park owes its creation to naturalist Charles Sheldon. During the winter of 1907-'08, Sheldon observed the slaughter of some 2,000 magnificent Dall sheep, killed by market hunters to be sold to railroad workers and gold miners. Realizing that this kind of pressure would quickly deplete the wild sheep herds, Sheldon joined with the Boone and Crockett Club, the country's oldest conservation group, and convinced Congress to protect this ecosystem.

In 1917, President Woodrow Wilson signed a bill establishing more than 2 million untouched acres along the Alaska Range as McKinley National Park. The park was enlarged to 6 million acres and renamed Denali National Park and Preserve in 1980.

Though originally established to protect Dall sheep, the national park status has benefited the entire Denali ecosystem. Herds of caribou and many smaller mammals (arctic ground squirrels, hoary marmots, snowshoe hares, wolverines, lynx, red fox and porcupines) await the watchful visitor. And the Denali Park Road is the best and safest place to view wolves and interior grizzly bears.

Birders will not be disappointed. Sightings of willow ptarmigan and golden eagles are guaranteed, but you might be lucky enough to see gyrfalcons, whimbrels, long-tailed jaegers, arctic warblers and rock and white-tailed ptarmigan.

Though Denali is in the heart of the Alaskan interior, wildlife is generally spread rather sparingly through it. But long summer days along the road offer many opportunities to witness

WEST

nature in the raw. As dramatic as the landscapes are, I return to this mountain for those in-your-face encounters with wildlife.

The images often return to me. For example, one spring, a mama bear was snoozing on the open brown tundra. Nearby, a rufous-colored yearling cub lazily nipped grass shoots. Her brother, a straw blond, nosy cub, had become an annoyance to the females and was kept away. He entertained himself.

As I shot video of the bears, my son Josh observed a young black wolf approaching the bears.

After a brief stare, the wolf loped off toward the bears. The rufous cub was eager for confrontation. As the wolf circled, the cub pivoted and kept her big rear end pointing away from the wolf. The grizzly's short fuse smoldered; wolf's golden eyes burned; bear exploded. In perfect sync, the wolf whirled and moved on.

Then, slipping up close behind the big, sleepy sow, the brazen wolf pressed her nose into the sow's fur. The annoyed bear slowly rose, swung her huge head and eased into position. Like a lightning flash, a crushing hook ripped out a thick swath of…fresh mountain air.

Frustrated, the sow began to graze, shadowed by the wolf. When the sow bedded down again, the wolf made her move. In a playful pounce, she nipped the grizzly on the behind. Satisfied, her coup complete, the wolf trotted off down the road.

I wonder whether pushing the mama bear's buttons was just reckless fun or survival. Either way, for memories that truly last a lifetime, the Denali Park Road delivers. ◆

*The Denali Park Road is the best place to view wolves and bears.* ◀

NATIONAL PARKS 15

WEST

STORY AND PHOTOS BY
LAURENCE PARENT

# JOSHUA TREE

FIND OTHERWORLDLY BEAUTY WHERE THE COLORADO AND MOJAVE DESERTS MEET IN JOSHUA TREE NATIONAL PARK.

**WHEN I TURN OFF** Interstate 10 east of Palm Springs, California, the traffic fades and the road climbs north toward the wrinkled Cottonwood and Eagle mountains. The stark Colorado Desert surrounds me. The terrain is harsh and so rugged that hardy plants like creosote bush struggle to survive in the heat and dry air.

After turning onto Cottonwood Springs Road, I stop briefly at the Cottonwood Visitor Center to pick up information and stroll through the small man-made palm oasis. Birds twitter in the trees, attracted, like me, to the water and shade.

I continue my drive, eventually turning northwest onto Pinto Basin Road. I stop at a garden full of Bigelow cholla cacti. The thick golden spines catch my eye, but I approach the plants warily. Cholla segments break off easily when brushed by careless hikers, and their barbed spines cling to clothes and skin.

From the garden, I leave the Colorado Desert and drive higher into the slightly wetter and cooler Mojave Desert. Here Joshua trees, a type of yucca, appear, their many limbs reaching upward as high as 40 feet. In some areas, the trees grow thickly enough to create a surreal, sparse forest among the giant tumbled granite boulders that dot the landscape at White Tank, Jumbo Rocks and other areas.

I pause at the Ryan Ranch turnout and walk a short trail to explore ruins left behind by miners and ranchers who eked out a living in the park's rough country.

There are five fan palm oases in the park, and my next stop is the 49 Palms Oasis. I leave the park to get to the trailhead. It's a 3-mile-round-trip hike to this gift of shade tucked away in a hidden canyon.

As I climb the trail, I wonder whether my efforts will be rewarded. After half an hour, I spot palm trees and soon reach them and relax in the shade, listening to fronds rattle in the breeze. The hike and the trip was worthwhile.

WEST

### NOT TO BE MISSED
Take in a beautiful view by following Keys View Road to the 5,000-foot-high overlook at Keys View. On a clear day you can see the San Jacinto Mountains and the Salton Sea.

### WORDS TO THE WISE
Be on the alert for flash floods from thunderstorms.

### SIDE TRIP
Just southwest of Joshua Tree National Park, drive part of the Palms to Pines Highway. Beginning at Palm Desert, the drive follows Routes 74 and 243 from palm-studded lowlands to the lofty pine woods of San Bernardino National Forest. At first, hairpin turns lead up the dizzying slopes of the Santa Rosa Mountains, followed by a smooth cruise through the grasslands of Garner Valley. Inviting trailheads await hikers at Idyllwild, and the last leg of the drive winds through the lushly forested San Jacinto Mountains, descending to the austere, boulder-strewn hills near Banning.

*Top: The Joshua tree is a member of the agave family. Bottom: Beware of Bigelow cholla cacti!*

NATIONAL PARKS   17

WEST

STORY BY
**DANA MEREDITH**

# LASSEN VOLCANIC

EXPERIENCE GEOLOGICAL WONDERS WITHOUT THE CROWDS AT THIS UNDER-THE-RADAR SPOT THAT HAS ROOM TO ROAM.

**FROM BUBBLING HYDROTHERMAL** mud pots to one of the largest plug-dome volcanoes in the world, these 106,452 acres look like the setting for a sci-fi movie, but they make up Northern California's least-visited national park. The steep and winding 30-mile Lassen Volcanic National Park Highway transports you through dense forest from one amazing scenic overlook to the next (many with picnic areas and lakes). You'll see unbeatable views throughout the park from the comfort of your car.

But hop out and see geology in action on Bumpass Hell Trail, a moderate 3-mile hike—one option of 150 miles of trails that wind through forests and past lakes—to the largest hydrothermal area of the park.

Rise at dawn in one of the park's campgrounds or the rustic Drakesbad Guest Ranch, and hike the easy 1.5-mile Manzanita Lake Trail to catch sublime morning views of Lassen Peak. There is no motorized boating on the park's 20 lakes, but you can rent a canoe or a kayak for your exploring. If you're adventurous, hike up to the summit of Lassen Peak. Stops at the Kohm Yah-mah-nee Visitor Center and the Loomis Museum showcase the park's history and highlight the area's eruptions.

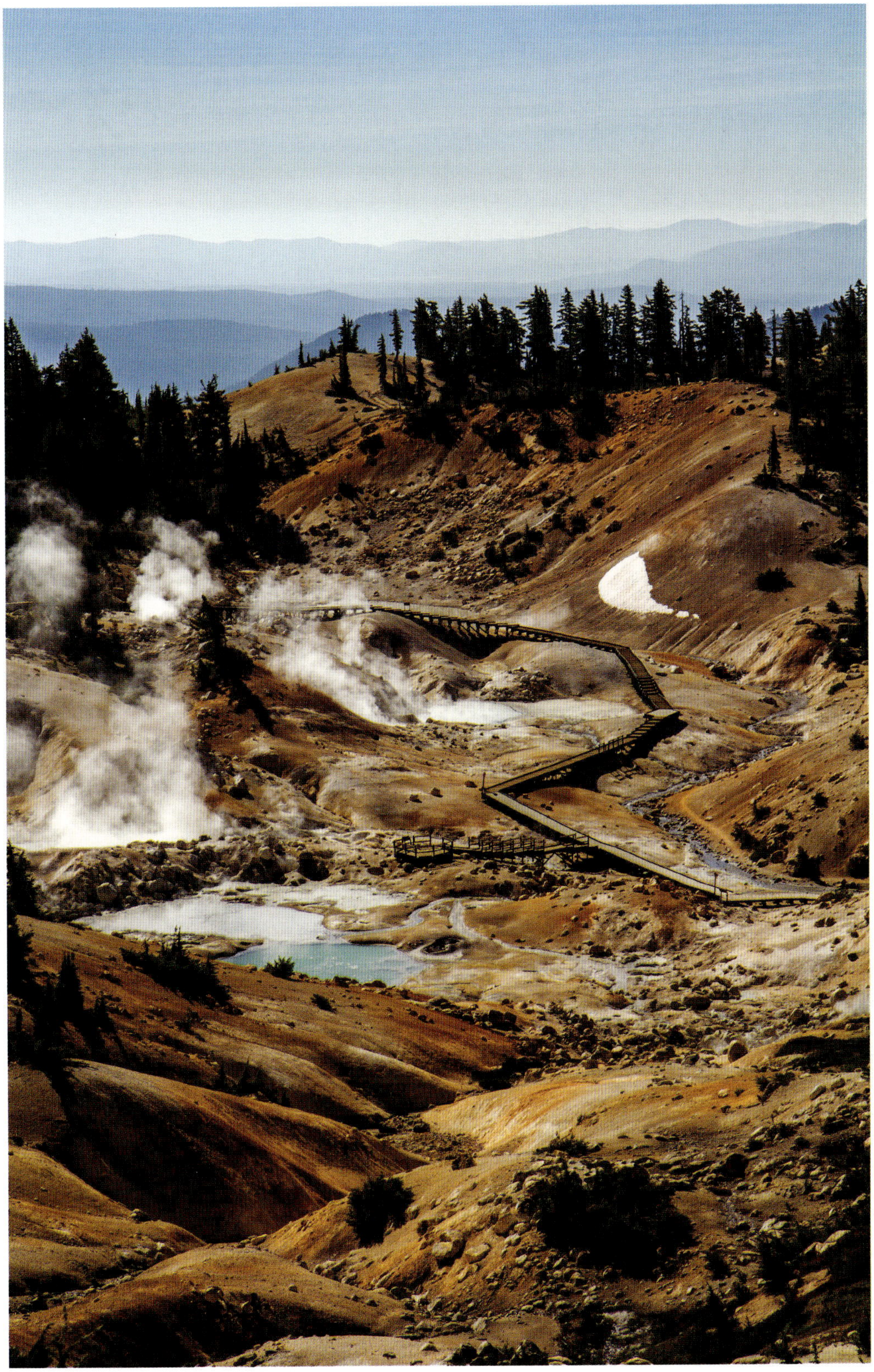

JOSHUA HAWLEY/GETTY IMAGES

*Rising steam mists the air at the Bumpass Hell hydrothermal area.*

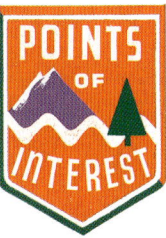

**NOT TO BE MISSED**

The Lassen Dark Sky Festival, held annually in August, provides a fantastic opportunity to learn about the stars. If you are looking for the best views during the daytime, visit Bumpass Hell and Manzanita Lake.

**FUN FACT**

Lassen Peak last erupted for seven years beginning in 1914 and is the park's tallest volcano, at 10,457 feet.

**WORDS TO THE WISE**

Boardwalks lead to many of the sites, and visitors are advised to stay on the trail, because parts of this region where the Earth's molten interior escapes to the surface have been known to collapse.

The best time of year to visit is July to October, but make sure to check for road conditions.

*The view of Machete Ridge on the Balconies Trail.*

WEST

STORY BY **DONNA B. ULRICH**
PHOTOS BY **LARRY ULRICH**

# PINNACLES

DELIGHTFUL ARRAYS OF PLANTS AND ANIMALS THRIVE AMONG TOWERING ROCK FORMATIONS AND WINDING CAVE TRAILS.

**HUGE MONOLITHS AND SHEER CANYONS** bear silent witness to Pinnacles National Park's dramatic ancestry as an ancient volcanic field. The San Andreas Fault lies east of the park in central California, and millions of years of faulting, tectonic plate movement and erosion have formed quite spectacular rock formations.

Pinnacles, which had been a national monument, became America's 59th national park in 2013. Situated east of the fertile Salinas Valley in the Gabilan Mountains, Pinnacles is far removed from California's much more famous destinations but is a boon to hikers and rock climbers looking to get away from the crowds.

In 1891 homesteader Schuyler Hain arrived here from Michigan. Over the next 20 years he became known as the "Father of Pinnacles" by leading tours through Bear Valley and writing articles urging preservation of the area. Set aside as a national monument in 1908, Pinnacles' roads and trails were greatly improved by the Civilian Conservation Corps in the mid-1930s.

In spring, when we took our first trip to Pinnacles in eight years, Larry and I were reminded that the area makes us think of Easter. Not only do wildflowers bloom that time of year, but the lichen-covered rocks are a soft pastel color, like Easter eggs nestled in a bed of grass. Blossoms of shooting stars, paintbrush and Johnny-jump-ups paint the green meadows in the exuberant hues of spring.

We hoped to see a California condor, a rare bird re-established at Pinnacles in 2003. With a wingspan reaching 9 feet and beyond, a condor can live for more than 50 years.

Our first stop was the Visitor Center, where we met Sierra Willoughby, an interpretive park ranger. He'd studied geology, so we were not surprised to hear his favorite feature of the park: "Definitely the rocks. There are

# WEST

**FUN FACTS**

In 2003 the park was designated as a national release site for the California Condor Recovery Program. Lucky hikers may spot one of these rare birds.

There are more than 30 miles of tended trails against a backdrop of the endlessly changing hues and textures of eroded volcanic rock.

**WORDS TO THE WISE**

So-called "wilderness treks" here are for experienced hikers and cave trails are for the would-be spelunkers (don't forget a flashlight). Scaling the Pinnacles' sheer pink cliffs demands experience and special equipment.

Several trailheads are accessible from Bear Gulch Visitor Center. The Moses Spring Self-Guiding Trail climaxes with a visit to the Bear Gulch Reservoir. Hikers who want even more of a challenge can take High Peaks Trail, a 2-mile ramble along the higher reaches.

The park is open year-round and admission is charged.

*Johnny-jump-ups and padre's shooting stars carpet a hillside.*

boulders the size of office buildings, and narrow canyons not unlike those found in Desert Southwest parks like Zion and Bryce. I also appreciate that the park's ecosystem is incredibly intact—the plants and animals have been protected here since 1908. There are about 450 moth, 400 bee and 14 bat species."

As the light faded at our campsite that evening, we watched a cottontail rabbit savor sweet young grass in the nearby meadow. Acorn woodpeckers tapped in the elegant old oaks, the rufous-sided towhee offered its simple tweet and crows cawed to let everybody know who was boss.

At dusk we saw turkey vultures land in a gray pine about 50 feet away. They circled overhead and came to roost one at a time until the tree held at least 50 birds.

We packed for a long day of hiking the next morning. Since the wildflowers were scarce this time, we took Sierra's advice and climbed up the Bear Gulch Cave Trail, entering the caves along the way. The talus caves, formed from narrow canyons crowned with fallen boulders, are famous for their stair-step, zigzag complexity. It's a stoop-and-slide-on-your-behind kind of hike. Bear Gulch Cave is closed from mid-May to mid-July to protect the bat colony as the parents raise their young.

Along the trail we heard one of my favorite birdsongs. The descending melodic trill of the canyon wren never fails to bring my soul into harmony with the boulders and canyons.

On the hike back I saw a big bird soaring in the distance and focused my binoculars—and hopes—on it. I called out to Larry, but he was taking a picture and was not to be distracted. When I saw the white shoulders and then the telltale identification tag on one wing, I knew it was a condor.

We saw only a few bees and didn't see the bats, but the boulders and birds were more than enough to fill our days with beautiful memories.

WEST

*A popular hiking trail leads to Bear Gulch Reservoir.*

*Boy Scout Tree Trail is in Jedediah Smith Redwoods State Park, part of Redwood National and State Parks.*

WEST

STORY BY
**GORDON AND CATHY ILLG**

# REDWOOD

TRAVEL BACK THROUGH TIME ALONG THE CALIFORNIA
COAST IN THE SHADE OF GIANTS.

**LARGE REDWOOD GROVES ARE DEEP,** green sanctuaries, where the light is often muted through fog and foliage. They are quiet spaces where normal voices seem harsh and out of place.

But they are also welcoming. These groves are refuges for the human spirit, places of rejuvenation for when the complexity and fast pace of modern living become too much for us.

A 35-mile stretch of U.S. Highway 101 in extreme Northern California is a time machine that transports drivers back millions of years to when ancestors of today's beautiful redwood trees grew all across the Northern Hemisphere.

Today, redwoods are found along the West Coast, starting near the Oregon border and reaching to just south of San Francisco, but the heart of their territory lies along the California coast between Crescent City and Orick. The ideal combination of longitude, climate and elevation helps the trees thrive.

Sixteenth-century Spanish and English mariners were probably the first Europeans to see this part of the world. However, because there were so few good harbors along the coastline, the native Yurok people were relatively sheltered from our young country's westward expansion until 1828, when

NATIONAL PARKS 25

# WEST

**NOT TO BE MISSED**
At Tall Trees Trailhead (where a free permit is required), a 3-mile loop skirts the 361-foot Howard Libby Tree.

**FUN FACT**
Signed into being by President Lyndon Johnson and later expanded to 106,000 acres by President Jimmy Carter, Redwood National Park also includes several California state parks, running the Pacific coastline for some 40 miles.

**WORDS TO THE WISE**
If traveling across the backcountry by bicycle, the Ossagon Trail combines with the Coastal Trail, Davison Road, Streelow Creek, Davison Trail and Newton B. Drury Scenic Parkway in a 19-mile loop.

**SIDE TRIP**
To see more redwoods, visit Avenue of the Giants. South of Eureka, a 31-mile stretch of old Highway 101 winds through Humboldt Redwoods State Park and the largest old-growth redwood forest in the world.

▼
*A curious elk stops to smell the lupines.*

Jedediah Smith pioneered an overland route to the redwood forests.

Gold miners also came to explore but found relatively little of the precious metal. The riches of this region are its trees, and by the late 1800s, the timber and lumber industry was king along the Northern California coast.

As entire groves of these giant trees disappeared, concerned citizens began efforts in the 1910s to preserve this scenery for future generations.

The Save the Redwoods League was set up in 1918 as a nonprofit organization committed to acquiring redwood plots for preservation. With private donations and matching state funds, the league purchased more than 100,000 acres of redwood forest from 1920 through 1960.

The California Department of Parks and Recreation created a network of state parks utilizing these lands during the 1920s.

Redwood National Park was established in 1968, and in 1980, the United Nations designated the Redwood national and state parks as a World Heritage Site and Biosphere Reserve.

U.S. Highway 101 runs through this reserve, past the national park and through the Del Norte Coast, Prairie Creek and Jedediah Smith Redwoods state parks, which contain most of the remaining giant redwood trees in the world.

While the entire drive is scenic, there are a couple of side trips that should not be missed. A few miles north of Orick, a short detour takes you to the Lady Bird Johnson Grove, which was dedicated to her in 1969 for her conservation efforts. The 1-mile trail winds through groves of mature redwoods looming out of the fog.

Another great detour is Davison Road, a narrow dirt passage not recommended for trailers or large RVs. What makes the road special is that it leads past Gold Bluffs Beach, where elk can often be seen, and ends at the Fern Canyon Trailhead.

This half-mile trail leads visitors along the bottom of a tight canyon whose 30-foot walls are covered with ferns. It's the sort of place where one would expect to see fairies and wood nymphs living.

One stop that's right on U.S. 101 is not particularly special for most of the year. But when the rhododendrons are blooming in late May and early June, there is no better hike than the Damnation Creek Trail, about halfway between Klamath and Crescent City. Here, the large pink blossoms vie with the trees for your attention, and you don't have to walk far before your senses are overwhelmed.

The oldest redwood trees in the parks sprouted 2,000 years ago, and the largest trees are about 10 feet longer than a football field and more than 65 feet taller than the Statue of Liberty. Humans understandably feel small in their presence.

Redwood groves are truly nature's cathedrals, where we can marvel at and give thanks for the old things, the giant things and the green things that remain.

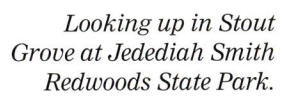

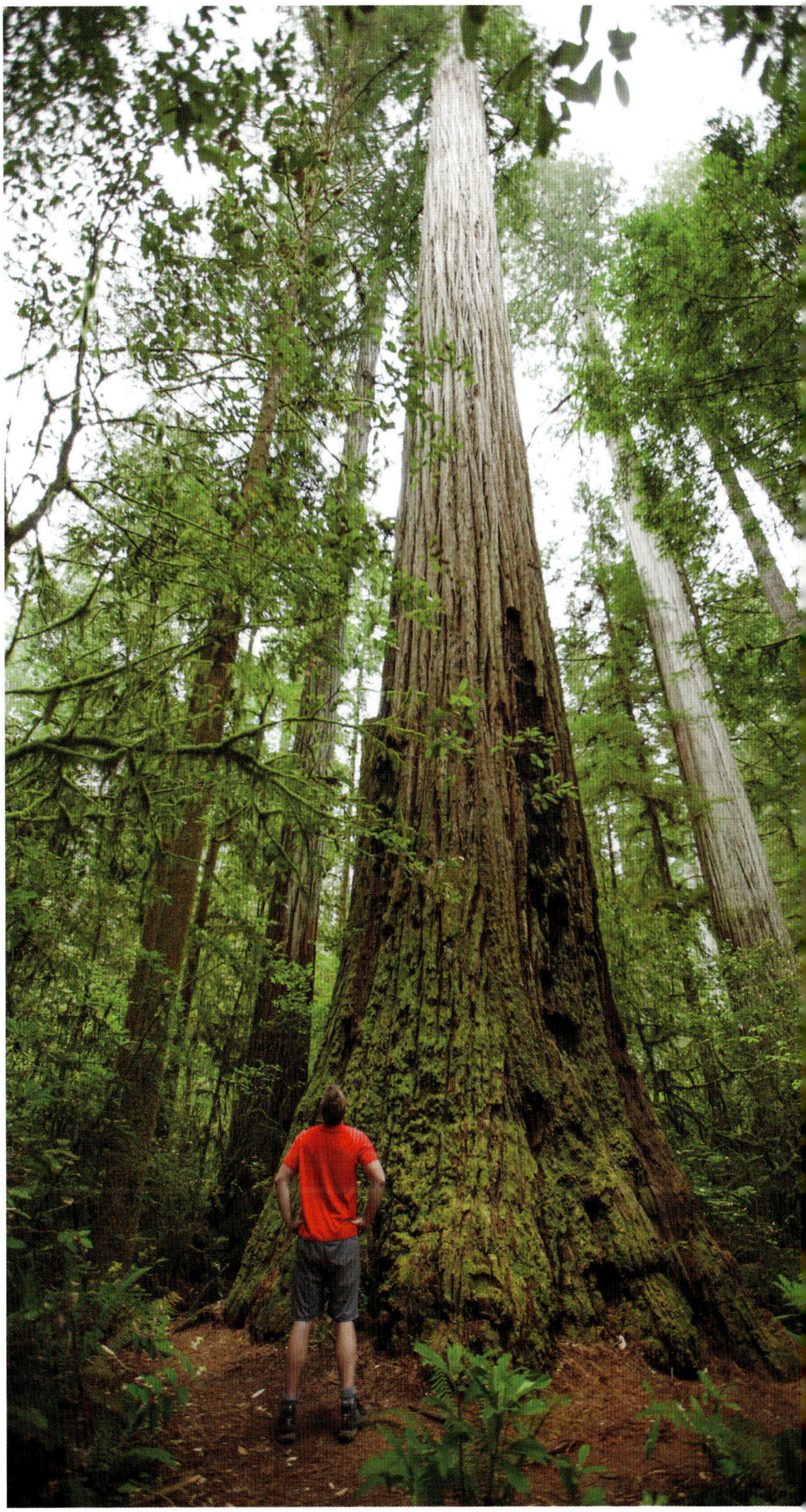

*Looking up in Stout Grove at Jedediah Smith Redwoods State Park.*

LEFT: CATHY AND GORDON ILLG; RIGHT: CHRISTOPHER KIMMEL/GETTY IMAGES

*Clearing storm over Sixty Lakes Basin in Kings Canyon.*

WEST

STORY AND PHOTOS BY
**LONDIE GARCIA PADELSKY**

# SEQUOIA & KINGS CANYON

THE WORLD'S LARGEST TREES RISE ABOVE PRISTINE
WILDERNESS IN THE HEART OF CALIFORNIA'S SIERRA NEVADA.

**PIONEER NATURALIST JOHN MUIR** called California's Sierra Nevada the Range of Light, and you'll still find 1,350 square miles of that dazzling wilderness in Sequoia & Kings Canyon National Parks. You'll also find much smaller crowds than at Yosemite to the north—partly because 90 percent of the park is accessible only on foot or horseback.

Through the years I've spent days, weeks and even months at a time riding and hiking those trails, trying to capture the Sierra Nevada's magic with my camera. But you can also enjoy spectacular scenery from well-tended walking paths or your car. I especially recommend going in April or May, when temperatures are cooler, grasses are greener and the wildflowers are blooming.

Sequoia National Park dates back to 1890, making it the nation's second-oldest national park. General Grant National Park, only a month younger than Sequoia, merged with Kings Canyon when it was named a national park in 1940, and Sequoia and Kings Canyon merged in 1946.

It's almost a full day's drive from my home to the Ash Mountain entrance on the park's southwest corner, and I always look forward to staying in the artists' colony of Three Rivers. The Kaweah River flows through the backyards of the town's stores and restaurants, which means coffee on the deck with a river view.

Heading into the park from the Ash Mountain entrance, Generals Highway climbs more than 5,000 feet on narrow

NATIONAL PARKS  **29**

WEST

*The waters run eerily clear in the remote High Sierra.*

**NOT TO BE MISSED**
Go caving! The park offers a variety of tours through the ornate marble passages of Crystal Cave from May through November. Buy tickets online at least two days in advance on the Sequoia Parks Conservancy website or at the Foothills or Lodgepole visitor centers.

**WORDS TO THE WISE**
Be aware that with an elevation range from 1,370 feet to 14,494 feet, weather can vary a lot by season, so dress in layers.

**NEARBY ATTRACTIONS**
Sequoia National Forest; Sierra National Forest

switchbacks to the edge of the Giant Forest, where four towering sequoias called the Four Guardsmen straddle the highway.

Giant Forest is home to more than 8,000 of these towering trees—half of all the sequoias on the planet. The largest of them, the General Sherman Tree, is 275 feet tall, 100 feet around at the base and an estimated 2,100 years old. Its 52,500 cubic feet of wood make it the largest living thing on Earth. A nearby walking path leads you past a phenomenal display of incredibly massive trees named after the likes of Abraham Lincoln, George Washington, Chief Sequoyah and Benjamin Franklin. I especially like to wander among them on spring weekdays, when there's almost no one on the path.

A short drive away, Moro Rock's granite dome soars above the treetops. A quarter-mile climb up a steep staircase rewards you with spectacular views across the snowcapped peaks of the Great Western Divide. The Moro Rock/Crescent Meadow Road also features a tunnel log you can drive through and the homestead of pioneer cattleman Hale Tharp. I once spent several lovely hours shooting starflowers here—until a black bear meandered by.

# WEST

From Giant Forest, Generals Highway heads northward to the Kings Canyon/Grant Grove section of the park. Along the way I like to stop at Lodgepole Visitor Center and take the short hike to Tokopah Falls, where the Kaweah River tumbles down a 1,200-foot staircase of granite.

In the park's northern section, you'll find still more idyllic trails through groves of towering sequoias—including the General Grant Tree, a national shrine to those who died in the Civil War.

But if you're looking for off-the-beaten-path beauty, drive 35 miles beyond Grant Grove on the Kings Canyon Scenic Byway to Cedar Grove. Here you'll find deep-cut canyons, meadows, waterfalls and towering glaciated granite mountains. This hidden paradise is a sampling of nature in the making and a tempting promise of what the Sierra Nevada offers after the road ends.

These backcountry trails usually don't open up until late June or July, and even then the snowpack determines how far you can go. From most of the trailheads, it takes at least two days of hiking or riding over rugged terrain to reach what I call the heart of the Sierra. You have to be self-sufficient in these parts; there are no concessions—only nature, and lots of it.

This wild country is a masterpiece sculpted by the last ice age. Polished granite peaks rise over 14,000 feet from a sea of valleys dotted with thousands of crystalline rivers and lakes. It's a place that continually lures you back, a scenic wilderness that refreshes the mind and rejuvenates the soul.

*The morning sun shines over giant sequoias and cutleaf coneflowers.*

NATIONAL PARKS 31

*This boardwalk invites visitors to hike through Yosemite Valley in the heart of the park.*

WEST

STORY AND PHOTOS BY
**LONDIE GARCIA PADELSKY**

# YOSEMITE

JAW-DROPPING MOUNTAIN VISTAS AND CLIFFHANGERS LINE THIS BYWAY THROUGH YOSEMITE NATIONAL PARK.

**THOSE OF US LIVING IN** the Sierra Nevada know that the heavy snows have begun to melt and spring is about to explode when Tioga Pass Road opens to Yosemite National Park.

At its peak elevation of 9,945 feet, Tioga Pass Road is the highest mountain highway in California. It cuts across Yosemite from the east entrance to Crane Flat in the west. You can drive the road in about two hours, but if you stop for a few excursions it can take all day!

Tioga Pass Road begins on Highway 120 just south of Lee Vining. Right from the start, the road is impressive as you leave the desert sage behind and drive straight toward the high Sierras. When the road weaves to the right, you have an incredible view of Lee Vining Canyon and the two-lane road cutting into a steep mountainside. I don't mind hugging the mountain on the way up—it's the drive down alongside a cliff's edge without any guardrails that puts me on notice.

Come late September, there's a definite nip in the air. That's when the leaves really sparkle in the sunlight. Looking down at Lee Vining Creek from Tioga Pass Road, you view a sea of aspens in vibrant yellow and orange, mixed in with the pine trees. The rich displays of autumn color lure photographers from afar to take pictures of the east side of the Sierra before Tioga Pass closes in November.

At the top of the pass, the road plateaus at Ellery Lake. In a campground nearby, you will find an easy trail to the site of Bennettville, a

NATIONAL PARKS  33

# WEST

## POINTS OF INTEREST

**REST STOP**
Get snacks, gas and music at the Whoa Nellie Deli. The view of Mono Lake is incredible.

**FUN FACT**
Tioga Pass Road is a fixture in the Sierras. Before John Muir made Yosemite and its environs famous, Native Americans used the road as a footpath. By the 1880s, it became the Great Sierra Wagon Road and connected mines to the railroad.

**WORDS TO THE WISE**
Depending on weather conditions, Tioga Pass Road usually closes in November and reopens in May. Road updates are available on the National Park Service website. Yosemite is popular in autumn, so plan your visit in advance to beat the crowds.

**NEARBY ATTRACTIONS**
The Sierra National Forest abuts Yosemite National Park. For a unique way to sample the forest, take the 45-minute ride on the Yosemite Mountain Sugar Pine Railroad, which hauled timber out of the woods beginning in 1899 but now restricts its load to visitors.

▼
*Ruins stand where the mine in Bennettville once boomed.*

historic mining town. From there you can hike to some stunning alpine lakes. It's worth the side trip.

Back on the road, continue to the Tioga Pass Entrance Station at the east end of Yosemite. Every time I go through here, I reminisce about legendary Yosemite ranger Ferdinand Castillo, who manned the entrance. For nearly 40 years he had greeted folks with a smile and a joke or some kind of historic Yosemite tidbit. As the story goes, a man once asked Ferdinand what he should do if he had only an hour to visit the park. Ferdinand responded, "See that rock over there? I'd go sit on that rock and cry!"

A sign posted at the entrance station reads "8 miles to Tuolumne Meadows." At 8,600 feet, it is one of the largest subalpine meadows in the Sierra Nevada. The meadows extend far beyond Tioga Pass Road, up the Lyell Fork of the Tuolumne River, where backpackers on the John Muir Trail and Pacific Crest Trail pass through.

My favorite times at Tuolumne Meadows are the early mornings and evenings of spring and summer, when the sunlight brightens and fades across the meadow, and the gray-silver domes and peaks become soft pastels. Few other wanderers are present then, but almost always deer are grazing, coyotes are howling and little pikas are skirmishing about.

Tenaya Lake is a short jaunt from Tuolumne Meadows, and the Tioga Pass Road is just steps from the lakeshore. The Yosemite Indians called it Lake of the Shining Rocks. Here you can fish, canoe, kayak, take an ice-cold dip, or relax on a beach chair and watch the climbers.

Another of my favorite stops is Olmsted Point. From there, a quarter-mile trail leads to an erratic boulder field that seems to have been perfectly placed for travelers who wish to sit and soak in the scenery.

Looking across at the peak known as Clouds Rest and down the valley to Half Dome is amazing; at first glance the distant rounded dome may be unrecognizable. Take your binoculars, as you might be able to see the stream of hikers going up the cables on Half Dome.

From Olmsted Point to Crane Flat, the road demands your attention as it curves with the mountains, although nearly every bend offers a magnificent view. Please be aware that a coyote, deer or black bear could be crossing the road at any time, day or night.

About a mile before Crane Flat at the old Big Oak Flat Road pullout, you can walk on the dirt road through the Tuolumne Grove of giant sequoia trees. One of the many highlights is a 60-foot-high stump with a vehicle tunnel that was cut through in 1878.

Whether you use this amazing mountain road as a mere drive or as a destination, I guarantee that it is one of the most consistently scenic journeys you will ever have the pleasure to experience!

*Fallen leaves rest on rocks next to Lee Vining Creek.*

WEST

STORY AND PHOTOS BY
**LAURENCE PARENT**

*Colorado*

# BLACK CANYON OF THE GUNNISON

**LEAVE THE LOGJAMS OF TRAVELERS BEHIND AND EXPLORE ONE OF THE MOST DRAMATIC PLACES IN AMERICA.**

**THE FAINT ROAR OF WHITEWATER** drifts up from the abyss at my feet as I cautiously lean over the railing and peer down at the Gunnison River 2,000 feet below. Just a single family shares the overlook with me on this summer afternoon, and I admit the extra elbow room helps make Colorado's Black Canyon of the Gunnison National Park one of my favorite places.

With its sheer, dark gneiss and schist walls shrouded in shadow even in brightest daylight, it's clear where Black Canyon gets its name. I continue along the South Rim Road, stopping at the many overlooks along the way. Each provides an inspiring, vertigo-inducing view of the canyon. At the Painted Wall View, newer molten rock has squeezed through cracks, coloring the massive cliff with pinkish streaks.

At Dragon Point I watch the sunset over the plateau and envy a raven as it dives into the depths, reaching the bottom in moments. The next morning I take a less dramatic trip down to the river along the steep, narrow East Portal Road to Crystal Dam and Reservoir. It's a beautiful drive, but I still yearn to stand beside the river as it rages through the deepest part of the gorge.

So I drive around to the nearly deserted North Rim. And after making sure to check in with a park ranger, I begin my descent—part hike, part scramble—down a narrow ravine. There's no trail, and the route drops 2,000 feet in less than a mile. At the bottom, canyon walls block all but a sliver of the sky and trap the deafening roar of the river as it crashes through rapids and over giant boulders.

I find myself wishing I were that raven, able to fly back to the top of these towering cliffs, but I'm going to have to climb. It's still worth it. That evening, as I once again enjoy the sunset over the canyon, I wonder why more people haven't discovered one of the most striking places in America.

WEST

*Top: A wind-sculpted juniper hangs on for dear life near Dragon Point. Bottom: Painted Wall plummets 2,250 sheer feet.*

## POINTS OF INTEREST

### NOT TO BE MISSED
The 7-mile South Rim Drive provides spectacular views at its 12 overlooks. Try to allow for 2-3 hours, but if you have limited time, make your stops at Gunnison Point, Chasm View, Painted Wall and Sunset View.

Six more overlooks await on North Rim Road. The canyon walls here are almost vertical. To see all the sights on this side at your leisure, allow 2-3 hours.

### FUN FACT
The Gunnison River has a Gold Medal Water & Wild Trout Water designation, which means angling for large trout here is a real treat. Make sure to check out Colorado Parks and Wildlife Fishing Regulations online.

### WORDS TO THE WISE
Be aware that many trails have steep drop-offs. Also, bears are in the area, so keep snacks within arm's reach at all times.

NATIONAL PARKS 37

WEST

*Colorado*

STORY BY **SUSAN QUAST**
PHOTO BY **TIM FITZHARRIS**

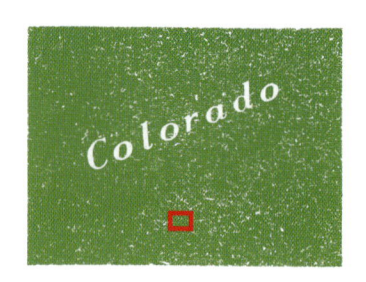

# GREAT SAND DUNES

CLIMB TO WHERE THE SAND MEETS THE SKY FOR AN UNFORGETTABLE TIME IN PARADISE.

**THERE'S AN INCREDIBLE SPOT** hidden in the mountains of Colorado. It's a place of adventure where kids of all ages can play in Mother Nature's sandbox.

Great Sand Dunes National Park & Preserve, in south-central Colorado, is home to some of the tallest sand dunes in North America. The Sangre de Cristo Mountains provide a dramatic backdrop for the dunes, which are the centerpiece of a diverse landscape of grasslands, wetlands, conifer and aspen forests.

The tallest dune, the Star Dune, is a mere 750 feet high. What a sand pile! It's about a 2.5-mile hike around the entire dune field, and there's no specific trail to follow. Sandboarding and sledding down the dunes are favorite pastimes in the park.

So, how were the dunes made? Most of the sand came from the San Juan Mountains, about 65 miles to the west. Larger grains and pebbles came from the Sangre de Cristos. Sand and sediment from both ranges washed into a huge lake that once covered the valley floor, and as the lake disappeared, winds from the southwest moved the sand into piles. Then winds coming through the mountain passes from the northeast kept piling the dunes back onto themselves, forming the tallest dunes in North America.

After you've hiked, stop and splash in Medano Creek. Depending on the time of year, the creek is just a 6- to 7-foot-wide stretch of damp sand. It begins in the snowfields of the Sangre de Cristos and then cascades down past meadows and into a wide, shallow field. The creek is famous for its surge flow, which creates waves of water on the sand. The creek recedes in July and August, but when its cool waters flow, the sight is just unforgettable.

Regardless of the season, the park offers much to see and do, including camping, hiking and watching for wildlife. With 200 bird species here, birding is another popular activity.

On any clear night, the sky is so dark you can see the Milky Way. Dry air, lack of light pollution and high elevation make the park an ideal spot for stargazing. And if looking up at the heavens is your passion, plan your visit around major astronomical events.

This park isn't as well-known as the Rockies or the scenic train to Durango, but the great dunes are a hidden gem.

WEST

*This creek's name, Medano, is Spanish for "sand dune."*

### POINTS OF INTEREST

**NOT TO BE MISSED**

Experience the park at night. It is certified as an International Dark Sky Park by the International Dark Sky Association. You can explore dunes, stargaze and listen to the sounds of nocturnal wildlife on your own or led by a ranger.

This unusual park appeals to sand skiers as well as hikers, backpackers, and campers who stay in a campground in an area of junipers and pines at the dunes' edge.

**FUN FACTS**

Not only are these ever-changing dunes ranked as the tallest in North America, but the dune field stretches over 30 square miles of high mountain-valley floor. The difference between the high and low points in the park (13,604 feet and 7,520 feet) is a whopping 6,084 feet.

**WORDS TO THE WISE**

The best weather is generally spring and fall. In summer, even though the air temperature is moderate, the sand can get uncomfortably hot.

▼ *Cliff Palace was discovered in 1888 by two cowboys looking for stray cattle.*

WEST

STORY AND PHOTOS BY
**CHRISTOPHER MARONA**

# MESA VERDE

BREATHTAKING VIEWS STRETCH FOR MILES, BUT A CLOSER LOOK REVEALS ANASAZI DWELLINGS.

**STOPPING AT THE ENTRANCE STATION,** I rolled down my window. A ranger leaned out and greeted me with a map and brochure. "Enjoy your visit," he said. Then, almost as an afterthought, he added, "Long House is open today."

Tucked in the southwest corner of Colorado, Mesa Verde National Park is 10 miles from New Mexico. The name is Spanish for "green table," and at 8,572 feet above sea level, Park Point is the highest spot of this very tall green table. It affords views stretching across the southwestern landscape to impossible distances.

Immediately to the west, Sleeping Ute Mountain, sacred to local tribes, looks like a napping chieftain with a fanned-out headdress and crossed arms. Farther west in Utah, the La Sal Mountains shimmer in the sun. Just a twist to the south stands Shiprock, New Mexico. Eastward, beyond the green patchwork pastures of the Mancos Valley, the snow-capped La Plata Mountains gleam like the silver for which they are named.

As beautiful as the vistas are, the real treasures of Mesa Verde are those engineered by ancestral Puebloans. These settlers built, occupied and left complex structures more than 300 years before the Pilgrims set foot on Plymouth Rock.

Sometimes called Anasazi, these people inhabited the region 1,400 to 700 years ago. Early structures, called pit houses, were dug into the earth and topped with wooden roofs. As their skills grew, the Anasazi built ceremonial kivas, interconnected rooms with windows and observation towers. In their last era, they created multistory cities perched on the sides of cliffs. Though some dwellings have only three or four rooms, Cliff Palace and Long House both contain more than 100 rooms.

In 1906, President Theodore Roosevelt designated the area a national park, and today UNESCO recognizes it as a World Heritage Site. The National Park Service has restored 35 to 40 structures, but officials estimate there may be 4,500 within park boundaries.

*Long House is open today.* I could just make the last tour, so I grabbed

NATIONAL PARKS **41**

WEST

## POINTS OF INTEREST

**NOT TO BE MISSED**
At the Chapin Mesa Museum, lifelike dioramas and various exhibits on basket weaving, pottery, masonry and other skills trace the evolution of Puebloan culture from its beginnings in settlements along the Colorado River to its demise nearly eight centuries later.

**FUN FACTS**
The dwellings were discovered in 1888 when two ranchers, Richard Wetherill and Charlie Mason, set off in a snowstorm in search of stray cattle. Instead they found the preserved Cliff Palace, which was once home to more than 200 ancient Puebloans. The next day, they found Spruce Tree House, naming it for the tree that grew beside the ruin, and Square Tower House, the tallest structure in the park.

The dwellings wisely face south-southwest to keep hot summer rays out but welcome low winter sun.

**WORDS TO THE WISE**
The park is open year-round, but many sites are closed in winter months.

*A yellow-headed collared lizard welcomes the rising sun.*

my camera bag, tripod and water and boarded the tram. The trail descends 130 feet by switchbacks, stone steps and two 15-foot ladders. Only when you turn the last corner can you see Long House. In the next moment, you are overwhelmed by a massive, overarching rock ceiling and layers upon layers of ancient stone buildings.

I looked down into a circular subterranean room used for political and religious ceremonies. With no windows or doors, the only access would have been through a hole in the roof pierced by a ladder. On the floor, precisely in the center, the Anasazi had dug a small hole. This *sipapu*, as it's called, is found in every structure and symbolizes the tribe's physical and spiritual connection to the earth.

Close examination of the masonry work revealed straight walls, square corners and tightly sealed joints. I peered down over a broken wall into a room that would have served as a home. It was tiny. My guide explained, "Smaller rooms needed fewer materials, took less work to build and were easier to heat."

I was packing my gear when the ranger began to herd the group up the trail. In that moment I realized I was kneeling at the fire pit, where as many as 150 people would have gathered 800 years ago.

On the mesa top, the ranger waited to lock the gate. I asked for his opinion about how large an area the ancestral Puebloans had roamed. He replied, "From here to there—we believe there are at least 40,000 unique archaeological sites," and he swept his finger across the horizon.

WEST

*Wildflowers bloom on ancient mesa-top ruins.*

*The sweeping view of Odessa Lake from the side of Joe Mills Mountain.*

WEST

STORY BY
**DAN BLACKBURN**

*Colorado*

# ROCKY MOUNTAIN

FEEL ON TOP OF THE WORLD VISITING THIS WELL-KNOWN MUST-SEE NATIONAL PARK IN THE MIDDLE OF NORTH AMERICA.

**IN THE ARMY, A BUGLER BLASTS** you out of bed at dawn. In Rocky Mountain National Park, you may also be awakened by early-morning bugling, but a large elk with horns on its head provides the music. My wife, Gloria, and I hear an elk and rise from our tent.

On Sept. 4, 1915, 200-300 people assembled in Colorado's Horseshoe Park to celebrate the dedication of a new American treasure. U.S. Rep. Edward Taylor and Gov. George Carlson joined naturalist Enos Mills, who was instrumental in getting the park developed. President Woodrow Wilson had signed the order into law in January of that year, designating another beautiful national park.

The park sprawls across 415 square miles of widely varied terrain, from alpine tundra to pine forests and even wetlands, and encompasses more than 100 peaks rising above 10,000 feet as it spans the famed Continental Divide. The tallest is Longs Peak, a towering 14,259 feet high, visible throughout much of the park and reflected in several crystalline lakes. Dream Lake is reportedly the most photographed, but there are plenty of breathtaking alternatives to explore.

Ninety-five percent of Rocky Mountain National Park is protected as wilderness. This makes it a hiker's paradise with scores of trails, many of them used by American Indian hunters centuries ago. On these largely unchanged paths, it is easy to become immersed in the forest and revel in the tumbling sounds of water from rushing mountain falls and streams.

Snow blankets much of the park in winter, but the arrival of spring usually sees the snow retreat back to higher

# WEST

### POINTS OF INTEREST

**NOT TO BE MISSED**
Intrepid visitors may choose to stay at the famous Stanley Hotel in Estes Park, which served as the inspiration for Stephen King's *The Shining*.

Hikers who explore the Colorado River District trails on the western side of the Continental Divide are rewarded with views of Grand Lake as they climb the Devil's Staircase.

**FUN FACT**
Ninety-five percent of the park's 265,873 acres is protected as wilderness, with more than 350 miles of amazing hiking trails to explore.

**WORDS TO THE WISE**
Beware of lightning along Trail Ridge Road. It is usually open May to October, weather permitting; other roads are open year-round.

*In the backcountry this bull moose quietly grazes in wetlands.*

elevations. Trail Ridge Road closes in mid- to late October and, thanks to plowing, can reopen in late May.

This famous 48-mile-long scenic drive, the highest continuous paved highway in the U.S., climbs above 12,000 feet, offering visitors spectacular vistas of the Rocky Mountains in all directions.

Summer means blooming wildflowers and herds of people, as it's time for family vacations, and the park's easy access from Denver beckons schoolchildren and their parents. The park is definitely popular and one of the most-visited national parks.

Gloria and I are enthusiasts of the national parks, steadily working on our goal of visiting as many as we can from the Rocky Mountains to the West Coast. We're also dedicated tent campers. As we researched our trip, we heard the five campgrounds here were very good, and I'm happy to report this is true.

We pitched our tent in Moraine Park campground, nestled in a ponderosa pine forest above meadows. We visited in the fall, when the crowds are much smaller. The Big Thompson River runs through Moraine Park, attracting a variety of wildlife. On several days, we had mule deer grazing within a stone's throw of our campsite.

This campground is a good home base for exploring some highlights

WEST

of the park. Bear Lake Road, another scenic drive, begins here and goes 9.3 miles into the core of the Glacier Gorge area to Bear Lake, a sparkling jewel surrounded by dramatic mountain peaks at the foot of the Continental Divide.

For hikers, the Fern Lake and Cub Lake trailheads, both near the campground, are pathways to gorgeous waterfalls, lakes and mountains. Go in autumn and revel in the brilliant golden glow as the leaves on the aspens turn.

Even though there's much to explore, the bugling of the elk kept calling us back to the meadows. The male elk use this distinctive sound to summon the females to join their respective herds. Occasionally a younger male will challenge an older bull, and the clash of their massive horns echoes through the forests and across the meadows. The winner gets the harem.

Sometimes a wandering moose strays into the elk meadows, but none of the elk is foolish enough to challenge those big bulls. A visiting moose will survey the scene much like a tourist before moving on.

Painters capturing nature's beauty with oils or watercolors often spread throughout the park, and we spend some time looking over their shoulders while they graciously share their work and thoughts with us.

After a week, we concluded that the park is simply too large and diverse to experience in just one visit. Its size and variety border on daunting. Rocky Mountain National Park simply will have to go back on our list to happily return to again and again.

*Yellow wild-flowers along Trail Ridge Road await the sun.* ◀

NATIONAL PARKS  47

# WEST PHOTO GALLERY

1.

2.

**1. TRAIL OF THE CEDARS**
Taken on a trip to Glacier National Park in the summer, this photo shows an inviting trail through giant evergreens. At one point the trail crosses Avalanche Creek as it winds through the forest.
– ELIZABETH BOULTER

**2. SCHWABACHER LANDING**
The sun rose behind me and illuminated the top of Grand Teton Mountain at Grand Teton National Park. Smoke from mountain wildfires contributed to the reddish skies. – KEN SMITH

**3. MESA ARCH**
A brilliant sunrise at Canyonlands National Park in southern Utah. From this spot it feels as if you're standing on nature's balcony and peeking under the canyon's covers. – JUDITH FULLER

**4. GRAND PRISMATIC SPRING**
One of the most color-filled locations in Yellowstone National Park, this is my ultimate favorite spot to see and photograph. It's as unique as a fingerprint and is constantly changing. – RENEE LUND

3.

4.

NATIONAL PARKS 49

1.

PHOTO GALLERY   WEST

2.

3.

4.

**1. BACKPACKING INTO THE DUNES**
The wind was fierce during sunset at Great Sand Dunes National Park and the temperature was quickly dropping. – **JON RUFFOLO**

**2. RUSHING WATERS**
My brother, standing on the log above the Sol Duc Falls in Olympic National Park, illustrates the scale of the scene. When someone well over 6 feet tall is dwarfed by their surroundings, you can imagine the magnitude in person. – **ELISE MORRIS**

**3. WATCHMAN**
I love this classic close-up of the Watchman at sunset in Zion National Park. I am in awe of the vibrant color and details in the rock formations. I think it would look different every evening.
– **THOMAS GUFFY**

**4. TUNDRA SWAN**
I waded through 3 feet of snow and was rewarded with this swan flapping its wings in Yellowstone National Park. – **BARRY SAMUEL**

NATIONAL PARKS   51

## WEST PHOTO GALLERY

### 1. HALF DOME
This recognizable rock face is at the eastern end of Yosemite Valley in Yosemite National Park. It was evening when the sun's rays fell on the dome, with the smooth Merced River in the foreground. —GEORGE WIEDENHOFER

### 2. LOGAN PASS
I spent about three hours at this location in Glacier National Park. As I hiked around the trails, I was amazed at the number of bighorn sheep, mountain goats and deer. —MICHAEL SASS

### 3. EARLY RISER
Canyonlands National Park offers the most stunning sunrises and sunsets I have ever seen. The colors are breathtaking. Definitely worth getting into the park early to take in a sunrise. —BARRY WILLIAMS

### 4. HISTORICAL HOMESTEAD
The Moulton family built this barn in Grand Teton National Park. I love to imagine what it must have been like for homesteaders over a century ago, building their homes with views of the Tetons. —JULIA BLANTON

### 5. MAJESTIC TREES
The beauty of Redwood National and State Parks is definitely underrated. Walking among these giant ancient trees was a humbling experience. —KATARINA BATES

1.

2.

3.

4.

5.

NATIONAL PARKS 53

▼ *Life is renewed as a'e ferns grow out of cracks in dried lava in Hawaii Volcanoes National Park.*

WEST

STORY BY **CATHY ILLG**
PHOTOS BY **GORDON ILLG**

# HAWAII VOLCANOES

THE BIG ISLAND OFFERS A FRONT ROW SEAT TO EARTH'S MAGNIFICENT TRANSFORMATION.

**OUR SURROUNDINGS WERE PITCH BLACK,** but in our headlamps we could see bits and pieces of rough, twisted terrain so sharp that any bare skin that touched it came away wounded

We were stumbling in the dark with our guides, photographers CJ Kale and Nick Selway, to see the expansion of new land formed by lava on Hawaii, the Big Island of the Hawaiian Islands. They own Lava Light Gallery in Kailua-Kona, and likely have more photos of running lava than anyone else in the world.

The cracks we were stepping over glowed orange, and the heat was intense. CJ and Nick led us through the darkness to the island's western edge, where we could go no farther.

Earth is a constantly moving jigsaw puzzle, and nowhere is that more evident than the Big Island. The tectonic Pacific Plate is inching northwest over a weak spot in the Earth's crust that is more or less continuously leaking magma. Over time, enough lava has flowed to create an archipelago, or chain of islands, in the middle of the Pacific Ocean, and the process is still ongoing.

At more than twice the size of all the other Hawaiian islands combined, the Big Island offers something for everyone. And it is home to the must-see Hawaii Volcanoes National Park, founded Aug. 1, 1916.

In contrast to our rugged journey on foot, it's easy to explore the park via car. Kilauea Volcano, which has been erupting pretty much continuously since 1983, should be on every visitor's list. Crater Rim Drive, an 11-mile road, provides access to scenic points and short walking trails. Be sure to stop at the Kilauea Visitor Center before you begin your trip, because road conditions around active volcanoes may change with little notice.

For much of the eruption, lava flowing out of Kilauea has crossed national park land toward the sea. But in 2014, a breakout of lava began to flow across private property to the east. If you wish to view the lava, make

WEST

*An i'iwi feeds on an ohia lehua blossom.*

### POINTS OF INTEREST

**NOT TO BE MISSED**

Kilauea Volcano, inside the park. Take scenic Crater Rim Drive, which encircles the volcano.

Mauna Loa (Long Mountain) is the largest volcano on Earth, covering half the surface of the Big Island. Located inside the park, it last erupted in 1984.

**NEARBY ATTRACTIONS**

To reach the top of dormant Mauna Kea (White Mountain) you can drive from sea level to 13,796 feet in 2 hours—or hike from the Visitor Information Station at 9,200 feet in about 8 hours.

Akaka Falls, with a dramatic drop of 442 feet, can be reached via a short, paved path. The loop also passes by Kahuna Falls. At nearby Rainbow Falls, the Wailuku River rushes over a rocky archway, and the morning sun creates rainbows in the mist.

sure you go with a guide who has permission to access this property.

We watched from a safe distance nearby as the molten rock oozed its way downhill. It popped and it crackled, forming ropes and ribbons of incandescent colors. Where the lava poured into the pounding surf, it hissed, sending up clouds of steam.

The island's twin volcanic peaks of Mauna Loa and Mauna Kea are the tallest mountains on Earth—if you measure them from the ocean floor. Reaching to nearly 14,000 feet above sea level, they give massive testament to the amount of magma that has leaked out of the earth.

We drove high up the mountains to where there was frost on the tropical vegetation. When most people think of Hawaii, they think of white sand, not white snow. But it's true: Mauna Kea and Mauna Loa are often snowcapped in winter. In fact, the name Mauna Kea means White Mountain, and the road to the summit has been closed due to heavy snow.

Because they block the trade winds, these mountains divide the island into one of the world's wettest places on the east side and a desert on the west.

Sun worshippers will flock to the beaches of the Kona and Kohala Coasts on the dry western side of the island. But the rainforests north of Hilo on the east coast are just the ticket for those drawn to verdant landscapes. Maybe it's because we live in the arid American West, but these densely forested slopes feel simply magical.

Some of the largest, most scenic and most easily accessible waterfalls in the state can be found in this area: the 442-foot Akaka Falls and 80-foot Rainbow Falls on the outskirts of Hilo. And if you enjoy colorful blooms and lush jungles, the Hawaii Tropical Botanical Garden is just a 10-minute drive north of Hilo.

While we were bouncing over a rough road on the eastern slopes of Mauna Kea, our guide and fellow photographer, Jack Jeffrey, told us he wanted to show us something special.

WEST

Jack is a retired wildlife biologist with the Fish & Wildlife Service, and he's directly responsible for returning a large chunk of this forest to its natural state. He was taking us to the Hakalau Forest National Wildlife Refuge.

Hawaii is the most isolated island chain in the world. Species had to travel immense distances to reach these cooling volcanoes, and the surrounding ocean is miles deep. As these bare rocks rose above the waters, they were visited by life that was probably lost at sea: a plant seed here, a bird there. And from these colonists, new native species developed. Hakalau is one of the best places in Hawaii to see the fabulous native birds, and having a guide like Jack, who knows them better than anyone, will help you spot them.

The flamboyant and brilliantly colored honeycreepers owe their existence to some long-ago marooned finches. With names like amakihi, apapane and i'iwi, their beaks come in sizes and shapes that boggle the imagination. Watching an i'iwi probe an ohia lehua blossom for nectar was a much bigger thrill than becoming another sunburned tourist on the beach.

When you do go to the shore, we highly recommend poking your head under the waves to check out Hawaii's native fish; many species are found only here. Our favorite snorkeling spots are all on the sunnier, west side of the island. Kahalu'u Beach has shallow water, no dangerous currents and a bounty of fish and green sea turtles.

All of the Hawaiian Islands are truly gifts from the sea. But only the Big Island offers the opportunity to see how these islands were formed, such as in a place like Hawaii Volcanoes National Park. Marvel at the metamorphosis that has transformed the black, twisted landscapes of molten rock into paradise! ◾

▼
*The beauty of Akaka Falls speaks for itself.*

▼ *A carpet of color contrasts with the snow on Garden Wall in Glacier.*

WEST

STORY BY **KARIN LEPERI AND CHUCK HANEY**
PHOTOS BY **CHUCK HANEY**

# GLACIER

FALL AND SUMMER COLORS REALLY ENHANCE THE TRUE BEAUTY OF THIS SPECIAL PLACE IN MONTANA.

**FOR DRAMATIC FALL LANDSCAPES,** it's hard to beat Going-to-the-Sun Road over Logan Pass in Glacier National Park. A snakelike highway that seems to melt into the sun, the 50-mile, two-lane road was named after a Blackfoot Indian spirit who came to earth and returned to the sky via the mountain.

Here in the northern Rockies, an explosion of color contrasts starkly against cedar, evergreens and snow-covered jagged peaks. The golds and yellows from aspen and western larch, oranges and reds from ash, and huckleberry crimson provide a blazing palette of nature's glory. Amid air as crisp as Winesap apples, expect to encounter wildlife such as mountain goats, bighorn sheep, elk, moose and even grizzlies along the way as they prepare for the long winter ahead.

September is the best month for viewing aspen, birch, cottonwood and huckleberry. Mid-October is best for western larch. You'll see yellow-gold (aspen, birch, cottonwood, western larch); orange (Rocky Mountain maple); orange-red (mountain ash); crimson (huckleberry);  and green (juniper, cypress, ever-greens) as well.

If you are looking for a hiking experience among yellowing larch (also known as tamarack), choose any of the trails from Sperry Trailhead near Lake McDonald Lodge. This is bear country though, so make sure to take safety precautions and dress for variable weather conditions.

For some pedaling, just outside of the park you'll find an easy bike ride along an old railroad bed that became a bike trail. The path follows the old rail route past several highlights in the Flathead Valley, including Whitefish and Flathead lakes. For more info, visit the website of the Rails to Trails of Northwest Montana organization.

# WEST

## POINTS OF INTEREST

**NOT TO BE MISSED**

Flowers to look for in summer include:
- beargrass
- glacier lily
- clematis
- purple aster
- western anemone
- lupine
- mountain lady's slipper
- Lewis's monkeyflower
- trillium
- blanket flower

**FUN FACT**

Glacier National Park is home to thousands of mountain goats, and with good reason. These sure-footed climbers prefer high elevations and can easily ascend steep, rocky slopes that are 60 degrees or more. You will often find them resting on the rocky cliffs, away from predators, or—to make up for the salt they lack in their diet—licking the mineral-rich rock in an area of the park known as Goat Lick.

**NEARBY ATTRACTION**

Waterton Lakes National Park, contiguous to Glacier, lies north of the U.S.-Canada border. The two together are known as Waterton-Glacier International Peace Park.

*Nature paints a vibrant still life with wildflowers in the park.*

To camp, fall is a fantastic time to sleep under the stars in Glacier. The only auto campgrounds open by Nov. 1 are the Apgar and St. Mary campgrounds, both of which have no fees during the winter.

If you really do want to avoid the crowds, fall is likely the best time. You will, however, have to be self-sufficient, as many concessions will closed down for the season.

For another kind of colorful display, Glacier, also known as the Crown of the Continent, bursts with vibrant stands of prairie and alpine wildflowers during its brief summer season. With more than 730 miles of hiking trails that provide access to soaring peaks, mountain meadows, lush tracts of forest and clear, fish-filled lakes, the park offers countless places to view summer blossoms.

By early July, a vast array of prairie wildflowers, including lupines and blanket flowers, appears along roadways in the St. Mary and many Glacier valleys. The blooms move higher in elevation as the summer progresses.

The alpine meadows at Logan Pass are among the most beautiful spots on the planet. The best bet to take in all the glory of the flora is to walk 1.5 miles from the Logan Pass Visitor Center to the Hidden Lake Overlook. Most of the path is on a boardwalk to help protect the fragile environment.

Heading north from the visitor center, the 11.4-mile Highline Trail leads hikers along the west side of the park's resplendent and aptly named Garden Wall.

In late July, yellow glacier lilies emerge as the lingering snowfields begin to melt and recede, and by early August, it is a bloom fest with a variety of colorful wildflowers spread across the meadows. My favorites are the stands of Lewis's monkeyflowers, which add a layer of vibrancy to the red rock outcroppings.

Whenever you decide to go, the majesty of Glacier will draw you in.

WEST

▼
*Aspens at peak color are hard not to notice.*

WEST

STORY BY **DONNA B. ULRICH**
PHOTOS BY **LARRY ULRICH**

# GREAT BASIN

WHEELER PEAK PRESIDES OVER LAKES, VALLEYS, LIMESTONE CAVES AND SOME OF THE OLDEST TREES ON THE PLANET.

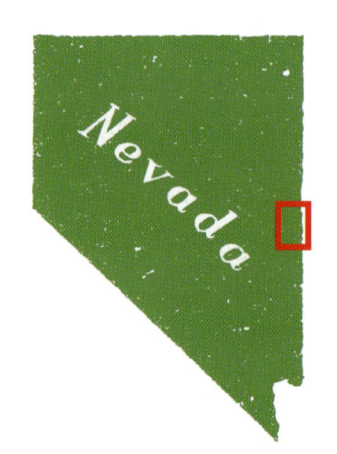

**GREAT BASIN NATIONAL PARK** has everything from snow-covered peaks and alpine lakes to trees as old as the hills. What it doesn't have is a major city nearby, unless you count Baker, Nevada, population around 60. If you like the thought of a park without cars and buses packed into parking lots, take this little side trip off what *Life* magazine once labeled "The Loneliest Road in America," Highway 50.

You'll find the park on the eastern edge of the Basin and Range Province, the region extending east from California's Sierra Nevada to Utah's Wasatch Range, and from southern Oregon to southern Nevada. A distinguishing feature is that all of the region's rivers flow inland, not to the ocean.

At 13,063 feet, Wheeler Peak soars above the desert valleys and dominates the skyline. The 12-mile Wheeler Peak Scenic Drive climbs nearly 3,000 feet from the park boundary to its terminus at 10,000 feet. At the road's end are a campground, trailheads for climbing, high mountain lakes and a bristlecone pine forest. The popular Alpine Loops trail passes by Teresa and Stella lakes, both above 10,000 feet.

Bristlecone pines are among the oldest trees on Earth; some were young when the Egyptian pyramids were under construction. In 1964, one pine tree on Wheeler Peak was determined to be 4,862 years old. Fantastically twisted, gnarled and fastened to the earth with roots like steel, bristlecone pines tell a tale of struggle for survival on barren, rocky, windblown terrain. The wood, worn smooth by the elements, has a sculpted beauty not unlike polished stone.

Down on Wheeler's flank are the Lehman Caves and the impressive Lexington Arch, carved out of limestone by ancient waters. It's thought that the arch was once part of a passage in a cave system.

When the high desert is awash with Indian paintbrush, desert dandelion and prickly pear cactus, all scattered in sagebrush, the park is a happy oasis off the Loneliest Road in America.

WEST

*Top: An aspen grove beneath the sheer rock face of Wheeler Peak. Bottom: The rugged landscape is no match for a hardy hiker at Lexington Arch.*

**POINTS OF INTEREST**

**NOT TO BE MISSED**
Stargaze in this designated International Dark Sky Park where you can see the Milky Way with the naked eye on a summer night. There's an annual Astronomy Festival, star train rides, a full moon hike and solar telescope viewing.

Spend a day fishing in Lehman Creek, or visit Upper Pictograph Cave to see ancient Fremont Indian rock art.

**FUN FACTS**
Sweeping across 77,000 acres, the park's drastic elevation changes—from desert valley floor to 13,000-foot Wheeler Peak—encompass springs, fossils, subterranean caves, a glacier, and dizzying arrays of plant, animal and bird species.

**WORDS TO THE WISE**
Visit in summer to early fall.

NATIONAL PARKS 63

▼ *The park has 400 species of plants, including penstemon.*

WEST

STORY AND PHOTOS BY
**DENNIS FRATES**

# CRATER LAKE

DIVE RIGHT IN TO THE SPLENDOR AND MYSTERY OF THIS NATURAL WONDER IN OREGON.

**THE FIRST TIME** my then-10-year-old daughter saw Crater Lake National Park, her jaw just dropped. Before her were the deep blue waters of a lake surrounded by jagged peaks—the remains of a mighty mountain known as Mazama.

"You told me this was a beautiful lake, but I had no idea it was this incredible," Nicki said at the time.

That is the Crater Lake effect. This magical and majestic place is the only national park in Oregon and the deepest lake in the United States. Though Crater Lake isn't among the most visited national parks, it should be. It is an awe-inspiring weekend getaway. Included here are things that I love to do at this scenic wonder.

Driving the rim is definitely tops. Crater Lake's rim rises 8,000 feet, allowing snow to remain until early summer. The best time to visit is in July and August when all the snow is mostly gone, the wildflowers are in full bloom and the historic Rim Drive is open. This 33-mile route is the easiest and most popular way to see the national park. It should take up to 40 minutes to complete the drive if you don't stop.

But you will stop, because beneath the serene dark blue waters sits a dormant volcano that literally blew its top more than 7,700 years ago, leaving behind the caldera we now see today.

Over time, lava cooled and sealed the bottom. Rain and snow melt filled the caldera with pristine and fresh water, creating the 1,943-foot-deep lake. The depth and clarity explain why the color of the lake is one of its most noteworthy attributes. As sunlight penetrates the lake, it absorbs all the colors of visible light except for blue, which it reflects back. The deeper and clearer the water, the more magnificent the reflected blue becomes. The hue is so unique that it is referred to as Crater Lake blue.

As you make your way around the lake, get peekaboo views of Wizard Island and Phantom Ship Island. There are a few places to see wildflower fields, too. You could easily spend the day on this leisurely drive. If you'd rather someone else take the wheel, hop on the Crater Lake Trolley, which makes

NATIONAL PARKS 65

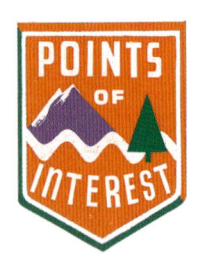

# WEST

*Historic Crater Lake Lodge is a landmark, charming visitors since 1915.*

### POINTS OF INTEREST

**FUN FACTS**

Crater Lake itself is 6 miles wide. It is the deepest body of fresh water in the U.S. with a depth of 1,943 feet.

**WORDS TO THE WISE**

Daybreak, when a remarkable shade of blue reflects from the water's surface, is the best time to see the lake.

There are two campgrounds, at Mazama and at Lost Creek, both accessible by road from Rim Drive. They are only open in the summer. With a permit you can camp in the backcountry.

Crater Lake is particularly beautiful in winter and, despite an annual snowfall of 533 inches, easy to visit. The road is kept clear, and a ski trail circles the crater rim. On weekends from Thanksgiving to April, you can join snowshoe hikes led by a park ranger.

up to seven stops along its two-hour tour of Rim Drive. Plus, a ranger is on board to share trivia and fun facts about the park.

Some visitors want more than a jaunt around the rim. These folks lace up their boots and trek the park's 90 miles of trails. Ranging from easy to challenging, these paths lead to amazing views.

Pinnacles Trail will have you thinking you are in the Badlands of South Dakota. In this truly unique geologic area, the spear-shaped pinnacles formed when hot ash cooled after the big eruption.

Watchman Peak Trail takes you to a fire lookout above Wizard Island, which is known as one of the best spots in the park to watch the sunset.

The rocky climb of the Garfield Peak Trail winds past wildflowers and unusual vegetation. You might even spot a marmot or two. If you are up for a bit of a more adventurous hike, consider the one to Mount Scott, the highest peak in the park. The 4.5-mile round-trip hike is best undertaken in the early morning hours. Another sunrise sensation is Discovery Point Trail. The breathtaking views of a blue sky filled with displays of orange and red are your visual reward for getting up before dawn.

Just one trail actually leads to the water's edge—the Cleetwood Cove Trail. It is moderately steep, but only about 2.2 miles long. Cleetwood Cove is the only shoreline where swimmers can enter the lake. The water is about 57 degrees in summer, so be prepared for a chilly reception.

If you'd rather not wade into the water or take a summertime version of a polar plunge, set sail on a boat tour of the lake. Eight tours depart Cleetwood Cove daily. There are a couple of options: a two-hour trip that will take you around the caldera or a longer trip that includes a stop at Wizard Island (the boat tour is the only way to get there). The latter gives visitors a chance to swim and explore the island, which is actually a cinder cone formed during later eruptions. It's a terrific outing for kids because they can experience one of the lake's standout volcanic features.

WEST

*Phantom Ship Island is a natural rock formation found within Crater Lake.*

WEST

*Rubber rabbitbrush, a popular snack with deer, blooms on the rim of Crater Lake.*

*A golden-mantled ground squirrel nibbles on an almond.*

Crater Lake and its surrounding forest filled with mountain hemlock and pine are home to an abundance of birds. Spot eagles and peregrine falcons along the rim cliffs or look for American dippers near streams. Wildfire-burned forests attract several species of woodpeckers, including the rare black-backed and three-toed woodpeckers. Common mergansers can be seen on the lake, and calls of songbirds permeate the forests and the meadows.

Mammal sightings are far less common, but a wide variety of animals inhabit the terrain around the lake, including bobcats, gray wolves, red foxes, cougars and several species of marten, to name but a few. Expect to encounter several white-tailed deer, since they seem oblivious to visitors.

Even if you opt to stay outside the park or in a campground, don't miss a visit to historic Crater Lake Lodge. Originally opened in 1915, the lodge takes you back to the rustic charm of the 1920s. If you do choose to stay, it is an experience you will never forget.

Located on the edge of the caldera and overlooking the lake, the lodge has fantastic views of this natural wonder. Rise with the sun in the morning and eat a hearty breakfast before heading out to the trails, or upon your return refuel with an elegant dinner and sip a glass of wine in the dining room.

As a landscape photographer, I have always been drawn to Crater Lake. I was delighted that my daughter Nicki recognized its beauty so many years ago. Although I don't know if our trip planted some kind of seed, today she is a landscape photographer, too. Crater Lake is truly a magical place.

*The stunning view from Green River Overlook.*

WEST

STORY AND PHOTOS BY
TIM FITZHARRIS

# CANYONLANDS

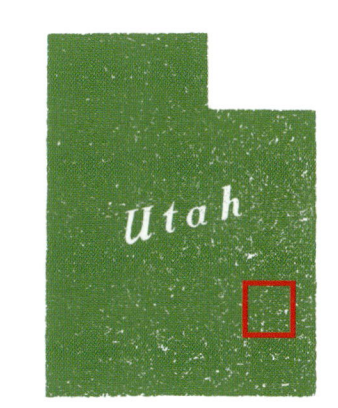

A MAJESTIC DESERT MARVEL RICHLY REWARDS TRAVELERS WHO HAVE THE GUMPTION AND FOUR-WHEEL DRIVE.

**THE DRAMATIC VISTAS** at Canyonlands National Park rival those of the Grand Canyon, while its exotic geology is first cousin to that of a nearby and better-known national park, Arches.

I've spent many very thrilling days chasing endless photo opportunities in this immense region of deep canyons, sheer-drop mesas, staircase benchlands and soaring sandstone spires.

A remote high-desert wilderness, with elevations ranging from 3,700 to 7,200 feet above sea level, Canyonlands is one of my favorite places to shoot Wild West landscapes.

The park sprawls over 337,598 sparsely populated acres in southeast Utah, not far from the town of Moab.

It is composed of three sections whose boundaries are loosely carved by the Colorado and Green rivers. The three sections are isolated from one another, and you reach them by separate dead-end roads that snake inward from the park periphery.

The Needles district is on the southeast side of the Colorado River, about 90 minutes from Moab. This is the most developed part of the park, with a small store, cafe, visitor center and campground.

Needles, named for the area's vibrantly colored sandstone spires, is also known for its steep canyons, towering arches and buttes.

Visitors can explore more than 60 miles of interconnecting trails, which can be challenging even for experienced hikers, or about 50 miles of backcountry roads for those in a four-wheel-drive vehicle. The incredible scenery is worth the extra effort.

Looming over the northern reaches of the park, Island in the Sky is a grand, flat-topped, tree-studded mesa about 45 minutes from Moab.

It's the easiest area of the park for visitors to reach and the best location for capturing those fabulous panoramic shots. A meandering paved road connects numerous overlooks of the river-carved terrain thousands of feet below. Facilities include a visitor center and small campground.

I love to spend the early morning in this part of the park hiking several of

NATIONAL PARKS 71

# WEST

*Mesa Arch, in the Island in the Sky region, offers fantastic sunrises.*

## POINTS OF INTEREST

**FUN FACTS**

Canyonlands is the largest yet the least developed of the national parks located in Utah.

Historic people of many cultures have visited the area over a span lasting more than 10,000 years—relying on and exploiting the rich resources that hide in the desert landscape. Many prehistoric campsites exist within the park's boundaries.

You'll find short trails leading to an ancient Anasazi granary and to an abandoned cowboy's camp that features century-old wooden and iron handmade furnishings.

**SIDE TRIP**

If you have time to venture outside the park on a brief side trip, you won't want to miss the dramatic view of Canyonlands from the adjacent Dead Horse Point State Park.

---

the short trails to discover how the light is mottling the exotic rock forms carved by the river.

The Shafer Trail Road leaves the mesa's rim and drops 1,000 feet in a series of jaw-clenching switchbacks to the White Rim, a massive bench of rock that encircles Island in the Sky.

The Maze district is Canyonlands' least-visited sector, and thorough preparation is a must before mounting any expedition there.

This labyrinth of multihued rock canyons is accessible only by four-wheel drive or by hiking over remote unmarked trails.

I have not ventured into the Maze, but this trek is high on my wish list, along with spotting and photographing the park's elusive desert bighorn sheep and mountain lions.

Spring, with its pleasant weather, light crowds and burst of wildflower color, is my favorite time to visit Canyonlands. Typically, daytime highs reach a comfortable 60 to 80 degrees.

May and early June offer flowering cacti and herbs, which I photograph on rare overcast days, when the landscapes lose some of their drama to the soft light.

Summer's high temperatures, frequently exceeding 100 degrees, make hiking difficult. But the heat also stirs up thunderstorms that add rainbows, magnificent sunsets and clouds of all shapes and colors to an already sumptuous array.

In autumn, aspens and cottonwoods along the rivers and streams put on a nice show of fall color, made even more enjoyable by clear October skies and pleasant temperatures.

I've also tested my cameras here in the winter, when snow dusts the tawny or rusty wilderness. Use caution when visiting during winter, however, as even a light snowfall can make roads treacherous to navigate.

Through the lens, and to my eyes, Canyonlands' raw, undisturbed beauty is remarkable all year-round.

WEST

▼
*Washer Woman Arch, in the distance here, looks just like its name states.*

▼ *An early morning rainbow appears at the Towers of the Virgin.*

WEST

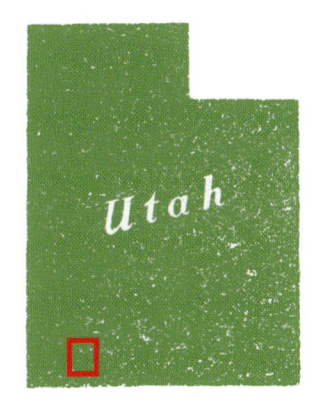

STORY AND PHOTOS BY
**TIM FITZHARRIS**

# ZION

WIND YOUR WAY THROUGH VIBRANT SANDSTONE MOUNTAINS, COTTONWOODS AND THE GLORIOUS VIRGIN RIVER.

**THE ZION-MOUNT CARMEL HIGHWAY,** a section of Utah's Scenic Byway 9, can be driven in less than 45 minutes, yet it draws some 3 million visitors yearly from all parts of the globe. You could spend months exploring the grand mountain and desert attractions that are peppered along the route. It is the main thoroughfare through Zion National Park and connects to the prime tourist draw of the region—Zion Canyon Scenic Drive. That drive follows the Virgin River northward through Zion Canyon to the Temple of Sinawava, an elegant 2,000-foot-high sandstone rampart with delicate groves of cottonwood and box elder interlaced around its feet.

It was 30 years ago that I first became intrigued with the area as I sat at my kitchen table planning my first photo trip into southern Utah's red rock country. Names on this part of the map seemed a little overblown: Great White Throne, Angel's Landing and Checkerboard Mesa, to mention a few. Apparently, the area made quite an impression on the European settlers.

Once I arrived, I had to admit I was mistaken. These names understate the majesty of these natural monuments. It's not just the colors (vermillion, rust, buff, ochre) but the immense scale, which tends to get muffled by its own grandeur until a raven passes high overhead, a black speck against the

NATIONAL PARKS 75

WEST

*These cottonwood trees hug the Virgin River.*

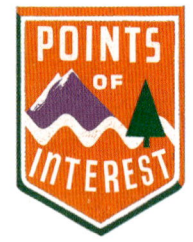

### POINTS OF INTEREST

**FUN FACT**
As the sun sets, photography becomes a social event for Zion visitors. You'll find fellow shutterbugs on the Pa'rus Trail happily snapping an iconic shot of The Watchman. Capturing Bridge Mountain is as easy as visiting the Zion Human History Museum and turning your camera east.

**WORDS TO THE WISE**
Even if you're just driving through, you'll need to pay the full park entrance fees. Also, the route's 1.1-mile tunnel requires a permit for big vehicles like motor homes. And from March to October, access to the 6-mile Zion Canyon Scenic Drive spur is by shuttle bus only. In winter, you're allowed to drive your own car.

red, which rises another thousand feet, perhaps, into the blue.

There are more than just natural marvels here. The Zion-Mount Carmel Highway is an engineering wonder in itself. It is listed in the National Register of Historic Places and designated as a Historic Civil Engineering Landmark. Construction was completed in 1930 as part of the Grand Circle Tour connecting southwest Utah's scenic spots with the north rim of the Grand Canyon in a quicker, easier route to lure visitors.

Photogenic views are stacked up in every direction, and I want to shoot them all right away. But eventually, I calm down enough to park, get out the camera and tripod and proceed on foot. Surprisingly, walking among these sandstone colossi (among the largest anywhere) seems as cinematic as viewing them at highway speed. The near-vertical walls, though enormous, are so tightly packed, so close, so varied in form and color that new compositions pass my eyes at a steady clip. I set up the tripod, frame a chiseled chasm that glows intensely red under reflected sunlight and then pad another hundred feet through river sand before I stop and do it again. This time, cottonwoods gracefully outline an opening in the canyon, which reveals another stone amphitheater within—dim, mysterious, inviting. When my shutter clicks, a mule deer raises its head from a brushy gold chamisa shrub nearby. A small flock of wild turkeys continues to forage, unconcerned except for a pair of toms that shake and fluff their formidable feathers into a courtship display. Zion National Park is home to an abundant variety of birds, mammals, amphibians and reptiles. Except for the latter—I spy many types of lizards basking in the hot midday rays—it seems that most of the inhabitants hunker down in shady places to keep cool.

The area's plant life is equally diverse, ranging from wetlands to arid grasslands to coniferous forest high up on sandstone crevices. How can a total of 900 different plant species exist here? The drastic changes in elevation, ranging from 3,600 to 8,700 feet, create multiple microhabitats in the park.

The river's murmur sets a soothing pace as I move past each new scene, each picture feeling different from the one before. The light changes, and cottonwoods photographed earlier along the Virgin River glow green compared to their muted cousins photographed at the foot of Bridge Mountain as the sky grows dark. As the color drops out of the canyon, I know it's time to call it a day. But I will be back along the road tomorrow, just as I will be next year and the year after. Why stop after three decades? The seasons and sunlight guarantee fresh perspectives. The excitement never fades.

*Prickly pear cactuses mimic Zion's iconic mountains.* ◂

WEST

STORY BY
**CAROL PUCCI**

# MOUNT RAINIER

EACH WINTER, ALMOST 600 INCHES OF POWDER FALLS IN THIS NATIONAL PARK, MAKING IT A PERFECT SNOW PLAYGROUND.

**WHEN YOU VISIT** Mount Rainier National Park, you will see splendid meadows of wildflowers give way to thick blankets of snow at the Paradise visitors area that sits at an elevation of 5,400 feet. Winter draws campers, hikers and snowshoers into wilderness areas like the Mazama Ridge, where white powder covers alpine meadows and crystalline frost coats the trees. Stunning views of the mountain reward downhill skiers at nearby Crystal Mountain Resort, nestled in the Cascade Range, a few miles from the park's northeastern entrance.

Named for the mirror views of Mount Rainier reflected in its subalpine lakes, the Reflection Lakes area attracts snowshoers and cross-country skiers to the edges of what look like frozen meadows in winter. Glissading—sliding downhill on one's feet or buttocks—is a fast and fun way to descend slopes here.

One of the few species of wildlife you might spot that thrives in winter at the park's higher elevations is the Cascade red fox. They have tails with white tips, and their legs are black.

And though snow falls early at Mount Rainier—blanketing meadows with deep drifts that can cover the ground into June—you may also find dark blue and black Steller's jays, along with crows and ravens.

Climbers use Emmons Glacier as a route to reach the summit of Mount Rainier. In winter, mountaineers believe it receives some of the best powder for backcountry skiing.

Though amazing all year, the park is a winter snow lover's dream.

WEST

### POINTS OF INTEREST

**FUN FACT**
Mount Rainier National Park's premier attractions—Longmire, Paradise, the Grove of the Patriarchs and Sunrise—are all linked by a single winding road that enters the park at its southwestern corner.

**WORDS TO THE WISE**
Visit in summer for wildflowers, early fall for foliage and fewer crowds, and in winter for snow fun. From November to April all park roads except the Nisqually-Paradise road are usually closed.

**NEARBY ATTRACTION**
For a close encounter with Mount St. Helens, the explosive neighbor of Mount Rainier that blew its top in 1980 and began erupting again in 2004, head south on Highway 12 to Randle along the White Pass Scenic Byway. Take S.R. 131, which leads to Forest Service roads 25 and 99, where visitors can stop for breathtaking pictures of St. Helens' crater from Windy Ridge. This route is only open in the summer months, but the views are certainly worth the wait.

*Top: A camper looks on at Mount Rainier in the distance from Mazama Ridge. Bottom: The ski lift at Crystal Mountain Resort.*

TOP: IMAGES BY T.O.K./ALAMY STOCK PHOTO; BOTTOM: DESIGN PICS/STUART WESTMORLAND/GETTY IMAGES

NATIONAL PARKS   79

WEST

STORY BY
**DANA MEREDITH**

# NORTH CASCADES

ALPINE JOY WITH LESS OF THE BUSYNESS FOUND IN OTHER NATIONAL PARKS MAKES FOR A PEACEFUL EXPERIENCE.

**WITH FEW VISITORS,** it's an easy choice to seek out the crystal clear glacial lakes, rugged mountains and gorgeous landscapes about three hours north of Seattle along North Cascades Highway (state Route 20). The road cuts across 684,237 acres of the North Cascades National Park Service Complex. This area stretches from the Canadian border through the Ross Lake National Recreation Area to Lake Chelan.

Start at North Cascades Visitor Center near Newhalem and drive east for captivating scenic overlooks, hiking trails of varying levels, campgrounds, climbing areas and riding trails. Take an easy hike to Ladder Creek Falls or a short walk on the fully accessible Sterling Munro Viewpoint Trail to see dramatic views of the remote Picket Range. And don't miss Diablo Lake.

The park's diverse ecosystem is home to elusive mammals such as the gray wolf, at least 28 species of fish and more than 200 bird species. In addition, 260 archaeological sites have been identified—some older than 8,500 years—including mining camps, fire lookouts and sheep herder camps. Scenery, wildlife, history and recreation—North Cascades National Park has it all.

WEST

### POINTS OF INTEREST

#### NOT TO BE MISSED
Ladder Creek Falls is lovely and definitely worth the stop. And you will get some of your best views in the park at Diablo Lake Overlook and Washington Pass Overlook.

The beautiful Skagit Valley Tulip Festival is held in April every year.

#### WORDS TO THE WISE
Plan to visit between mid-June to October.

Be aware that no fuel is available on the 70-mile stretch of S.R. 20 between Marblemount and Mazama.

#### NEARBY ATTRACTIONS
San Juan Islands (via ferry from Anacortes); Space Needle, Seattle.

*Rising more than 9,000 feet, Mount Shuksan overlooks pristine Picture Lake.*

*Sol Duc Falls is surrounded by a forest of 200-year-old hemlock trees.*

WEST

STORY BY
**LESLIE FORSBERG**

# OLYMPIC

WITH LUSH FORESTS, WATERFALLS AND SANDY BEACHES, THIS DRIVE IS FOR NATURE LOVERS.

**CHLOROPHYLL RULES** in the damp Pacific Northwest. Experience it firsthand on a drive around Washington state's Olympic Peninsula loop, where logging trucks have given way to SUVs loaded with bikes and kayaks. You'll easily see the green in the Hoh Rain Forest, where bigleaf maples stoop like old men under the weight of thick pads of mosses and epiphytes (plants that grow on other plants for support). And you can almost taste it in the salt-tinged air of the area's pristine Pacific shore, where hemlock and red cedar forests trail down to beaches pounded by ocean waves.

With high mountain peaks, dense forests and ocean beaches, Olympic National Park—an UNESCO World Heritage Site—is the heart of the peninsula. It's flanked on three sides by Highway 101, which ribbons through small towns on a loop drive of more than 300 miles.

When you first lay your eyes on the peninsula, it will likely be from Seattle. From there, the snow-tipped Olympic Range forms a jagged outline on the western horizon. You'll aim straight for those peaks on board a Washington State Ferry from downtown Seattle to Bainbridge Island, an exciting start.

Make Port Townsend your first stop. This historic seaport features a fleet of painted ladies—beautifully restored and painted Victorian homes. Its downtown is filled with boutiques in old brick buildings. On its northern flank, Fort Worden Historical State Park is the site of year-round arts and culture festivals, and its lovely sand beach is marked by the 1914 Point Wilson Lighthouse.

After rounding a couple of tranquil bays, you'll arrive at the lavender capital of North America: Sequim. Spring and summer bring sweet scents to visitors strolling the grounds of the area's lavender farms. Many of the farms have gift shops where you can buy elixirs, potions and culinary items made from the fragrant herb.

Port Angeles, the largest town on the peninsula, is the gateway to Olympic National Park and a good spot to pull

# WEST

### POINTS OF INTEREST

**NOT TO BE MISSED**
Roll along the Olympic Discovery Trail, a bike path that goes past farmland, forest and ocean.

**FUN FACT**
Olympic National Park protects the largest unmanaged herd of Roosevelt elk in the world. Olympic was almost named "Elk National Park" and was established in part to protect these stately animals.

**WORDS TO THE WISE**
Bring adequate rain gear for hiking and camping. When beach walking, consult a tide table.

**SIDE TRIPS**
Watch wildlife at Dungeness Spit Recreation Area, home of the nation's longest natural sand spit at 5.5 miles. The spit is part of the Dungeness National Wildlife Refuge, which lies on the Pacific Flyway.

Paddle out of Freshwater Bay to sea caves and harbor seal haul-outs with Adventures Through Kayaking. Rent equipment or take a guided tour.

*Kayaks rest on the shore of Lake Crescent in Olympic National Park.*

in for the night and have a leisurely dinner. Next Door Gastropub, known for using fresh and local ingredients, is one of my favorite establishments.

Just beyond town, kick into low gear for the 17-mile climb to the 5,242-foot Hurricane Ridge. Here you'll experience jaw-dropping vistas of glaciated mountains. Alpine meadows are the home of black-tailed deer and Olympic marmots—adorably chubby rodents with shrill whistles.

Farther west, Highway 101 hugs the curves of the 12-mile-long Lake Crescent, whose cobalt depths are legendary. Also sparking stories is Lake Crescent Lodge, an arts-and-crafts-style resort perched on the shoreline. Some say President Franklin Roosevelt's overnight stay here in 1937 played a role in the creation of Olympic National Park.

Across the highway, a short hike leads to Marymere Falls, a 90-foot cascade in a rock alcove draped with delicate maidenhair ferns. Just a few miles farther, the Sol Duc Hot Springs beckon with relaxing thermal soaking pools and a spectacular nature walk through a mossy old-growth forest to Sol Duc Falls.

Just past the former timber town of Forks, the Hoh Rain Forest owes its existence to moisture-laden weather systems rolling off the Pacific that drop an average of 12 feet of rain annually. You see the rain's effect along the Hall of Mosses nature trail, where you will find massive, primeval trees covered with moss, and every square foot hosts an exuberant tangle of plant life.

Highway 101 finally reaches the Pacific at Ruby Beach, one of the crown jewels of Olympic National Park. The sensory experience here is full-on, with the tang of salt air, sea gulls mewling over the roar of the ocean and a broad sandy beach to sink your toes into. It's a visual feast as well, as seabirds swirl about sentinel-like sea stacks and brilliant anemones and sea stars glisten at the bottom of tide pools. The sun-bleached driftwood piled high is just one more reminder of the vast forests on this verdant thumb of land jutting into the Pacific Ocean.

WEST

*The trail to the top of Mount Angeles has steep switchbacks through meadows of flowers and fresh alpine air.*

WEST

*Wyoming*

STORY BY
TIM FITZHARRIS

# GRAND TETON

MULTIPLE TURNOUTS, OVERLOOKS AND TRAILS REVEAL THE GRANDEUR OF SOARING PEAKS AND MOUNTAIN LAKES.

**NO TERRAIN IN AMERICA'S** Lower 48 states surpasses the Grand Tetons for sheer eye-popping splendor. The upward thrust of these ice-crowned peaks, rising abruptly from surrounding prairies, is simultaneously inspiring and soulful. You feel good being around them.

The Tetons lord over their territory like abiding grandfathers. And at their base is a flurry of activity—tourists aplenty, but this place is preserved for moose, elk, bison, bear, coyote, squirrels, chipmunks, eagles and owls that confidently roam Wyoming's Grand Teton National Park.

Teton Park Road, a 43-mile loop drive, winds through lakes, forests and meadows as it snuggles against the mountain foothills. Highway 26/89/191 completes the circle and provides a more distant perspective on Teton grandeur. Branch off on Schwabacher Landing Road for an iconic photo at Schwabacher Landing.

The warmer seasons are my favorites for circling the Tetons. In spring and summer, the fields of wildflowers—particularly brazen patches of lupines and sunflowers—and newborn bison, elk and moose are what lure me to photograph here. You can snap them from your car window or hike into the fields (avoid meadows with bison to avoid being the target of a charge).

Autumn is when the elk and moose are in rut and antlered champions beg for challengers. I use a telephoto lens to keep my distance from these bulls—an unpredictable but thrilling bunch.

I like to alternate these gripping sessions with quiet work along the shores of String and Leigh lakes or Oxbow Bend, where still waters catch the reflection of Mount Moran or Grand Teton warmed by a rising sun. Fall is also aspen season, and the lower slopes and watercourses flash gold and bronze tints.

The meandering route through the park is peppered with wildlife, historic ranch buildings and grand views, and the trip never disappoints.

WEST

*Top: A route into the magical lands between the mountains and beyond. Bottom: Bison are sturdy icons at Antelope Flats.*

### POINTS OF INTEREST

**NOT TO BE MISSED**
Take Jenny Lake Scenic Drive off Teton Park Road for a spectacular view of the peaks. While there, don't miss Hidden Falls and Inspiration Point.

**FUN FACT**
In the very heart of Grand Teton National Park, Jenny Lake formed from melted glaciers about 60,000 years ago.

**NEARBY ATTRACTIONS**
Fossil Butte National Monument, WY, (fossil displays); Lava Hot Springs, ID, (known for its hot mineral pools); Periodic Spring, WY, (the spring gushes every 18 minutes from an opening in a canyon wall); Bridger-Teton National Forest, WY.

NATIONAL PARKS 87

*In the early evening, steam seems to drift endlessly from the West Thumb Geyser Basin.*

WEST

*Wyoming*

STORY BY
PEGGY KONZACK

# YELLOWSTONE

THERE WAS GOOD REASON TO GO THEN, AND SO MANY
AMAZING REASONS TO COME BACK TO MAKE MEMORIES.

**I HAVE SO MANY FOND REMEMBRANCES** of Yellowstone National Park that I feel as if I grew up there.

In the late 1920s and '30s my family lived in Butte, Montana, where my father owned a grocery store. We traveled to the park each summer. I remember one holiday weekend we spent in Yellowstone. I was 10 years old and excited to see my first geyser coming out of the side of the banks of the Firehole River. It wasn't long before we saw Emerald Pool, Morning Glory Pool and the (at the time) famous Handkerchief Pool, where a hankie would disappear and then reappear a few seconds later much cleaner and whiter. Unfortunately, people put so many things in the pool the debris damaged the "plumbing." Now the pool is all but forgotten.

Our next stop was the Old Faithful Inn to reserve a cabin for the night. Our cabin was simple and clean with two double beds separated by a curtain. We spent our evening listening to the park rangers lecture at the outdoor amphitheater, all the time watching and waiting for a bear to walk by.

At 6 the next morning we heard a knock on the door, and it opened (there were no locks on the doors). A young man declared "fire boy" and came in to build our fire. It took about three minutes and soon we had a cozy, warm room (he used a mixture of sawdust and coal oil to get the fire going in a hurry).

After the thrill of watching the famous geyser Old Faithful, we saw the thick, gray and bubbly mudpots, or mud pools. How they did smell like rotten eggs!

Then we headed to the Canyon Hotel (which is no longer), to reserve a cabin, and we received the same hospitality as we did at the Inn.

After a hearty breakfast the next day, we headed to Uncle Tom's Trail to walk to the bottom of Lower Falls. We walked down 900 steps, as I recall. Going down was fairly easy, but going

WEST

### POINTS OF INTEREST

**FUN FACTS**

Some geologists believe that the Norris Geyser Basin, named after a former superintendent of Yellowstone, may be the hottest place on Earth.

The floor of Yellowstone's Hayden Valley is covered with clay and lake sediments left from the most recent glacial retreat, 13,000 years ago, which is why the area is mostly marsh and lacks any trees.

**WORDS TO THE WISE**

Food, fuel and lodging are available at Canyon Village, Grant Village, Mammoth Hot Springs and Old Faithful.

Most park roads are closed from November through April, but park snowmobiles can be rented in winter.

**NEARBY ATTRACTIONS**

Beartooth Highway (Route 212); Grand Teton National Park.

*Lower Falls is by far the most popular waterfall in the park.*

back up we made use of the landing at every 50 steps and rested on a bench. It was quite a good feeling to accomplish such a great hike.

We then drove to Mammoth Hot Springs, which at that time was a very beautiful sight. Of course, those older than me had to visit Devil's Kitchen, a dried-up spring that the park service closed after discovering that carbon dioxide sometimes filled it. It was a scary place for a child.

Driving through the gate in Gardiner, we headed home to Butte with many happy memories of a long weekend!

Many years have passed since those visits to Yellowstone National Park. My husband and I have made six trips together. As I write this, I am in my 90s now and remember every single trip. Those were exciting and sometimes scary experiences. Summer or winter, Yellowstone is the perfect place to be out in nature.

WEST

*Well-known Old Faithful blows off a little steam.*

WEST **THEN AND NOW**

92  NATIONAL PARKS

THEN AND NOW  WEST

# LASSEN VOLCANIC NATIONAL PARK

### 1934
A woman stretches as she gets ready for a swim while standing at the edge of Manzanita Lake in Lassen Volcanic National Park. Looming in the distance is Mount Lassen.

### 2010
You can still swim in Manzanita Lake in Lassen Volcanic National Park today, and the color photograph here shows how dazzling a reflection of Mount Lassen in its waters really can be.

THEN: GEORGE A. GRANT/U.S. NATIONAL PARK SERVICE; NOW: MBRUBIN/GETTY IMAGES

NATIONAL PARKS  93

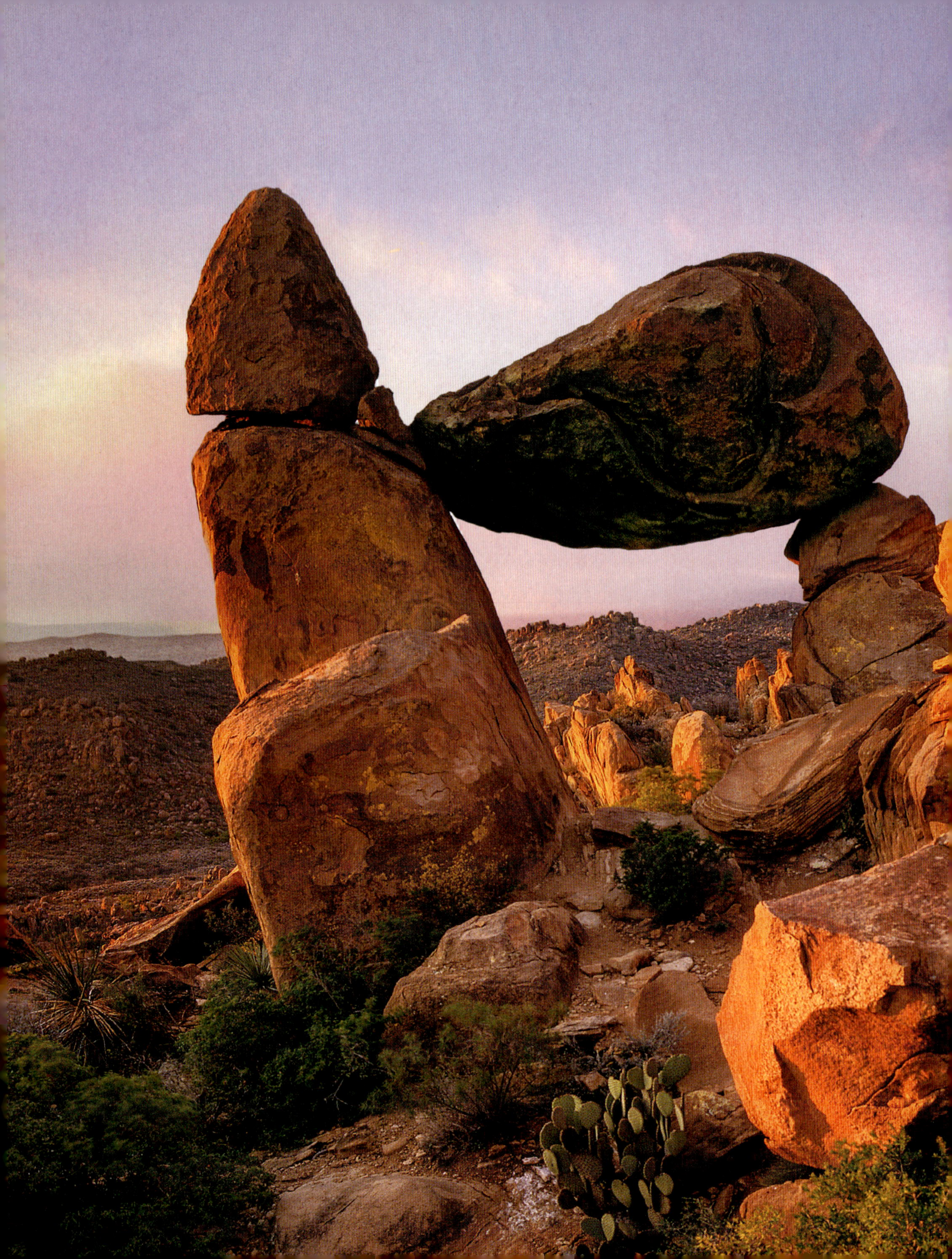

# SOUTHWEST

CANYONS · DESERTS · CLIFFS

▼ A sunset paints colors on the Colorado River and the surrounding landscape deep in the Grand Canyon.

SOUTHWEST

STORY AND PHOTOS BY
**LORA LUCERO**

# GRAND CANYON

GRANDFATHER'S MOTTO, "I THINK I CAN," SPURRED THIS FIRST-TIME HIKER TO THE TOP AT THIS WELL-KNOWN SPOT.

**I MADE RESERVATIONS** 13 months ahead for the popular Phantom Ranch, located at the bottom of Grand Canyon National Park in Arizona. As this adventure drew near, my hiking partner canceled. Doubts crept in—could I handle a 4,860-foot elevation drop from the rim to the Colorado River, and then hike back out? A sign on the South Kaibab Trail warns hikers: Hiking down is optional; hiking back up is mandatory.

I was a newly minted senior citizen who had been to the Grand Canyon many times before, but had never hiked to the bottom by myself. If I didn't do it now, I doubted I'd get another chance.

The night before my descent, I slept like a baby at Bright Angel Lodge. I didn't have any second thoughts. I think I can do this!

The next morning, the young man at the front desk related his experience slipping and sliding down South Kaibab Trail—the one I was set to embark on! A waitress who served me a hearty breakfast at the Harvey House Cafe told me she had tried to hike down, but turned back when she realized how difficult it was. Both of them were in their late 20s or early 30s. Uh-oh!

At 8:30 a.m., I made one last check of my backpack, clicked my walking sticks together, and started down the trail.

The day was bright and sunny and the Grand Canyon looked just like any postcard I'd ever seen. The 6.3-mile South Kaibab Trail is all downhill and appeared easy to negotiate. Nearly everyone I passed asked me if I was hiking alone.

Though I took my first step solo, I never felt alone with people of all ages hiking in both directions, watching out for each other.

My naive notion of a peaceful, meditative hike was promptly discarded when I realized the trail was narrow, rocky and dangerous in many spots. Since I was one of the slowest hikers, I frequently stepped aside as others approached from both directions.

Halfway down the trail, I felt strong and confident. I certainly didn't think about turning back. The temps rose as I continued down. I peeled off layers, sipped my water and ate a protein bar.

SOUTHWEST

*Day hikers savor the panoramic views along the South Kaibab Trail.*

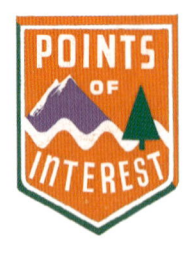

**POINTS OF INTEREST**

**WORDS TO THE WISE**

If planning to hike the Grand Canyon, assume it will take you twice as long to hike out as it does to hike in.

Hike with a sturdy pair of shoes and walking sticks.

Carry a headlamp and lightweight flashlight with extra batteries and bulbs in case you end up on the trail after dark.

Bring moleskin for any blisters.

Pack an emergency blanket should temperatures drop.

Keep a whistle where you can reach it easily in case you fall.

Most important: Have drinking water with you at all times.

**NEARBY ATTRACTIONS**

Meteor Crater, east of Flagstaff; Museum of Northern Arizona.

A ranger approached me, hiking up. He called out, "You must be Lora!" Female hikers I had seen earlier must have alerted him to my solo hike. He asked if I was OK. I told him I was quite thirsty and mistakenly thought that I could refill my water bottle along the way. Although there is potable water on Bright Angel Trail, there's none on the South Kaibab Trail.

The ranger offered me some of his water, convincing me that he carried extra water and wouldn't need it. He reassured me that Phantom Ranch wasn't far—and then I saw the Colorado River in the distance.

Crossing the river felt like a huge achievement. I wasn't sure how much farther Phantom Ranch was. Now I was really tired. The park service brochure estimates this hike down takes four to five hours, but for me it was nine to 10 hours.

At the ranch, I shared a cabin with nine women. Taking off my boots and socks, I saw the blisters. At dinner in the main mess hall, I sat next to a semiretired attorney celebrating her 81st birthday. Down the table, a young girl of 10 or 12 was also celebrating a birthday with her family.

The stars in the sky that night were the brightest I've ever seen. I climbed into my top bunk with cramped legs, took some Tylenol and was asleep before the cabin lights went out.

The next morning, after 4:30 a.m. breakfast, I headed out to climb the 7.8-mile Bright Angel Trail back up, my blisters covered with moleskin. When I crossed the Colorado River, knowing this was probably the last time I'd ever see it so close, I said a prayer of thanks.

The Bright Angel Trail is easier than the South Kaibab Trail, and my goal

SOUTHWEST

*A woman hikes in Blacktail Canyon.*

SOUTHWEST

*As it soars above, this raven seems to have the best view of a Grand Canyon sunset.*

*Crossing the Colorado River is a milestone for hikers trekking into the canyon.*

was to make it to the top before dark. I had to cross streams, and at one point I thought I'd even lost the trail. Many hikers passed me, all sharing some encouraging words.

At about 1 p.m., I realized that I wouldn't make it to the top before dark. A friend had warned me not to look up, just look back down the trail I'd traversed—good advice.

About 3 miles from the top rim, while I didn't feel any pain, I was very tired. The trail became steeper and steeper, almost like a difficult staircase to climb. I started moving more and more slowly.

At sundown I thought maybe I'll be stuck on the trail tonight, maybe I can't make it to the top. Then my grandfather's motto came to mind: I think I can, I think I can.

And then I saw a young woman, Annette, coming toward me. She said she was headed down the trail a bit to refill her water bottle, but she offered to carry my backpack for me when she returned.

Annette is the head housekeeper at Bright Angel Lodge, where she has worked for 20-plus years. I'm sure she could have hiked the final 1.5 miles up the trail in less than an hour, but she stayed with me for the next two hours, shining her flashlight ahead on the trail and chatting as we hiked. I wore my headlamp and had a flashlight, too.

I tripped once and had difficulty breathing. Annette never left my side. We finally reached the top at about 8 p.m. I know Annette's conversation and encouragement made the final ascent memorable and safe for me. So in the morning, I made a donation to the Grand Canyon Conservancy, a nonprofit organization that helps to preserve and protect the park, in Annette's name.

▼ *Hikers often find petroglyphs along Signal Hill Trail in the park's west district.*

SOUTHWEST

STORY AND PHOTOS BY
**RON & JANINE NIEBRUGGE**

# SAGUARO

AN ABUNDANCE OF CATUSES WELCOME HIKERS, CYCLISTS AND NATURE LOVERS TO THIS DESERT PARADISE.

**SAGUARO CACTUSES** stand out in the Sonoran Desert of Arizona. Tall with their treelike arms turned up to the sky (you could say they look like spiky green candelabras), they're an icon of the American Southwest and the star attraction at Saguaro National Park.

Let's start by learning how to pronounce this tricky word "saguaro." Remember that the "g" is silent: *sa-WAH-row*. Saguaros can live for up to 200 years, and the only place in the world where they grow is the Sonoran Desert. While growth rates may vary depending on precise location and weather, it takes about 35 years for the saguaros to produce their first signature flowers (the saguaro bloom), 50 to 100 years to grow their first arms and about 150 years to reach full height—up to 50 feet.

Split into east and west districts by the city of Tucson, Saguaro National Park preserves and protects this vital part of the desert. Though both districts feature visitor centers, picnic areas and plenty of opportunities for hiking and cycling, the terrain differs somewhat, so visiting both is a must.

With area elevations ranging from 2,180 to 8,666 feet, the plants and wildlife vary widely throughout the

NATIONAL PARKS 103

## SOUTHWEST

*Cactus Forest Scenic Loop Drive winds past plenty of prickly pears.*

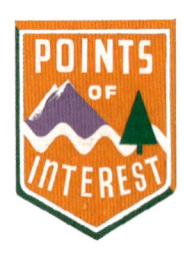

### POINTS OF INTEREST

**FUN FACTS**

The saguaros are a great boon to desert birds. Woodpeckers drill holes in the fleshy arms for nests, which are often used later by screech-owls, purple martins and sparrow hawks.

Over 50 miles of hiking and horseback-riding trails traverse a 58,000-acre wilderness and ascend to the summits of the fir-forested Rincon Mountains at an altitude of 8,700 feet.

**NEARBY ATTRACTION**

Though technically outside the park, the Arizona-Sonora Desert Museum will inspire you to find beauty and life in the surrounding desert.

park. Desert newcomers will find the landscape to be surprisingly lush.

The real treasure of the west district, which sits amid the Tucson Mountains, is the sheer volume of saguaros. The forest here is dense and astounding. Begin with a stop at the Red Hills Visitor Center and take in the super view from the picture window.

To truly appreciate the park, take the time to hike a trail or two (or three). Both districts have accessible trails, so there's something for everyone here. For example, the west's half-mile Desert Discovery Trail is paved and dotted with signs about the natural features of the Sonoran Desert. Valley View Overlook is another short, fairly easy trail with a stunning view of the Avra Valley and beyond. From here one can see how development has crept up to the park's boundary over the years.

The Signal Hill Trail is a must-do. It features iconic desert sunsets as well as petroglyphs etched by the Hohokam, an ancient, highly advanced Native American tribe whose disappearance in the 15th century remains something of a mystery.

If you'd rather explore the area on wheels, take the 5-mile Scenic Bajada Loop Drive by bicycle, motorbike or car. The road winds through a thick saguaro stand and has plenty of spots to pull over and take a photo.

The saguaros are not as dense in the east district. Rather, the draw here is a cactus forest, home to an abundance

# SOUTHWEST

of desert plants including teddy bear (or jumping) cholla, barrel and prickly pear. Numerous trails on this side of the park wind through the desert terrain. Keep your eyes open for young saguaros growing under a "nurse tree" (usually a palo verde or mesquite).

Another feature of the east district is the Rincon Mountain range. These sky islands are isolated and surrounded by a lowland climate that varies radically, with forest at the top and desert at the bottom. In fact, the east district encompasses five different biomes.

The east district has its own visitor center, and we suggest starting there. Take a look at the water feature out back and see if any animals stop by for a drink. Then, drive along Cactus Forest Drive in the foothills of the Rincons. There are many trails and overlooks along this one-way loop road. Desert Ecology Trail, for example, is paved and wheelchair-accessible. For something a little longer, the Loma Verde Loop is a solid choice.

Our favorite time to visit Saguaro National Park is in the spring, from mid-March through May. The weather is perfect at this time of year and the cactuses and wildflowers bring the desert to life. In May the saguaros will bloom, producing the lovely white blossom that is Arizona's official flower.

At a minimum, allow one full day for each section of the park. Always bring water and sunscreen, even in the winter or on a cool or cloudy day. And remember to bring a comb to remove cactus spines that may attach to you.

Explore Saguaro National Park and encounter a landscape teeming with life and the spirit of the Southwest.

*Saguaros steal the show in this Sonoran sunrise.*

# SOUTHWEST PHOTO GALLERY

1.

2.

### 1. TRANQUILITY
On a visit to Big Bend National Park in Texas, I took a hike to the river. About half a mile along the sun started to set. I turned around and this is the awesome view I was blessed to see. —HEATHER GROSJEAN

### 2. MORNING GIFT
There was a passing storm at Grand Canyon National Park and I was trying to photograph some lightning strikes off in the distance. But, as soon as the sun broke the horizon, a double rainbow appeared instead. —CHUCK ROBINSON

### 3. ANCIENT TREES
It is fascinating that these red colored blocks of stone at the Petrified Forest National Park in Arizona were once an enormous living tree in a lush forest. The tree was nearly 3 feet in diameter. —JOHN NUTILE

### 4. LAST LIGHT
My wife and I decided to hike around Yaki Point at the Grand Canyon so we'd be ready for the sunset. This tree and the sun captured the scene as well as the heat we felt that day, which topped out at 118 degrees. —BRAD KAVO

3.

4.

NATIONAL PARKS 107

## SOUTHWEST PHOTO GALLERY

### 1. CASCADING WONDER
Mooney Falls is the tallest of the three waterfalls in the Havasupai Indian Reservation near Grand Canyon National Park. I thought it would be interesting to get a picture from above, showcasing both the waterfall and the majestic drop into the canyon below. I included my feet in the photo to give some perspective.  — GRANT CLOUD

### 2. STRIKING
I'd been dreaming of going to the North Rim of the Grand Canyon for years, having been to the South Rim. I was hoping for beautiful clouds. The afternoon I arrived, the clouds came rolling in and to my surprise lightning flashed!  — TERRY WOOD

### 3. BEACON OF HOPE
I think this image looks like a lighthouse overlooking the Grand Canyon, perhaps leading people to safety and giving them hope. (This is the Desert View Watchtower.)  — KITTA DORY

### 4. BALANCED ROCK
It was amazing to see the rock formations and sit near this massive one called Balanced Rock at Big Bend National Park in Texas.
— SARA CRENWELGE

### 5. BLOOMING
The desert of Saguaro National Park comes alive after a wet winter. I drove through the park once a week during spring to see what was blooming next. Here, it's a prickly pear. — CAROLYN OWEN

1.

2.

3.

4.

5.

NATIONAL PARKS 109

SOUTHWEST

STORY BY
TIM FITZHARRIS

# BIG BEND

**THIS ECOLOGICAL CROSSROADS PACKS A PLETHORA OF NATURAL BEAUTY INTO A SINGLE NATIONAL PARK.**

**HERE IN THE 800,000-PLUS-ACRE** Big Bend National Park, the Chihuahuan Desert meets the Rio Grande. The U.S. meets Mexico. Northern species meet southern ones as the boundaries of many plant and animal ranges overlap, making this remote treasure as famously diverse biologically as it is geologically.

Each year I visit this place in the great south-dipping curve of the Rio Grande, where brittle desert gives way to badlands. The land undulates with jagged rocks, flat mesas and jutting plateaus, falling and rising until finally, at its heart, soaring more than 7,000 feet skyward into the Chisos Mountains. This is my destination. By squatting low among clumps of agave and filling the frame with rising rock formations, I capture some majestic desert photos.

Everywhere, subjects appear, from the sunbaked and cactus-studded Chihuahuan Desert to the Rio Grande winding a green ribbon between dark, narrow canyons. Inside the Chisos basin, a steep waterfall fools you into forgetting that you're deep inside an arid region. Mexico's mountains dominate the southern horizon.

Each season lends a distinct flavor to the terrain. A winter dusting of snow adds zing to the desert landscape. As spring rains arrive, wildflowers and cacti burst into bloom. Springtime also means bird migration, and Big Bend hosts more bird species than any national park in the country. By late summer, visitors are treated to afternoon thunderstorms, with lightning, rainbows and rolling cloud banks embellishing an already spectacular landscape. By autumn, the fiery colors of trees and shrubs ignite mountains and bottomlands.

Yes, deciduous trees grow alongside the southwestern pinyon pine and juniper, which—like many other northern and southern, eastern and western species—meet in this central region. Straddling subclimates, Big Bend might be the foremost place to experience the best of North, Central and South America combined.

SOUTHWEST

*Top: Looking out on an expansive view in the basin at Big Bend. Bottom: Black-tailed jack rabbits nibbling grass often venture close to campsites.*

### POINTS OF INTEREST

**NOT TO BE MISSED**

A must-see if you are up for a hike is the Lost Mine Trail.

Best views can be had at Santa Elena Canyon and the Chisos Mountains.

**FUN FACTS**

Big Bend Country is named for the great curve of the Rio Grande where it rounds the southern elbow of Texas.

The diverse habitats support 1,200 types of plants, around 450 bird species and varied wildlife, including mountain lions and javelinas.

**WORDS TO THE WISE**

You can't see everything in one day, but take the paved Ross Maxwell Scenic Drive for a sampling of what the park has to offer. Dirt roads crisscross the park, and gravel roads are open to horse riders.

When hiking, wear cool, rugged clothing for protection from prickly plants and take along at least 1 gallon of water per person per day.

NATIONAL PARKS 111

▼

*Years of wind and rain have eroded the massive limestone face of El Capitan.*

SOUTHWEST

STORY AND PHOTOS BY
**LAURENCE PARENT**

# GUADALUPE MOUNTAINS

UNCOVERING THE SECRETS OF THIS REMOTE RANGE REQUIRES STURDY BOOTS AND A LITTLE SWEAT.

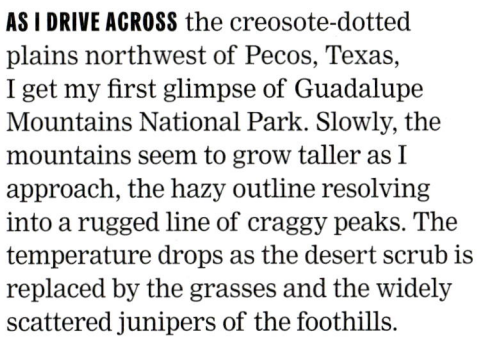

**AS I DRIVE ACROSS** the creosote-dotted plains northwest of Pecos, Texas, I get my first glimpse of Guadalupe Mountains National Park. Slowly, the mountains seem to grow taller as I approach, the hazy outline resolving into a rugged line of craggy peaks. The temperature drops as the desert scrub is replaced by the grasses and the widely scattered junipers of the foothills.

By the time I pull into the visitor center parking lot, the peaks tower almost 3,000 feet above me. The steep slopes and cliffs look quite harsh and unforgiving, although a few scattered pines, junipers and even red blotches of maples tucked into ravines high above give a small hint of what lies hidden here.

Guadalupe Mountains National Park is an isolated place with 86 miles of trails and three different ecosystems. The nearest town is 55 miles away, and gorgeous scenery abounds. The only thing missing is the crowds.

I set up my tent in the park campground and drive over to the historic Frijole Ranch house, where early settlers built their home at a spring that they used to water a fruit orchard and a vegetable garden. After studying the exhibits in the restored house, I begin the easy loop hike to Smith Spring. I quickly reach Manzanita Spring, where clear water fills a cattail-lined pond.

From Manzanita Spring, I follow the trail toward a canyon, where the mountains begin their abrupt rise into the high country above. I walk into a grove of ponderosa pines, alligator junipers and other trees. Thick trees harbor the hidden waters of Smith Spring. Bigtooth maple trees, their

## SOUTHWEST

*The last light of day illuminates ripples in the sand dunes.*

### POINTS OF INTEREST

**NOT TO BE MISSED**
Guadalupe Peak is also known as the "Top of Texas." A hike up the side is tough, but definitely rewarding. It's about an 8.5-mile round trip that may take you 6 to 8 hours. You'll encounter different ecosystems along the way, including high desert and high elevation forests.

**WORDS TO THE WISE**
The rough dirt road leading to Williams Ranch is the one place in the park where mountain biking is permitted.

**NEARBY ATTRACTIONS**
Hueco Tanks State Park and Historic Site; McDonald Observatory; Fort Davis National Historic Site

leaves aflame with gold, orange and scarlet, arch over the small stream that trickles through the woods.

The next morning I rise early and drive to the McKittrick Canyon trailhead. Although many call the canyon the "most beautiful spot in Texas," you might miss it because the canyon walls are mostly covered with hardy desert vegetation. The easy trail follows the canyon bottom upstream.

I crisscross the dry canyon bottom, its surface covered with rounded limestone cobbles. A few junipers and oaks appear as I move deeper into the canyon. At about 2 miles I pause at the stone house built by Wallace Pratt, the petroleum geologist who donated much of the canyon to the National Park Service. From there I walk up into South McKittrick Canyon, admiring the maple trees that grow thickly with other trees in the lush canyon bottom and dot the steep slopes above with bright colors. At the trail's end I relax in the shade and listen to a tumbling stream as the breeze blows colorful leaves off the maples. I now understand the canyon's reputation.

For my last day, I awake early and begin the long climb up the 8,749-foot Guadalupe Peak, the highest point in Texas. The steep yet excellent trail soon has me sweating and breathing hard. Three thousand vertical feet and 4.2 miles later, I collapse onto the craggy summit. Sheer cliffs line the west edge of the peak, dropping 5,000 vertical feet to the desolate Salt Flats below. West Texas and southern New Mexico sprawl out in every direction.

Looking at the horizon, I see limestone cliffs all around me. The white stone was created 250 million years ago when these mountains were a reef in a vast, ancient sea. To the north lies the mountain high country, a relict forest of ponderosa pine, Douglas fir, white pine and even a few aspens. None of this is visible from below. At Guadalupe Mountains National Park, I have to work to discover its secrets.

SOUTHWEST

*Hiker Heather Dobbins explores a slot canyon.*

SOUTHWEST THEN AND NOW

116  NATIONAL PARKS

THEN AND NOW **SOUTHWEST**

# GRAND CANYON NATIONAL PARK

### 1930s
The view from the steep cliff at Toroweap Overlook on the North Rim of the Grand Canyon is timeless, as seen in this vintage photo.

### 2015
Not much has changed with the spectacular scene overlooking the Colorado River, 3,000 feet below. It is still difficult to access, but visitors in both these photos know exactly what to do when they get there: take it all in at just the right spot.

THEN: EIVIND T. SCOYEN/
U.S. NATIONAL PARK SERVICE;
NOW: PIRIYA PHOTOGRAPHY/
GETTY IMAGES

NATIONAL PARKS 117

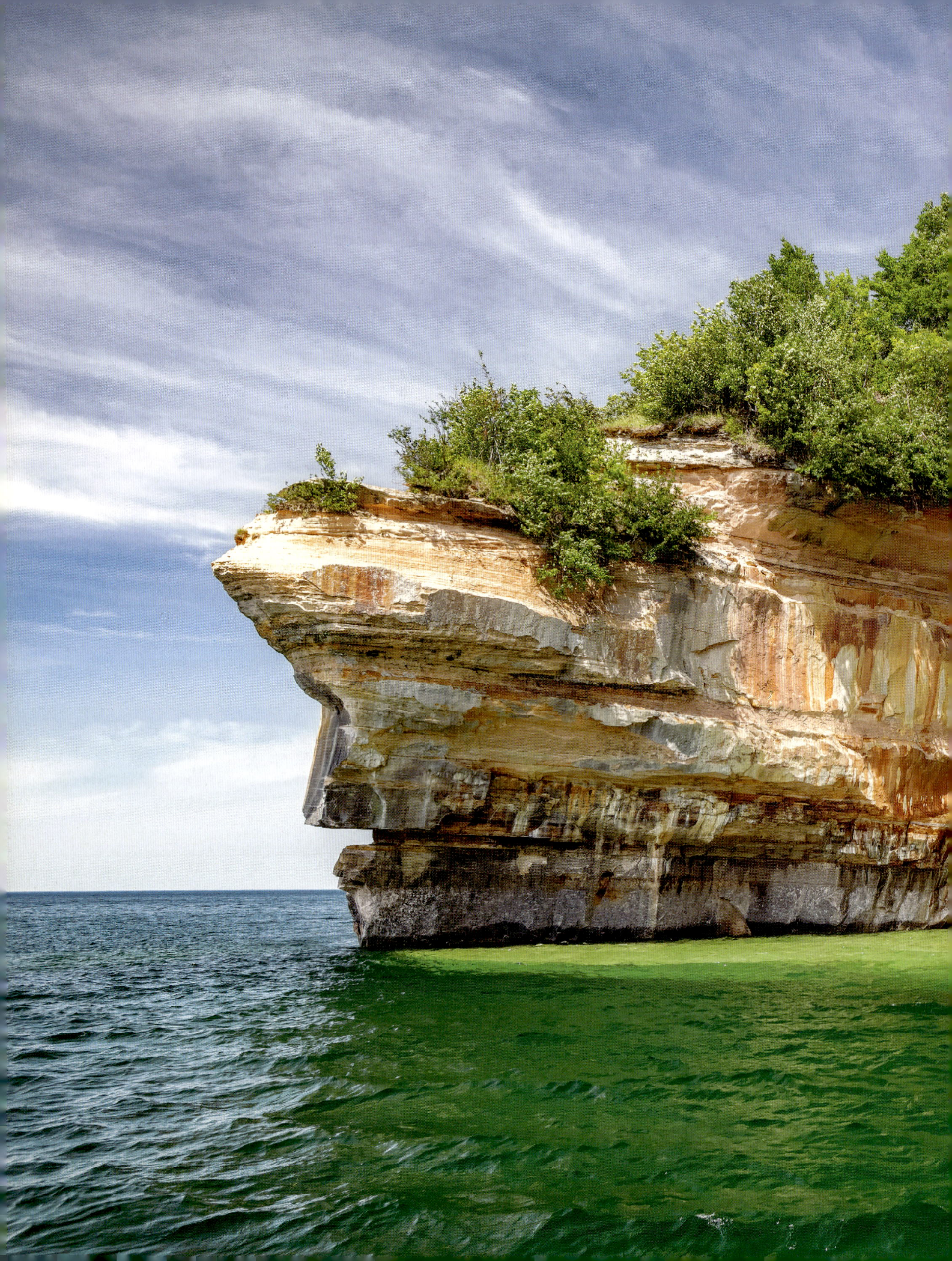

# MIDWEST

DUNES · LAKESHORES · PRAIRIES

▼
*The sand dune Mount Baldy stands 120 feet above the beach.*

MIDWEST

STORY BY
**MARSHA WILLIAMSON MOHR**

# INDIANA DUNES

CLEAR WATER, SANDY BEACHES AND ABUNDANT WILDLIFE CREATE AN OASIS ON THE SOUTHERN TIP OF LAKE MICHIGAN.

**THE WEEKEND AFTER** Labor Day, my husband, Larry, and I go to Indiana Dunes National Park to camp with friends. We set up tents about 4 miles from our favorite beach, so bringing bikes is a must.

With a day's supply of towels, coolers and toys, we pedal hard to the shore. Larry takes floating noodles, and one friend packs a bubble maker on their bike. It's a truly idyllic way to see and experience Indiana Dunes.

The park is an oasis with 15 miles of beaches surrounded by tall sand grass, and a lakeshore that is one of the most biologically diverse sites in the national park system. It has about 15,000 acres of natural terrain, with marshland and jack pine forest, hundreds of flower species, and many animals such as egrets, white-tailed deer, great blue herons and red fox, to name a few.

The Indiana Dunes lakeshore area is so beloved that it became a national park in 2019, as the latest step in an ongoing effort to save these pristine dunes that began in 1899, when industry and preservationists battled to control this shore. In 1966, the ecosystem won when the area was declared a national lakeshore.

Today, visitors climb to the top of the big sand dunes and then run back to the bottom. It's a tradition loved by children most of all. The clear waters invite a swim—one of my favorite things to do, especially at sunset.

Larry and I have hiked most of the 50 miles of trails. We love seeing the array of plant and animal life. Tamarack trees, floating mats of sphagnum moss, and blueberry bushes grow along the Pinhook Bog Trail System. Rare flowers like pink lady's slippers and yellow orchids

# MIDWEST

## POINTS OF INTEREST

**FUN FACT**
Indiana Dunes National Park has 352 species of birds—even more than Great Smoky Mountains National Park, which has 240.

**WORDS TO THE WISE**
Because of the hidden dangers of shifting sands that could be covered by snow in winter, sledding, inner-tubing, tobogganing, skiing and snowboarding are prohibited in the park.

**NOT TO BE MISSED**
You can experience Indiana Dunes by train! This park is part of a parternship the National Park Service has with Amtrak and the Texas A&M Department of Recreation, Park & Tourism Sciences. Passengers can experience the beauty of nature in a completely unique way, as volunteers lead the tour aboard the train and explain why certain sites along the route are meaningful.

*Visitors can hike up and down the dunes on boardwalk steps.*

dazzle hikers. (Sandy conditions on the trails require a bit more exertion, so bring plenty of water.)

The 4.7-mile Cowles Bog Trail winds through a pristine beach habitat, an 8,000-year-old fen (open wetland), a lowland forest of red maple, and a yellow birch and black oak savanna. This part of the park is named for Henry Cowles, whose plant studies led to its designation as a National Natural Landmark.

Birders flock to the Great Marsh Trail to spot coots, sandhill cranes and wood ducks. During migration, warblers, kingfishers, tree swallows and rusty blackbirds come to rest. Animal activity is a huge draw along the Great Marsh.

On our way back to camp we have to stop at a local gas station for soft-serve ice cream. It's the perfect, refreshing end to a day of exploration in one of Indiana's natural treasures.

122 NATIONAL PARKS

MIDWEST

*Indiana Dunes National Park offers stunning views of Lake Michigan*

*Kamloops Point was named for a ship that sank a couple of hundred yards away in 1927.*

MIDWEST

STORY AND PHOTOS BY
**CARL TERHAAR**

# ISLE ROYALE

FEW VENTURE OUT TO THESE ISOLATED ISLANDS, BUT THOSE WHO DO CAN'T WAIT TO RETURN.

**SURROUNDED BY WATER,** this unsung national park is truly a hidden gem. Those who make the trip to Isle Royale are drawn to the beauty of 337 miles of shoreline along Lake Superior and the peacefulness of one of the country's more isolated areas east of the Mississippi River.

Fewer visitors does not mean that Isle Royale and the 400 islands in its archipelago aren't beautiful or delightful. It only means this park is a little harder to get to than most. You can't drive there, and you'll find no roads after you arrive.

And once visitors fall for the park's unspoiled serenity, many come back time and time again. It's not unusual to hear conversations on the ferry boats about who can boast the most trips to the island.

After you disembark, the only way to travel through the archipelago is along hiking trails or waterways—on foot and in small boats—just as French fur trappers, known as voyageurs, explored the area hundreds of years ago.

Positioned about 15 miles off the shore of Canada, the 45-mile-long island is the largest in the "Big Lake." Setting off from Michigan or Minnesota adds a boat or seaplane ride to the adventure. Isle Royale National Park is served by ferries that depart from Grand Portage in Minnesota or Copper Harbor and Houghton in Michigan, and

NATIONAL PARKS **125**

# MIDWEST

*The waters of Tobin Harbor catch the sunrise.*

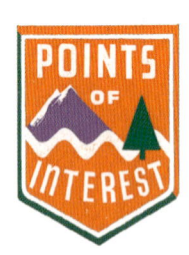

**FUN FACTS**

More than 600 flowering plants grow at Isle Royale National Park, including over 40 endangered or threatened species.

During the exceptionally cold winter of 1948-49, an ice bridge formed between Canada and Isle Royale, and a small pack of Eastern timber wolves crossed over to the island. Offshoots of the original pack became established there at one point. The wolves are important to maintaining a healthy moose population on the island by preying on the very old, sick or injured.

**WORDS TO THE WISE**

No pets are allowed on the island.

also by seaplane from the Houghton County airport.

This remoteness is one reason the average length of stay at Isle Royale is four days. After going through the effort to get there, you will definitely want to stay awhile to bask in the surroundings and the solitude.

Lake Superior not only contributes to the mystique and the sublime scenery with its rocky shorelines; it also has a major influence on the weather. Slow to warm up in the spring, it can cause a great deal of fog, especially in early summer. The water keeps the air cooler near the shore, while air in the higher ridges away from the lake can often be 20 degrees warmer.

The clear lake water provides excellent visibility for fishing for fresh trout or scuba diving to explore Lake Superior's many shipwrecks.

The size of the lake has also affected animal life on the island. Only half of the species on the mainland have been able to cross over. There are no bears, skunks or raccoons, and only two snake species.

With fewer ice bridges forming to the mainland in the last few decades, the possibility of new blood making its way to Isle Royale is slim.

Animal lovers who visit the island hoping to see wolves and moose might be rewarded with moose sightings. That population has increased. The wolf population has declined through the years. The National Park Service, however, is carefully reintroducing new wolves to sustain the ecosystem.

Many come to backpack the 165 miles of marked trails. Scattered throughout the park and along its inland lakes are 36 designated campgrounds, accessible by foot, canoe or kayak.

Kayakers and canoers also venture out onto Superior; some sites on Superior's shore have docks for sailboats or motorboats. Each year, a handful of expert paddlers take a week or two to circumnavigate the island, with a few extra days allotted in case of bad weather.

But most kayakers take shorter trips and stick to the more protected harbors in the island's long, narrow bays. The *Voyageur II* out of Grand Portage and a water taxi operated by the Rock Harbor Lodge can ferry you and your canoe or kayak to and from the campgrounds, trailheads and docks along their circuits around the island.

If you are looking for comfort and a soft bed, you can find them at Rock Harbor Lodge on the east end of the island. Rent a room, cottage or cabin. The lodge also operates a restaurant, stores that offer groceries and camping supplies, and a marina with gasoline and diesel fuel.

Rock Harbor is where you can get camping permits and rent canoes or small outboard boats to go exploring on your own. Guided tours on the MV *Sandy* offer a chance to see the historic Edisen Fishery and the Rock Harbor Lighthouse, the oldest on the island. Other cruises head off to Lookout Louise, with views of Ontario and Isle Royale's north side, or to Raspberry Island at sunset. You also can charter a fishing trip to catch salmon and trout.

Surrounded by the world's largest lake, feel the enormity of the universe and dance with the Northern Lights while you plan your return trip to the glorious Isle Royale.

*As Lake Superior's water level rises, daisies on Johnson Island get their feet wet.*

MIDWEST

STORY BY **MARY LIZ AUSTIN**
PHOTOS BY **TERRY DONNELLY**

# PICTURED ROCKS

MOTHER NATURE BLENDED HER MOST BREATHTAKING COLORS AND TEXTURES TO CREATE THIS NORTHERN MASTERPIECE.

**PICTURED ROCKS NATIONAL LAKESHORE** on Michigan's Upper Peninsula is one of our favorite autumn destinations. The northern forest's brilliantly colored leaves combine with the clear blue waters of Lake Superior to paint some spectacular fall scenes.

But when we stop for supplies, my husband and I can't help overhearing excited chatter about an impending snowstorm. The Yoopers, as locals are known, eagerly anticipate the prospect of early skiing, but Terry and I hope the snow won't end up burying our entire photography season.

The lakeshore is named for 200-foot bluffs colored by mineral-rich water seeping through layers of sandstone that have been sculpted into dramatic columns and caves by winds, waves and ice. With a backdrop of Superior's blue waters and autumn leaves, it's quite a show. The trail to Miner's Castle, the most famous formation, offers incredible views of the shoreline and lake.

But that's just the beginning. Two quaint towns anchor either end of the national lakeshore. On the western end, Munising boasts Munising Falls, a 50-foot ponytail waterfall in a beautiful sheltered canyon of yellow sandstone. On the eastern end, the town of Grand Marais offers easy access to Au Sable Point Lighthouse, Grand Sable Dunes and Sable Falls. And rolling, winding County Road H-58, which connects the two towns, ranks among the most scenic drives in America.

The overnight storm brings only a dusting of snow, so we get out early to see if we can capture some sunrise light, and it is cold. I'm shivering in my winter parka and every bit of wool I own when I notice several Yoopers hiking by. They're easily recognizable by the light nylon jackets they wear, as if it's a warm fall day. You have to be a hardy soul to live up here, but I guess that's part of what helps preserve the unspoiled beauty of this very special place.

MIDWEST

*Top: A gorgeous sunset decorates Miners Beach. Bottom: Chapel Rock, embraced by fall foliage.*

### POINTS OF INTEREST

#### FUN FACTS
The cliffs at Pictured Rocks draw many visitors, but they're not the only habitat worth exploring in the park. Inland lakes, bogs, marshes and pools are great places to see some of Pictured Rocks' 60 identified species of fish and amphibians.

Painted Rocks' Au Sable light station was built in 1874 as a way to keep boats afloat—and away from the jagged coast—during inclement weather. Originally called "Big Sable," the name was changed in 1910 to better reflect its proximity to Lake Superior; "Au Sable" means "of the sand" in French.

#### SIDE TRIP
A trip to upper Michigan wouldn't be complete without taking a trip to the Tahquamenon Falls State Park, a notable destination for both Michigan residents and tourists.

NATIONAL PARKS 129

▼
*Sunny beaches littered with Petoskey stones invite travelers to stop and relax.*

MIDWEST

STORY AND PHOTOS BY
**DARRYL BEERS**

# SLEEPING BEAR DUNES

THE WORLD'S LARGEST FRESHWATER DUNE SYSTEM SETS THE STAGE FOR THE CHARMING TOWNS AND STUNNING SCENERY ON MICHIGAN'S WEST COAST.

**I WAS ABOUT 10 YEARS OLD** when I joined my peers for a day of frolicking in the waves at an expansive beach on lower Michigan's western shore. I don't remember exactly where that beach was, but I vividly recall how much fun we had. I've been visiting that splendid shore as often as I can ever since.

The coastline's signature attraction is known as the singing sands, for the squeaky sound you'll hear as you walk across them. Visitors and locals alike delight in endless miles of swimming, beaches and over 300,000 acres of dunes—the largest freshwater dune system on the planet.

The most prominent of these dunes is found in Sleeping Bear Dunes National Lakeshore, on the northern tier of lower Michigan. The dunes there tower as high as 400 feet and are ideal for hiking, biking, climbing or sightseeing. Sleeping Bear Dunes is also home to lush forests, clear inland lakes and unique flora and fauna, all of which combine to make it the most beautiful place in all of America.

Do you doubt the authority of such a statement? Well, consider this: In 2011, Sleeping Bear Dunes won that exact title in a vote by almost 100,000 viewers of ABC's *Good Morning America*.

My favorite city on Michigan's western shore is Ludington, because it's fun to get there—via a four-hour cruise aboard a refurbished car ferry, SS *Badger*, which first set sail in 1953. From mid-May through late October, the ship carries passengers and vehicles between Ludington and Wisconsin. The focus for recreation in Ludington is Stearns Park Beach, which offers 2,500 feet of sandy shore.

My favorite drive in the area is Highway M-116 north out of Ludington. Though only about 6 miles long, the road hugs the shoreline with its sand beach on one side and stretches of dunes on the other.

The road ends at Ludington State Park, which by most accounts is Michigan's most popular. I've spent countless hours combing the beaches here and hiking to the historic Big

NATIONAL PARKS **131**

# MIDWEST

## POINTS OF INTEREST

*Lake Michigan meets Sleeping Bear Dunes National Lakeshore.*

**FUN FACT**
The name "Sleeping Bear" comes from a Native American story about the largest dune in the park, called Mother Bear; at that time, the dune looked like a bear at rest.

**WORDS TO THE WISE**
Bring a pair of shoes if you plan to hike on the dunes. While the sand might feel nice on your bare feet at first, the National Park Service warns the sand can be hot and abrasive.

**NEARBY ATTRACTIONS**
Cruise down the 7-mile Pierce Stocking Drive to soak up the scenery, especially at the Lake Michigan Overlook. At nearly 450 feet above the lake, the overlook offers breathtaking views of the Sleeping Bear dunes far away in the distance. And, for those who aren't keen on a long walk, the overlook is just a short hike from the parking lot.

Sable Point Lighthouse. At 112 feet, this light is one of the tallest in Michigan. From May through October, it's open to the public for the strenuous, but rewarding, climb to the top.

But there's much more to lower Michigan's west coast than singing sands and sparkling water. The city of Holland hosts its Tulip Time Festival each May, when millions of brilliant beauties bloom at once. I fondly recall childhood trips here, where I was dazzled by the display of colors and patterns in both the tulips and the Dutch costumes of the performers.

Two additional nods to Holland's heritage are Nelis' Dutch Village, which re-creates the Netherlands of the 1800s with 10 acres of authentic architecture, canals and gardens, and the city's DeZwaan Windmill. Built in the Netherlands in 1761, the remarkable historic mill was dismantled, then shipped here in pieces and carefully reassembled in 1964. It's the only authentic working Dutch windmill in the U.S. And it's still grinding flour, which is sold to tourists, bakers and numerous restaurateurs.

Not far from the site of all this Dutch influence, Michigan's west coast also boasts more than its share of elegant Victorian architecture. In the later 1800s, steamships brought a huge influx of visitors from Chicago. Seeking a summer refuge on this breezy shore, many built ornate second homes here. Scores of these 19th century houses survive, and many have been converted into cozy bed-and-breakfasts.

A bit to the south, many Chicago painters and sculptors were drawn to the communities of Saugatuck and Douglas. The art colony continues to thrive, with so many galleries and outdoor sculptures on display that the area proudly calls itself Michigan's "art coast."

# MIDWEST

During my first visit to these twin cities, I was fascinated to witness the *Saugatuck Chain Ferry* in action. Built in 1838 to haul horses across the Kalamazoo River, the boat—said to be the only hand-cranked ferry still running in the U.S.—is now a tourist attraction, carrying passengers and bicycles. The ferry is still run by a crank attached to a chain along the river bottom; it takes about 200 cranks and five minutes to cross the 100-yard-wide river.

Farther to the north, Traverse City, which is nestled at the base of Grand Traverse Bay, lays claim to being the world's cherry capital. Its weeklong National Cherry Festival, held every July, draws a crowd of about 500,000 with everything from pie to parades.

The city is also home to three tall ships: the schooners *Manitou* and *Madeline,* and the sloop *Welcome.* Through educational and recreational programs, these three working replicas of 19th century vessels submerge visitors in maritime history.

My favorite scenic drive here follows Highway M-37 north from Traverse City through Old Mission Peninsula, which last year made *USA Today's* list of the nation's most scenic coastal routes. The trip is especially grand in the spring, when both sides of the roadway are awash in a sea of beautiful cherry blossoms.

The same climate that makes cherry trees thrive here is also a good one for European grapes, so vineyards abound along the route. The 18-mile drive through the peninsula ends at Mission Point Lighthouse, a magnificent place to photograph.

Northeast of the peninsula, not far from the tip of lower Michigan, is the

*Historic DeZwaan Windmill is part of Holland's Dutch heritage.*

NATIONAL PARKS 133

MIDWEST

▼ *The South Manitou Island Lighthouse is a tricky climb, but the views are worth the effort.*

*Michigan's Leelanau Peninsula boasts brilliant cherry blossoms.*

fisherman's paradise of Walloon Lake, where the young Ernest Hemingway spent many summers at his family's cottage. Devoted readers can follow in the writer's footsteps on a self-guided "Hemingway tour" of the area.

Accolades for Michigan's west coast would be incomplete without bringing up three islands off the northern shore. North and South Manitou islands are part of the Sleeping Bear lakeshore and are accessible by ferry service from Leland, a historic fishing community. They have no permanent residents, and no vehicles are allowed—but hiking, backpacking, picnicking and rustic camping are permitted.

I cherish the memory of the two peaceful nights I spent camping on South Manitou. I was planning to get to bed early so I could photograph the island's lighthouse at dawn, but I was utterly unable to resist one of the most incredible nights of stargazing one could imagine. A good night's sleep had to wait.

Then there's the very different but also inviting Beaver Island, Lake Michigan's largest island, with a cozy year-round population of about 650 that swells to some 3,500 on summer weekends. A ferry running out of Charlevoix takes people and cars to and from the island. The isle has a history of Mormon settlement and an influx of Irish fishermen.

There are many great attractions at Sleeping Bear, but it's those beautiful beaches that keep luring me back to this special part of Michigan. I have no doubt that anyone who, on a warm summer evening, strolls barefoot on the sand and basks in the glowing light of a Lake Michigan sunset will realize they're standing in God's Country.

MIDWEST PHOTO GALLERY

1.

2.

**1. SPECTACULAR SUNSETS**
One of our favorite parks in northern Michigan is Sleeping Bear Dunes National Lakeshore. From stop 9, you can look over Lake Michigan—and you might be able to spot one of the many Great Lakes freighters. —JERRY STUTZMAN

**2. NEVER THE SAME TWICE**
Theodore Roosevelt National Park is in my home state. I try to go there at least once a year, and sometimes I am lucky enough to go there more often. —KATHERINE PLESSNER

**3. PEACEFUL GRAZING**
I saw this pronghorn in Theodore Roosevelt National Park. They're the fastest land animal in North America, but this one paused for a moment on the grass. —LISA DOUGLASS

**4. MICHIGAN'S GLORY**
This is one of my favorite views in Sleeping Bear Dunes. Lake Michigan in all her glory—with colors that rival the Caribbean—along with the dunes and perfect blue sky make this the epitome of a Michigan summer "up north." —RENEE TOWNSEND

3.

136 NATIONAL PARKS

4.

NATIONAL PARKS 137

1.

## PHOTO GALLERY MIDWEST

### 1. BEYOND BEAUTIFUL
Pictured Rocks has gorgeous cliffs with a beautiful forest. You can go hiking, kayaking, snowshoeing and cross-country skiing. – **DIANE CUNNINGHAM**

### 2. DON'T MISS IT
We visited Theodore Roosevelt National Park in July. Someone told us to go to the Painted Canyon to see the sunset. Wow—so beautiful!
– **KIRSTEN BUSSE**

### 3. UNEXPECTED COLOR
I always envisioned the Badlands to be a vast monochromatic terrain—a dry and dim scene. Boy, was I ever wrong! We discovered sunbathing bison, bluebird skies, and lush greenery hugging the base of these incredible rock formations.
– **AMY MUIR**

### 4. SUPER CUTE
This photo of a prairie dog was taken in Badlands National Park. Trying to catch this picture was quite a feat! They appear cuddly, but I know they have quite the temper. – **MARY HENDERSON**

NATIONAL PARKS 139

# MIDWEST PHOTO GALLERY

**1. STARRY-EYED**
This is a self-portrait taken on the beaches of the Sleeping Bear Dunes in Michigan. After I hit the shutter to start this 25-second exposure, I ran into the frame, froze in place and pointed my flash light to the core of the Milky Way. —JOHN BERRY

**2. PRETTY COLORS**
I snapped this photo on an evening cruise of the Apostle Islands National Lakeshore. I loved how the late-day sun made the rocks light up with a soft, warm glow. —ADAM SMITH

**3. WHAT ON EARTH?**
Where am I? Am I walking on the moon? I didn't know what to expect as to the lay of the land at Badlands National Park, but I was certainly surprised. —WALT MATHER

**4. UNTAMED BEAUTY**
During this difficult season of COVID-19, Theodore Roosevelt National Park was empty and the wild horses abounded. —SABINA ROBBINS

**5. RETURN TRIP**
Pictured Rocks National Lakeshore is relatively close to me, yet I hadn't visited for decades. So last fall my wife and I spent a week re-exploring the area. Even though the upper observation deck was crowded, I waited for my opportunity to set up and capture this image. —DAVID HEILMAN

1.

2.

140 NATIONAL PARKS

3.

4.

5.

NATIONAL PARKS 141

▼

*A herd of bison graze near Scoria Point.*

MIDWEST

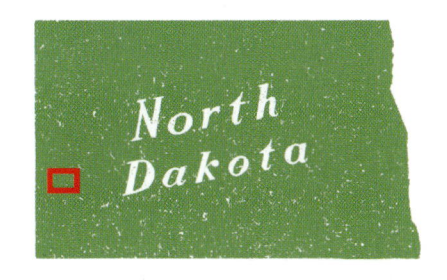

STORY AND PHOTOS BY
**TIM FITZHARRIS**

# THEODORE ROOSEVELT

THIS LAND OF "VAST, SILENT SPACES" INSPIRED AMERICA'S
BULL MOOSE TO BEGIN SAVING WILDERNESS TREASURES.

**LOST IN THE VAST** Great Plains in western North Dakota, Theodore Roosevelt National Park encompasses 70,467 acres of protected prairie wilderness. Here deer and antelope play, delighting wildlife photographers like me.

Described by its namesake as "a land of vast, silent spaces," the park extends a modest welcome to visitors at first, with an undulating expanse of green.

But look closer: This serene land is gouged by a mysterious badland architecture of jumbled gullies, valleys, buttes, pinnacles and spires painted with a truly remarkable color palette.

The Little Missouri River links the two main sections of the park. Its waters support trees and shrubs that make this expanse of pristine wilderness a hot spot for viewing wildlife.

Teddy Roosevelt traveled to Dakota Territory from New York to hunt bison in 1883, but he found that their once-great numbers had dwindled quite alarmingly. As he spent more time in the region, he grew more concerned about the damage to the land and the loss of wildlife.

His observations from that trip shaped a conservation policy that benefits America to this very day.

Theodore Roosevelt National Park is the largest protected mixed-grass prairie ecosystem in the U.S. It is home to bison, wild horses, elk, bighorn sheep, white-tailed and mule deer, prairie dogs and nearly 200 species of birds, including golden eagles, sharp-tailed grouse and wild turkeys.

Wildlife photography is challenging if you are intent on capturing a shot of a special bird or drawing close to the wary pronghorn or wild horses. But the bison, elk and deer are accustomed to people, and I shoot them at my leisure right out the side door of my motor home. I can grab close-ups of wildflowers, cacti and small critters like chipmunks and prairie dogs by hiking numerous trails.

Both sections of the park also offer scenic drives that allow for easy wildlife observation and panoramic views up and down the Missouri River valley.

In May and June, a trio of attractions lures me here with my camera—lush prairies dotted with wildflowers; frisky

# MIDWEST

### POINTS OF INTEREST

**NOT TO BE MISSED**
Make sure to stop by Elkhorn Ranch Site. Theodore Roosevelt once considered it his home ranch. Now, only the foundations are still standing.

If you're a birder, you'll want to take a trip to the park during spring or fall migration. According to NPS, more than 186 species of birds, including sandhill cranes and warblers, either live in the park year-round or pass through on their yearly journeys.

**FUN FACT**
While in Mingusville, 35 miles west of Medora, Theodore Roosevelt once got into a bar fight! He didn't start it, of course, but he certainly finished it.

**NEARBY ATTRACTIONS**
Stop by the North Dakota Cowboy Hall of Fame in Medora to learn more about the state's rich western heritage; the 15,000-square-foot space hosts traveling and permanent exhibits. And there's a gift shop, too.

*This sanctuary shelters many species of wildlife, like pronghorns.*

newborn bison, pronghorns and prairie dogs; and thunderstorms that light up the sky.

July marks the beginning of the bison rut, when gigantic bulls bellow, plow up the prairie with horns and hooves, and battle one another in dust-raising head-to-head battles.

September offers the nicest weather, with fair skies and mild temperatures that provide relief from the sweltering humidity of August.

While the scenery and wildlife bring in plenty of photographers, the park's well-preserved attractions, including Roosevelt's original ranch cabin and several Civilian Conservation Corps projects—a legacy of the other President Roosevelt, FDR—appeal to history buffs.

In and around the restored frontier town of Medora, museums, displays, live theater and historic sites provide insight into the challenges of settling this wild country.

Tales of legendary personalities like the Marquis de Mores, a French entrepreneur who named Medora after his wife, make the past come alive.

Medora offers plenty of shopping, restaurants and lodging, but I prefer to remain in the park's campgrounds, surrounded by nature, keeping my camera handy so I can capture each breathtaking detail of the High Plains.

MIDWEST

*Wind Canyon on the Little Missouri River.*

MIDWEST

STORY AND PHOTOS BY
**GREG LATZA**

# BADLANDS

MIGHTY ROCK FORMATIONS ATTRACT EVERYONE FROM FAMILY VACATIONERS TO STORM CHASERS.

**MY FAMILY OFTEN CHOSE** South Dakota's Black Hills for summer vacations and our excursions were never complete without a cruise along the 40 miles of Highway 240, commonly known as the Badlands Loop Road, which meanders through Badlands National Park.

Since the late Cretaceous Period, multiple layers of seafloor mud, river bottom sediment, tropical swampland and volcanic ash compressed upon each other and created formations of sedimentary rock. The Cheyenne River watershed drained this very erodible area and formed the rough, dried-mud terrain and jagged valleys that are the Badlands' signature.

I loved the drive, but most of our time there was in afternoon, along with thousands of other tourists. It wasn't until a few years later that I understood the true mystique of the Badlands occurs at the beginning and end of the day—times when the landscape comes alive with color.

Warm-colored sunlight, mixed with the various striations of colored earth, creates a palette of hues. In spring, the formations are dressed with emerald grasses that contrast against the warm earth tones. In fall, the dying grasses amplify the same warm tones and create a rich burst of yellows, oranges and reds. Set against a blue sky, the color contrasts can be almost startling.

My favorite addition is a prairie thunderstorm. Nothing adds more drama than thunderheads rolling across the horizon. Getting in position for a fast-moving storm front is more a matter of luck than planning. But, oh, what rewarding photos might occur—lightning strikes, rainbows and retreating cloud banks painted pink and orange by the sunset are just a few of the side benefits of Badlands thunderstorms.

My advice to Badlands newcomers? Try being there for the first or last hour of daylight, and avoid the flat midday sunlight. And if you see dark colors on the radar headed that way? Step on it!

MIDWEST

*Early morning sunlight casts the Badlands in warm, colorful hues.*

### POINTS OF INTEREST

**NOT TO BE MISSED**
Make sure to check out the Ben Reifel Visitor Center at the park's eastern end. The center offers museum exhibits where visitors can discover more about the park's history, as well as a fossil preparation lab and a 25-minute film about the park.

**FUN FACT**
The name "Badlands" honors the Lakota people, who lived on the land and referred to it as *mako sica*, which means "bad lands." When you imagine having to travel over the jagged cliffs and vast, waterless prairies by foot or in a wagon, it's not hard to imagine why early settlers would've thought the name was fitting.

**WORDS TO THE WISE**
Rattlesnakes call the Badlands home, but they're usually hiding during the day. To make sure you don't disturb them, don't stick your hands or feet in shady places or areas with limited or obscured visibility.

MIDWEST

STORY AND PHOTOS BY
**CHUCK HANEY**

# APOSTLE ISLANDS

EXPLORE A WORLD OF MAGICAL SEA CAVES, OLD LIGHTHOUSES AND MARITIME TREASURES TUCKED INTO LAKE SUPERIOR.

**PADDLING A SEA KAYAK** through Lake Superior to the islands at Wisconsin's northern tip had been on my bucket list for a long time. So I was excited about getting to spend the majority of a week getting to, camping on and exploring the wilds of the Apostle Islands National Lakeshore.

Eighteen of the park's 21 islands boast campgrounds. The chain also appeals to lighthouse lovers, with eight historic towers on six islands. But the highlight was the chance to paddle through the chain's fascinating series of sea caves, formed by wave after wave crashing into the islands' sandstone cliffs and carving out hollows barely big enough for a person to navigate a narrow kayak.

Our Devils Island campground was up on a bluff at the southern end of the island. A mile-long forest trail bristling with ripe blueberries led to an old lighthouse on the northern end. An older couple manned the structure in summer; it was delightful to visit and hear their stories and share a cup of coffee.

Winds mean everything here, and they're very unpredictable. One day I discovered that fierce winds kicking up whitecaps off the southern end of the island were totally blocked by the island itself. I rushed back to camp to tell my companions, and we were soon paddling calm waters on the island's leeward side, exploring the nooks and crannies of the handsomely eroded sandstone caves.

The best place to start exploring the Apostles is the charming town of Bayfield, with its many lodging choices and restaurants serving fresh local whitefish. Book a Lake Superior boat tour from here. I'm so glad I finally got to know Devils, Manitou, Sand and York islands—but there are many more lighthouses, magical caves and secluded sandy shores left for me to explore.

MIDWEST

*Top: Wave-carved sea caves in the sandstone cliffs of Devils Island. Bottom: A kayaker enjoys a quiet Lake Superior sunset.*

## POINTS OF INTEREST

### NOT TO BE MISSED
Apostle Islands offers cruises that allow visitors to marvel at the beauty of the islands, the cliffs and the lighthouses from the water. The most popular cruise, according to NPS, is the Grand Tour, which takes visitors on a 55-mile journey through the heart of the archipelago.

### FUN FACT
In the 1950s and '60s, the Apostle Islands were designated as one of the biggest migratory flyways in the Great Lakes region. Plenty of birds make their homes there, whether temporarily or on a permanent basis. One such bird is the endangered piping plover—just one of the shorebirds that can be found living around the islands.

### WORDS TO THE WISE
If you're planning a trip to the islands specifically to visit the ice caves, be advised that a 2-mile round-trip hike on the ice of Lake Superior is required. In addition, the caves might not be open every year; park staff monitors them for safety.

NATIONAL PARKS 149

MIDWEST THEN AND NOW

150  NATIONAL PARKS

THEN AND NOW **MIDWEST**

# BADLANDS NATIONAL PARK

### 1936
Visitors enjoy traveling down the Badlands' winding road near the park's east entrance and taking in the scenery.

### 2016
Today, visitors still find joy in driving down the park's scenic routes—like Loop Road, pictured here. The road offers 12 scenic outlooks and plenty of chances to spot park wildlife.

THEN: GEORGE A. GRANT/U.S. NATIONAL PARK SERVICE; NOW: PETER UNGER/GETTY IMAGES

NATIONAL PARKS 151

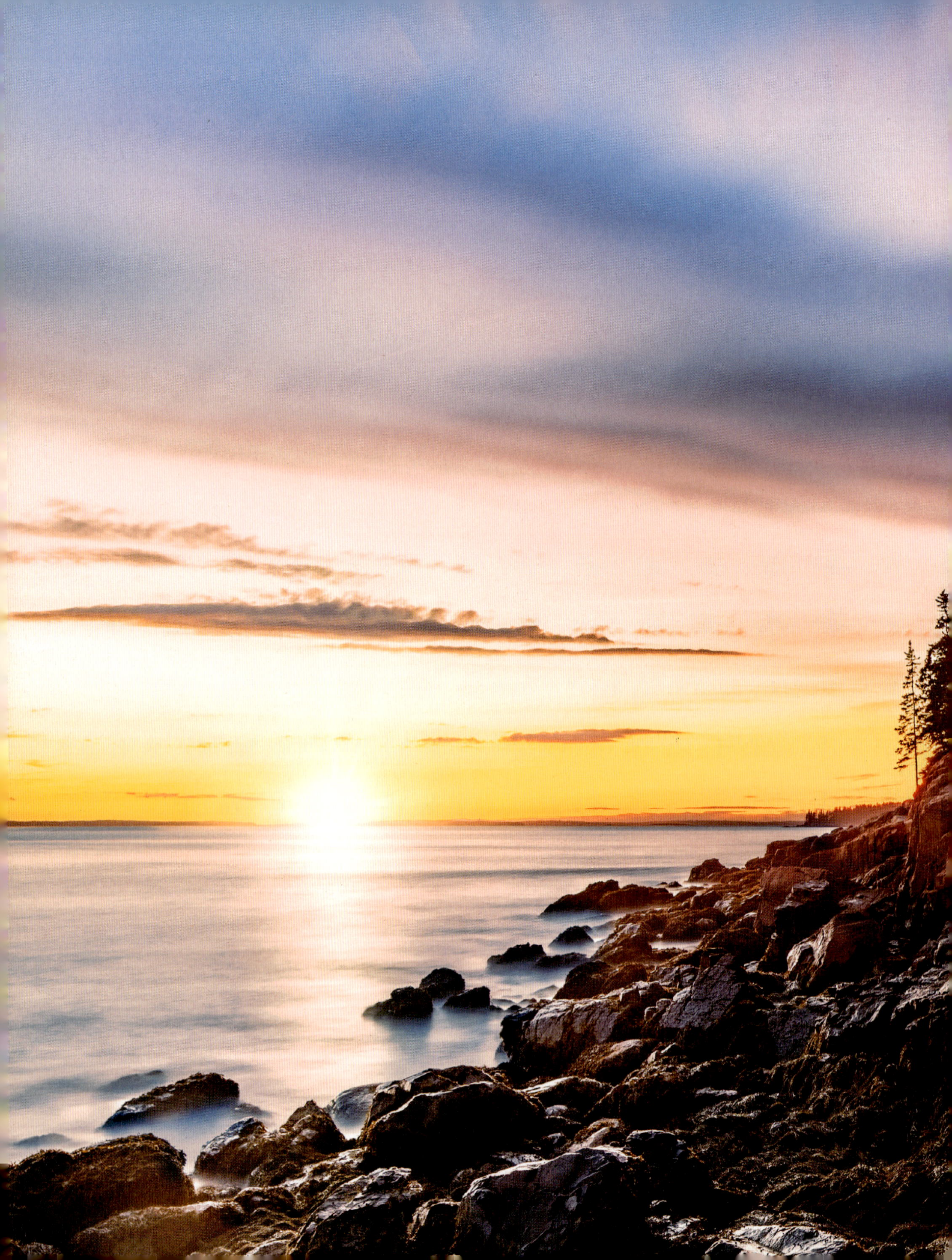

# EAST

SEASHORES · CAVES · FORESTS

*Early morning at Eagle Lake.*

EAST

STORY BY **PAULETTE M. ROY**
PHOTOS BY **PAUL REZENDES**

# ACADIA

FROM ROCKY COASTS TO MAGICAL FORESTS, YOU WILL CATCH YOUR BREATH AT EVERY TURN.

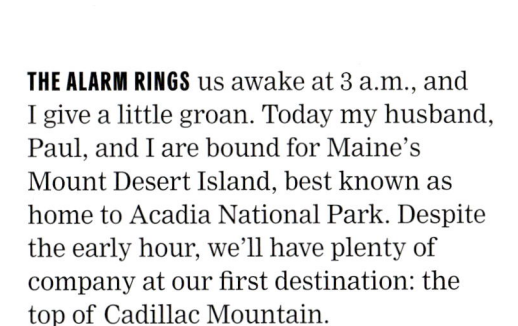

**THE ALARM RINGS** us awake at 3 a.m., and I give a little groan. Today my husband, Paul, and I are bound for Maine's Mount Desert Island, best known as home to Acadia National Park. Despite the early hour, we'll have plenty of company at our first destination: the top of Cadillac Mountain.

At 1,530 feet, this time-worn granite dome is the highest point along the North Atlantic seaboard, and from October through March it's the first place in the U.S. touched by the sun's morning rays. According to today's weather forecast, which calls for lowland fog and partly cloudy skies, we have the perfect conditions for a dramatic summer sunrise. Soon, despite the early hour, we're raring to go.

After a spectacular sunrise shoot, we pull onto Park Loop Road, which offers 27 miles of stunning scenery. But we drink in only part of it, making a detour for a 2-mile hike down Ocean Path, which skirts the rocky coastline. Between the trail and the waterline, a sprinkling of stepping-stone boulders offers a more adventurous route. The path ends atop 110-foot Otter Cliffs, one of the highest headlands along the eastern coast.

West and inland, the Jordan Pond House Restaurant is a tradition, not just for its famous popovers but for its scenic view overlooking the pond. We intend to stop and take a break from photography. But with the North and South Bubble Mountains casting reflections across the water, we can't resist taking a few more photos. Then, all too soon, it's time to move along.

We haven't planned our afternoon itinerary in advance, and now we pause. If this were autumn, there would be no shortage of inland waters hugged by foliage—scenes that simply take your breath away as the million hues of summer greens burnish into autumn's vivid golds, russets and reds. Our personal favorites are Duck Brook Bridge and New Mills Meadow Pond.

Asticou Azalea Gardens offers the same spectacular show, but we prefer to stroll its winding paths in spring, when we can gaze at endless shades of pink, orange and red blooms reflected in the placid pond as birds serenade us

NATIONAL PARKS 155

EAST

## POINTS OF INTEREST

**FUN FACTS**
There's no shortage of ways to appreciate nature in Acadia. This park—one of the top 10 most-visited in America—boasts 27 miles of historic motor roads and 158 miles of hiking trails.

If you're determined to spot wildlife on your visit, check out the "Tour de Wildlife" page on Acadia's website. There you'll find which trails not to miss.

**WORDS TO THE WISE**
You can bring your pet to Acadia! Plenty of hiking trails (more than 100 miles) allow pets on a leash no longer than 6 feet.

**SIDE TRIP**
Visit Maine Coastal Islands National Wildlife Refuge for more opportunities to hike shorter trails and bird-watch.

**NEARBY ATTRACTIONS**
Several museums are located in the area around Acadia, including the Mount Desert Oceanarium and the Great Harbor Maritime Museum.

*One of six carriage road bridges.*

with their sunny songs. More than 80 avian species call the gardens and its surrounding area home.

Today being a warm summer day, however, we turn south for a drive along Northeast Harbor. With his Portuguese sailor's blood, Paul can't help pausing to check out the sailboats before we head back north. Sargent Drive follows the shore of Somes Sound, a narrow, 7-mile body of water that nearly bisects the island.

Route 102 circles the western peninsula of the island, known as the "quiet side," an easygoing escape from the busier parts of the islands, like Bar Harbor. You won't find the typical tourist amenities here, but you also won't find traffic, overpriced food or crowded hiking trails. Instead, fishing villages, farmland, peaceful coves, picturesque harbors and scenic roads fill the landscape.

We reach the north end of the Sound at Somesville, the oldest settlement on the island. We pause to photograph the famous white wooden walking bridge and colorful flower boxes. Down and around to Southwest Harbor, we detour onto the shore-hugging southern Route 102A loop. Mansett treats us to fields of lupines arrayed before an Atlantic Ocean backdrop.

Further south, we pass Wonderland, a magical forest where silvery moss drips from spruce boughs as the path leads you through a long and shady corridor before opening to a dazzling view from the coast. In autumn, the forest's huckleberry bushes blaze a fiery red. Next up is Bass Harbor, shared by the charming fishing villages of Bass Harbor and Bernard, and the historic Bass Harbor Head Lighthouse perched atop its rocky cliff.

After all this, we hurry back to Cadillac Mountain to grab a sunset from a different vantage point. Satisfied but exhausted, I sigh. Another 3 a.m. wake-up will come much too soon. But as I watch the sun disappear, I think it can't come soon enough.

EAST

*Bar Harbor and Porcupine Islands, as seen from Cadillac Mountain.*

*Bearfence Mountain on the Appalachian Trail.*

EAST

STORY AND PHOTOS BY
**PAT & CHUCK BLACKLEY**

# SHENANDOAH

PICTURESQUE FARMS, MISTY MOUNTAINS AND HISTORIC SITES AWAIT IN VIRGINIA'S LEGENDARY VALLEY.

**WE WERE BORN AND RAISED** in Virginia's beautiful Shenandoah Valley, and we consider ourselves blessed to live here.

According to legend, the name Shenandoah derives from a Native American word that means "clear-eyed daughter of the stars." With its gentle mountains, rushing waters and green meadows, the spot fits its name well.

Nestled between the Blue Ridge and Allegheny mountains, the valley lies in the Shenandoah River watershed. Isolated from the rest of the Virginia colony by the Blue Ridge Mountains, the valley remained largely unsettled by Europeans until the early 1700s, when farmers of German and Scots-Irish descent began making their way from Pennsylvania in search of land suitable for farming. English settlers from the coastal Tidewater region followed in the mid-1700s.

These early settlers discovered fertile soil, a moderate climate, and abundant rainfall, wildlife and natural resources. Their farms yielded bountiful crops of grains and vegetables; their orchards produced bushels of peaches and apples. Sheep and cattle fattened in lush green pastures.

Today, many valley residents earn their living on family farms established by those who came before, growing the same crops and raising the same livestock. Agriculture is an important part of the regional economy: Four of Virginia's top five agricultural counties are in the Shenandoah Valley, and numerous small farms grow vegetables and fruits to sell at farmers markets. In season, especially in Mennonite country, roadside stands sell melons, corn, strawberries and other produce.

The region is also one of the nation's largest exporters of apples. When the orchards bloom in spring, it's a truly awesome sight. Known as Virginia's apple capital, the city of Winchester celebrates its agricultural heritage every April and May by hosting the Shenandoah Apple Blossom Festival, an immensely popular weeklong event that draws thousands. This family-friendly fair features music, dancing, an arts and crafts show, parades and a carnival.

In addition to agriculture, the valley brims with history. There are plenty of museums and other sites to explore. One favorite is Winchester's Museum of the Shenandoah Valley, which features a multitude of interesting exhibits that tell stories of the valley and its residents. Another is Staunton's Frontier Culture Museum, which features a complex of original and reproduction 17th and 18th century farmsteads from England,

NATIONAL PARKS 159

EAST

### POINTS OF INTEREST

**FUN FACT**
Shenandoah National Park blooms with abundant flora and wildlife. Skyline Drive runs through the park for 105 miles, with numerous overlooks along the way.

**SIDE TRIP**
Natural Bridge State Park is home to a 215-foot limestone arch that once was owned by Thomas Jefferson. The 1,500-acre state park is also a National Historic Landmark.

**NEARBY ATTRACTIONS**
The Museum of the Shenandoah Valley in Winchester has many exhibit-filled galleries. On the grounds is the Glen Burnie House, built in 1794 by Winchester's founder, James Wood. Six acres of gardens surround the house.

Luray Caverns are the largest caverns in the eastern United States. Visitors follow lighted, paved paths through cathedral-sized spaces, which rise 10 stories high, to see massive stone formations.

*The Baylor Mill in Swoope.*

Ireland, Germany and West Africa. The West African farmstead is based on an Igbo household in land that is now Nigeria, home of some 40 percent of enslaved people brought to Virginia. Here, visitors will learn about their origins, customs and contributions to American culture.

Of course, the best way to get to know and appreciate the beauty, history and friendly people of the valley is to travel its roads and visit with folks. There are many scenic drives that take it all in, especially in the spring.

Skyline Drive, in Shenandoah National Park, is one of them. Its 105-mile route offers a bird's-eye view of the valley from the park's overlooks. There, visitors can enjoy springtime blooming flora and watch for fawns and black bear cubs.

We love looking for wildflowers along the park's 500-plus miles of hiking trails, including a 100-mile section of the famous Appalachian Trail. These trails also lead to the park's stunning waterfalls, which are at their best in the spring.

At Waynesboro, Skyline Drive ends, but the road continues as the Blue Ridge Parkway, winding 469 miles through the Blue Ridge Mountains all the way to the Great Smoky Mountains National Park in North Carolina.

The area west of the little town of Dayton is home to a Mennonite community. We love driving the back roads and admiring the tranquil beauty of this area, with its tidy farms and pretty white houses, handsome barns, silos and grazing cattle. We always welcome and return waves and smiles from the occupants of the horse-drawn buggies we pass.

Another fantastic drive is U.S. Route 11, which takes you through the valley's past and present. This road—the main highway through the valley before construction began on Interstate 81 in the late 1950s—has a long, storied history. Once a Native American trail, it became the Great Wagon Road, used by early settlers making their way to the western frontier. Now known as the

Valley Pike here in Shenandoah, the road opened up travel and commerce, and was a key transportation route for both the northern and southern armies during the Civil War.

Connecting the towns of Winchester, Harrisonburg, Staunton and Lexington, Route 11 passes through charming villages and gorgeous countryside with idyllic farms and grazing livestock.

Like Skyline Drive, Route 11 is scenic in the spring, with lambs and calves frolicking in intensely green pastures; farmers on tractors plowing up rows of rich, dark soil; and blooming dogwood, redbud and fruit trees painting the hillsides, with those blue mountains standing as a backdrop. The air is filled with the smells of mown hay and turned soil. During this time, puffy clouds float from the west in a magical, turquoise blue sky.

This drive is like a trip back in time, passing by old stagecoach stops, taverns, mills and covered bridges and Civil War battlefields and museums. Of special interest is the Virginia Museum of the Civil War in New Market.

On May 15, 1864, New Market saw the arrival of 257 cadets from Virginia Military Institute—the youngest of whom was just 15. Having marched 85 miles from their school in Lexington, they joined the forces of Gen. John Breckinridge. Ten of them died and 45 were wounded, including Chuck's great-great-uncle.

Each year, people come from all over the country to take part in the New Market battle reenactment. Held on the weekend closest to the battle's anniversary, the event is the longest

*Virginia's Dark Hollow Falls are a short 1.4-mile round-trip hike off Skyline Drive near Big Meadows.*

EAST

▼
*Lush pastures make for a tasty dinner near Middlebrook.*

*Autumn's sunrise glows bright at Shenandoah National Park.*

continual reenactment in the United States that is still held on the field where the battle was fought.

In Rockbridge County at the southern end of the valley, Route 11 crosses over the Natural Bridge of Virginia. This National Historic Landmark in a state park is a 215-foot mammoth limestone arch that once belonged to Thomas Jefferson, and George Washington claimed to have surveyed it when he was a young man.

The valley's cities and towns feature lovingly restored structures from the 18th, 19th and early 20th centuries and numerous historic sites. In Winchester, visit both a log cabin that briefly served as an office for George Washington, and the house Stonewall Jackson used as his headquarters.

About 95 miles south is the small city of Staunton, birthplace of President Woodrow Wilson and the location of his Presidential Library and Museum. Lexington, further along Route 11, is a historic college town with many Civil War sites. Everywhere you go in the valley, there's a history lesson waiting to be learned.

Perhaps our beautiful valley's greatest assets, however, are its residents. They are incredibly warm, friendly, kind and generous, as well as hardworking, industrious and always eager to help a neighbor or a stranger in need. When out photographing one day, Chuck got his Jeep stuck in a ditch. A passing farmer stopped and, after assessing the situation, told him he'd be back in a jiffy.

He went down to his farm and returned shortly with a winch that he used to pull the Jeep out. Chuck thanked him, and the gentleman just told him he was glad to help. That's typical in these parts.

For those of us who call it home, the Shenandoah Valley is truly God's country. From its gentle, misty blue mountains, picturesque farms and lively towns to its exciting history and wonderful people, it's a little slice of heaven, and there's no place we'd rather be.

EAST

STORY BY
**DANA MEREDITH**

# CONGAREE

**EXPLORE HISTORY AND NATURE IN A PARK THAT HAS SUPPORTED LIFE FOR 13,000 YEARS.**

**GAZE SKYWARD** through towering bald cypress, loblolly pines and tupelo trees in the middle of the largest and tallest old-growth bottomland hardwood forest east of the Mississippi. The cacophony of buzzing insects, croaking frogs and hooting owls is joined by the rustling of turkeys, deer and wild boar in the brush. The amazing biodiversity of Congaree National Park reveals itself in nearly 27,000 acres of flood plain 20 minutes east of Columbia.

This free park is not a swamp, but the nearby Congaree and Wateree rivers flood around 10 times annually, leaving behind nutrients that refresh this eerie ecosystem. Check the Harry Hampton Visitor Center for trail maps and current conditions.

Hike the easy 2.4-mile Boardwalk Loop Trail through the forest, or take the Weston Lake Loop Trail around the lake. Explore the Cedar Creek Canoe Trail in your canoe, or paddle the 50-mile Congaree River Blue Trail from Columbia to the park.

From mid-May to mid-June, Congaree hosts one of only three species of synchronous flashing fireflies in North America. Check with the park for dates and times of the annual Fireflies Festival.

EAST

*Bald cypress trees reach for the sky along Boardwalk Loop Trail.*

## POINTS OF INTEREST

### NOT TO BE MISSED

If you enjoy canoeing or kayaking, you'll want to check out the Congaree River Blue Trail. This paddling path stretches from the state capital, Columbia, to Congaree National Park and provides access to several hiking trails.

If you're looking for the best views in the park, check out the Boardwalk Loop Trail (2.6 miles) and the Weston Lake Loop Trail (4.4 miles).

### WORDS TO THE WISE

Planning to make the trip for the Fireflies Festival? The best time to see the bright bugs is between 9 and 10 p.m. Dogs aren't permitted on the Fireflies Trail.

### SIDE TRIP

While you're in South Carolina, consider heading to Fort Sumter and Fort Moultrie National Historical Park, about 100 miles southeast. There, you can learn about the forts' American Revolution and Civil War history.

EAST

STORY AND PHOTO BY
**PAT AND CHUCK BLACKLEY**

# MAMMOTH CAVE

DESCEND INTO A GARDEN OF EDEN AT THIS PARK WITH HUNDREDS OF CAVES AND PLENTY OF HIKING.

**THIS DESTINATION IS KNOWN** for over 400 miles of caves, but there's also much to see aboveground, and in mid-April, the Cedar Sink Trail is a wildflower enthusiast's dream. At first we found the hike there to be pleasant, but a bit unremarkable. Then, after descending into a large depression, we arrived at a platform and gazed down into a Garden of Eden.

Filled with native trees and lush vegetation, the sink was surrounded by cliffs of layered sandstone and limestone. A stream emerged from a cave and babbled on the surface before disappearing into another cave. The forest floor and cliff faces were draped with colorful wildflowers.

Well-kept paths wind through large clumps of red and nodding trilliums, blue phlox, larkspurs, fire pinks, yellow celandines, Dutchman's breeches and more. Hikers can reach the floral wonderland by way of a 1.6-mile loop trail that's rated moderate, although there's a steep set of stairs to the sink. The reward is absolutely worth taking the climb.

EAST

*Delicate phlox and trilliums decorate the Cedar Sink at Mammoth Cave.*

### POINTS OF INTEREST

#### FUN FACTS
During the War of 1812, the mineral saltpeter was mined from the caves to use in black gunpowder. Today, visitors can see remnants from Mammoth Cave's mines, including vats and wooden pipes.

Visitors can explore several historic churches and cemeteries at Mammoth Cave. Some churches are open, inviting visitors to imagine what life was like for settlers in the area.

#### SIDE TRIP
Mammoth Cave is located less than an hour away from Abraham Lincoln Birthplace National Historical Park. There, visitors can step inside the Memorial Building, constructed where the Lincoln cabin is believed to have been built.

#### NEARBY ATTRACTIONS
Close-by towns and communities offer plenty of chances for dining, lodging and exploration; Bowling Green, Brownsville, Cave City and more are all a short drive from the park.

# EAST PHOTO GALLERY

1.

2.

**1. BEAUTY ALL AROUND**
Roughly a 3-mile round-trip hike in Shenandoah Valley leads you to the summit of Sharp Top Trail, near Bedford, Virginia. It's the perfect place to behold amazing 360-degree views. —ASHLEE NEMETH

**2. CHANGING SEASONS**
I took this photo at an entrance area to Great Smoky Mountains National Park near Bryson City, North Carolina. Gorgeous fall colors are reflected in the water, a calming reminder of the beauty that occurs here every year. —ANTHONY GIACOMINO

**3. A SURPRISE VISITOR**
While driving in Great Smoky Mountains National Park, I am typically moved by the beauty of the mountains, waterfalls and wildflowers. But to my surprise I spotted this bull elk in the Oconaluftee River. —CINDY YOUNT

**4. GLORIOUS NEW DAY**
This photo showcases the serenity of an early morning sunrise as witnessed atop the summit on Cadillac Mountain in Acadia National Park. —TODD ERB

3.

4.

NATIONAL PARKS 169

1.

PHOTO GALLERY  EAST

2.

3.

4.

### 1. NATURE'S MAJESTY
My family and I visited Acadia National Park in Maine last summer. The beauty and untouched nature was so overwhelmingly breathtaking.
– KELLY DEAN

### 2. INNER PEACE
This is the type of sunset we get in Everglades National Park. The calm water transports me to a quiet place and reminds me it's going to be OK.
– JESSE WILSON

### 3. PERFECT PICTURE
While heading home after an amazing day at Cades Cove in the scenic Great Smoky Mountains, we spotted this lone coyote.  – BARBARA HOUSTON

### 4. FIRST RAYS OF LIGHT
Catching the sunrise in Acadia National Park is a popular activity, as it offers the first sight of the sunrise in the continental United States (at least for part of the year). It is always beautiful.
– KAREN CHRISTMAN

NATIONAL PARKS  171

# EAST PHOTO GALLERY

### 1. *WHOO* IS IT?
This gorgeous barred owl resides right outside Congaree National Park in South Carolina. I carefully approached the field where the bird sat to photograph it in the setting autumn sun.
—DANIEL RIDDLE

### 2. GORGEOUS AND GREEN
I took this photo at the Great Smoky Mountains in May. I am amazed by the beauty of the many trails throughout the Smokies—more than 800 miles of them. —PATTY BARNES

### 3. ACADIA'S SPLENDOR
This photo is of Jordan Pond in Acadia National Park, Maine. The greens and blues are truly magnificent; this park and the state of Maine have so much loveliness to offer. —BRIAN WILLEY

### 4. IN THE MOMENT
While my vacation in Virgin Islands National Park was incredible, I found it challenging to live in the moment. One morning, while snorkeling with my husband, all the fish seemed to disappear. As I looked around, I was shocked to see this turtle gracefully swim by. It reminded me of how small my problems were and put things into perspective for me. —LEAH NICHOLSON

### 5. THE END OF A BEAUTIFUL DAY
I captured this stunning sky at Bar Harbor in Acadia. There are many excellent places to watch the sun set in the park. —MIKE COHN

3.

4.

5.

NATIONAL PARKS   173

▼
*Waterfall at Hot Springs National Park.*

EAST

STORY BY
**DONNA B. ULRICH**

# HOT SPRINGS

ARKANSAS' RESTORATIVE SPRINGS GAVE BIRTH TO STATELY BATHHOUSE ROW IN THE GOLDEN ERA OF "THE AMERICAN SPA."

**FOR THOUSANDS OF YEARS,** Native American tribes gathered in what some called the "Valley of the Vapors," searching for relief from common ailments through soaking in mineral-rich hot springs. In modern times, the area has become a mecca for people "taking the waters" in Hot Springs, Arkansas.

Early European settlers came to the waters at Hot Springs Mountain in hopes of relieving problems ranging from sinus, muscle and joint pain to afflictions of the skin. They built simple platforms over the outflow to inhale the vapors.

Crude brush huts and log cabins came next, and, as the place known as "the American Spa" grew in popularity, bigger and better accommodations sprang up. Today a row of luxurious stone and masonry bathhouses beckons visitors at Hot Springs National Park.

The natural thermal springs are fed by ancient rainwater filtering down to areas deep in Earth's crust, where it's slowly heated. Then it rapidly rises to emerge from 47 local springs as steaming-hot water.

Congress first gave federal protection to the area's natural features in 1832, 40 years before Yellowstone became the first national park. Designated as Hot Springs National Park in 1921, it is the smallest in the park system. The promenade, called Bathhouse Row, was constructed by wealthy entrepreneurs and is preserved as a National Historic Landmark District to provide a peek into the city's grand past.

And a colorful past it was! Gambling, prostitution and bootlegging were as much a part of everyday life in this peaceful valley as the spas. Las Vegas-style amenities and a secluded location attracted gangsters from the late 1800s to the mid-1900s.

Al Capone used the remote town in the Ouachita Mountains as a base for making and shipping moonshine during Prohibition. Hot Springs and its surrounding forest provided cover for the stills; from there Capone struck deals to ship the contraband to his clubs in Chicago.

National Park Ranger Coby Bishop, born and raised in Hot Springs, worked

# EAST

**POINTS OF INTEREST**

*The Arkansas wilderness at twilight.*

### FUN FACTS
The springs in the park are all grouped around the base of Hot Springs Mountain. They release a flow of over half a million gallons of water every day.

You might think of Hot Springs for its waters, but it's a notable archaeology site as well. People have been on the park's land for more than 10,000 years.

### WORDS TO THE WISE
Forgot your water bottle? You can drink the water at Hot Springs. At the thermal and cold spring fountains, you are able to fill up jugs of drinking water from the springs.

### NEARBY ATTRACTIONS
There are plenty of museums and things to do in the city of Hot Springs. One notable attraction is The Gangster Museum of America, which features exhibits about mobsters who used the springs.

---

in the park for six years. "I loved the variety of architecture," he says. "Each of the bathhouses reflects the builder's sense of style. My favorite was the Maurice, because of its simple yet elegant lines, beautiful tile work, Mediterranean style and spectacular stained-glass skylights and windows."

Concessionaires run the bathhouses, with payment made to the federal government for the spring waters, which are now considered recreational rather than therapeutic in nature. Renovations continue.

The Buckstaff, which has operated continuously since 1912, and Quapaw are still open for a relaxing soak and spa experience. The Fordyce now is the national park's visitor center, and the Ozark Bathhouse currently houses the Museum of Contemporary Art.

The surrounding Ozark landscape features 26 miles of trails meandering through oak, hickory and pine forests.

Spring is an especially lovely time, with wildflowers, azaleas and flowering dogwoods brightening the lovely forest. Hikers might even come across a natural cold spring and easily forget that a bustling city is just out of sight.

In that sense, Hot Springs is ideal both for "taking the waters" and taking in the history that endures.

176 NATIONAL PARKS

EAST

*A stone bridge in the Gulpha Gorge Creek.*

*The hike to Lynn Camp Prong is an easy one with huge rewards.*

EAST

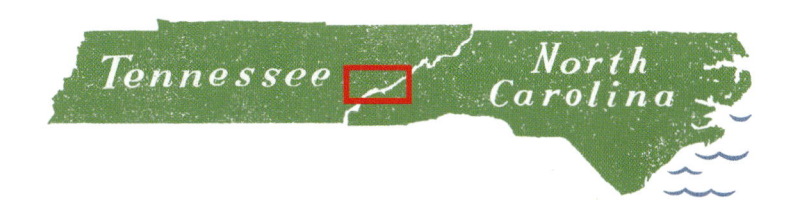

STORY AND PHOTOS BY
**PAT AND CHUCK BLACKLEY**

# GREAT SMOKY MOUNTAINS

SOMETIMES HAVING THE GREAT SMOKY MOUNTAINS TO YOURSELF MEANS RISING BEFORE THE SUN.

**THE GREAT SMOKY MOUNTAINS** have captivated us for more years than we would admit. Nonetheless, we never tire of the misty mornings in its coves, the explosion of rhododendron bloom along its streams or the riot of fall color among its trees.

Affectionately called the Smokies, this mountain range is mostly preserved within the 800-square-mile Great Smoky Mountains National Park, straddling the Tennessee-North Carolina border. The Cherokee called these mountains "place of the blue smoke" in tribute to the mist that perennially envelops the landscape here.

However, the very things we love about the place beckon the masses. Today, with 11 million visitors per year, the national park is one of the most-visited in the country. Over the years we have learned that the best time to avoid the crowds is the early morning, as the park and its wild residents awaken to a new day.

When we want a quiet vacation, Chuck and I head over to Townsend,

# EAST

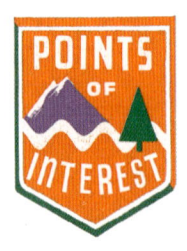

## POINTS OF INTEREST

**NOT TO BE MISSED**

Known for lovely wildflowers in the spring, Greenbrier is rarely crowded. The hike along Porters Creek Trail is a colorful wildflower trek that rambles past a historic log cabin and a barn.

At Foothills Parkway, west of Gatlinburg, you'll find more than 32 miles of scenic parkway stretching from Wears Valley to Chilhowee. The road boasts spectacular mountain views around every bend.

Discover Roaring Fork Nature Motor Trail, which was named for a loud and fast stream. This 5½-mile drive winds past clear streams, waterfalls and pioneer structures.

**FUN FACT**

In Elkmont, the clubhouse and cabins of the Appalachian Club still stand along with abandoned resort homes once frequented by the well-to-do from Knoxville. Remnants of logging operations here include an early 20th century railroad bed repurposed as a hiking trail.

*Fog lifting at the Henry Whitehead Cabin.*

Tennessee, which calls itself "the peaceful side of the Smokies." We find it true to its claim—and an ideal spot to dine, refuel and settle in for the night. From here, we can access the most beautiful spots on the Tennessee side of the Smokies without encountering the crowds a few miles away.

Townsend is not a village as much as it is a short and linear group of motels, restaurants and stores connected by a main road that is parallel to a well-maintained walking and biking path. We frequently see folks enjoying the path as the cool of the evening sets in. The town offers opportunities to tube or swim in the Little River, visit a cultural museum or explore caverns.

But it's the mountains we've come here to see. Staying in Townsend is most convenient to Cades Cove, our favorite spot in the park. Here, in this valley surrounded by high mountains, lived a community of pioneers who embodied the Appalachian spirit.

Today their churches, cabins and barns are preserved and their fields are still tended. We love stepping back in time in such a tranquil setting, which is one of the most popular places in the park.

We've found that Cades Cove is best visited early in the morning, so we line up at the entrance gate for the dawn opening to relish one of the valley's magical sunrises. In these early hours, fog usually drifts within the cove and wildlife is plentiful near the roads. It is typical to see deer sparring, turkeys strutting and, maybe, a bear browsing not far from our car.

After sunrise, we travel the mostly empty cove roads until midmorning or so, when visitors begin to flock in from Gatlinburg, a tourist town known as the gateway to the Smokies. Since the early fog has dissipated and wildlife are back in the woods, it is now that we take our leave of the valley.

From May to September, Cades Cove is restricted to bicycle or foot traffic until 10 a.m. on Wednesdays and Saturdays. This is the best time to take your bike ride here. We aren't cyclists, so on these mornings, we have a lovely breakfast at our favorite place for old-fashioned country cooking: Riverstone Restaurant in Townsend.

At midmorning, we explore some of the park's more than 800 miles of hiking trails, including several former railroad beds that the hardworking Civilian Conservation Corps converted to trails in the 1930s. These hikes vary from strenuous mountain climbs to easy peaceful strolls. Whatever your skill level might be, each hike leads to breathtaking beauty.

The Little River Trail, our favorite repurposed railroad bed, follows its namesake east from Elkmont, a former logging camp. This gently sloping path passes beside the tumbling waters of the river as it flows through the heart of the Great Smoky Mountains.

With several places to turn around, this trail can be an easy, relatively short walk or a full day's trek through land that changes with the seasons: delicate wildflowers in springtime, colorful rhododendrons in summer and vibrant leaves in fall.

Also at the Little River trailhead, we have the option to change our course and follow the Jakes Creek Trail, which ascends the mountain to the Cucumber Gap Trail and its majestic stand of tulip poplar trees.

Closer to Townsend, at Tremont, is Middle Prong Trail, another converted railroad bed that follows the Middle Prong of the Little River. This is an easy hike of a half-mile to the Lower

*White-tailed deer forage in the fields.*

EAST

▼ *Dawn breaks beside Sparks Lane in Cades Cove.*

*A hiker on the Cucumber Gap Trail treks past fantastic fall color.*

Lynn Camp Falls, which cascade dramatically from the left. The trail extends beyond the falls at a steep grade for several more miles on the rail bed, then proceeds on a strenuous stretch up the mountain.

Even if we're not hiking, we find the drive to Tremont beside the Middle Prong—on a road that is half paved and half well-maintained dirt—to be among the loveliest in the park.

Another of our favorite midmorning destinations is Newfound Gap Road, which rises 3,000 feet in 14½ miles. While soon-to-be-bustling Gatlinburg is just beginning to yawn and stretch, we're admiring the park's famous overlooks, including Chimney Tops, a craggy bare double peak the Cherokee call Forked Antler.

If there is time, we drive the 7 miles to Clingmans Dome, the highest peak in the Smokies. Even if we don't hike the trail to the observation tower, the view from the parking lot is a must-see. By noon, the crowds arrive, and soon the overlook parking lots are filled.

Planning ahead, we picked up lunch in Townsend earlier so we can eat at a picnic area along the route. Our favorite is Chimneys, deep in the woods and not far from its namesake mountain on Newfound Gap Road. We find a spot near the stream and bask in the afternoon sunshine.

Knowing when and where to find peace and stillness makes the entire experience here just perfect for us. We hope you fall in love with the Smokies as we have.

EAST

STORY BY
**CINDY JORDAN**

# CANAVERAL

**EXPLORE AND SIGHTSEE AT CANAVERAL'S SANDY BEACHES AND IN ITS BLUE OCEAN WATERS.**

**THE SEA LURED US** to Canaveral National Seashore, where we explored the 24-mile stretch of powdery white sand, laughing at funny little birds (sanderlings), running from the blue-gray waves and breathing in the salty air.

Home to more than 1,000 fish and bird species and even more plant and wildlife species, Canaveral sits on a barrier island complex. The Atlantic Ocean is on one side, the Indian River (really a lagoon) is on the other, and in between lies Mosquito Lagoon, which covers about two-thirds of the park.

We made our first stop at the Apollo Visitor Center, picked up a map, learned about the history of the island and set off to find the nesting sea turtles that lay their eggs under the sand.

My family and I scoped the dunes and peeked through railroad vines and sea oats, hoping to catch a glimpse. Then we turned to the lagoon, where turtles spend their adolescent years sheltered among the mangrove roots and seagrasses.

The waters are alive with oysters, clams, manatees, dolphins and more. At Indian River, the salty ocean water meets and mixes with fresh water. Such complex estuary ecosystems are often called cradles of the ocean because they're the spawning grounds for so much life.

With such beauty and abundance, I can see why the ancient Timucua tribe lived here. Archaeological sites, including Turtle Mound (one of the tallest Native American shell middens in Florida), abound.

Canaveral is a year-round destination with places to fish, swim, boat, canoe, camp or just relax on the beaches. There are no high-rise buildings, restaurants or cars, but paved roads and boardwalks lead to numerous historic sites, pristine beaches and hiking trails.

Today Canaveral National Seashore remains much as Mother Nature intended it to be—a peaceful refuge.

EAST

*A wooden boardwalk, among palmettos and sabal palms, leads to the Atlantic Ocean.*

### POINTS OF INTEREST

**FUN FACT**

Canaveral's name is one of the oldest geographical names on record in America. It means "place of Cane."

**WORDS TO THE WISE**

Look out for jellyfish! NPS warns that during the summer, men-of-war and jellyfish can wind up on the shore. They recommend carrying vinegar on the beach to use in case of a sting. Hot water (and an abundance of caution when walking) helps, too.

**NEARBY ATTRACTIONS**

You'll want to check out Kennedy Space Center on your trip, too. Featuring exhibits about everything from the moon landing to the next phases of space travel today—as well as the Astronaut Training Experience—the Kennedy Space Center is a must for anyone interested in exploring the stars.

EAST

STORY AND PHOTOS BY
**MARILYN BAGGETT**

# EVERGLADES

FIND PEACE IN THE EVERLASTING BEAUTY AND ABUNDANT NATURE OF AMERICA'S LARGEST SUBTROPICAL WILDERNESS.

**FOR MOST OF MY YEARS** I have lived less than an hour away from an American treasure: the Florida Everglades. As I found my life increasingly stress-filled, I sought a place of solitude and beauty to revive my spirit.

One day, I recalled that Everglades National Park was near, so I ventured out with a full tank of gas, a light lunch, water, my camera, tripod and bug spray. What I found was a timeless place I had all but forgotten. My every sense was intrigued by the wonder and majesty of it all.

At first I felt the quiet, but I soon realized the air was alive with sounds and devoid only of the noise of people. The constant buzz of insects was topped with the cries of tropical birds. And the air vibrated with the grunts and bellows of the great alligators. My eyes feasted on sunsets, ablaze with pinks, oranges and reds, crowning the sawgrass prairie and the pineland forests.

During dry season flocks of birds, including iridescent purple gallinules, snowy egrets and roseate spoonbills, congregate around watering holes. In wet season I hear the low rumbling of thunder in the distance. Warmed by the sun and refreshed by the rain, the cycle of life here hangs in a delicate balance.

After each visit, I am renewed and ready to face any challenge. I'm so very thankful for those who possessed the foresight to protect and preserve such a rare natural wonder. I look forward to my next visit when I will once again find something new to appreciate in my big backyard.

EAST

## POINTS OF INTEREST

**FUN FACT**

Many early national parks were founded to preserve scenery, but Everglades National Park was created to preserve habitat for a variety of animals. Residents include red and gray foxes and black bears, as well as birds like wood storks, herons and egrets.

**WORDS TO THE WISE**

Protect your car from vultures! NPS has let visitors know that vultures living in the park are often drawn to windshields and windshield wipers. To keep yourself from getting a nasty surprise when you return from your hike, the park service recommends using tarps and bungee cords to cover cars when parked; these items are available for free at some visitor areas.

**SIDE TRIP**

Take a day trip to Big Cypress National Preserve. Located just a half-hour away from the Everglades, it features plenty of opportunities for hiking, canoeing, stargazing and more.

*Top: Marilyn finds serenity in a cypress grove in Everglades National Park. Bottom: Roseate spoonbill.*

NATIONAL PARKS 187

▼ *Trunk Bay is the home of the park's underwater trail for snorkelers.*

EAST

STORY BY **DONNA ULRICH**
PHOTOS BY **LARRY ULRICH**

# VIRGIN ISLANDS

SNORKEL, SAIL AND SMILE IN A TROPICAL PARADISE WITH ONE OF THE WORLD'S BEST BEACHES.

**YOU CAN DRIVE** to most of America's national parklands, while some others require an airplane flight. But on our first visit to Virgin Islands National Park, we sailed in.

Located on St. John, in the Caribbean Sea, this treasure of the park system is a legacy of conservationist Laurance Rockefeller, who donated more than 5,000 acres for it in 1956. Park officials acquired 5,650 undersea acres off the northern and southern coasts in 1962, and today the park covers more than half of St. John's 19 square miles and nearly all of tiny Hassel Island.

Imagine a luxurious tropical paradise with easy access to beaches—and we own the place! The U.S. purchased St. John and many smaller islands from Denmark during World War I. Virgin Islands is one of just two national parks not located within the 50 United States, the other being the National Park of American Samoa in the South Pacific.

Weather in the park averages a balmy 79 degrees, with very little temperature change between summer and winter.

My husband, Larry, and I spent 11 memorable days exploring Caribbean waters on a 42-foot sailboat before anchoring off the park's Trunk Bay, consistently voted one of the 10 best beaches in the world. The long strip of white sand, framed by lush tropical plants, stretches invitingly for a quarter of a mile.

Offshore, an underwater snorkeling trail through the Caribbean invites the visitor to linger and enjoy dazzling coral formations and fish of colors unfamiliar in our terrestrial world. Signs along the 225-yard underwater path tell snorkelers about the coral and other life forms they may see, including the coral-munching parrot fish, moray eels and trumpet fish. Farther out in the bay you may see green turtles, stingrays and eagle rays.

Serious snorkelers can also explore many other interesting reefs and bays along St. John's north coast. In fact, coral reefs surround much of the island.

Though you can camp in the park, we hadn't brought the necessary equipment to do so. There are cottages available for rent, but we chose to rent a bungalow complete with resident anoles—quick-moving lizards that eat bugs.

# EAST

*Turk's cap cactuses keep watch over Salt Pond Bay.*

### FUN FACTS

Sea turtles come to St. John Island's beaches to nest. Several species have been spotted there, including hawksbill, leatherback and green sea turtles.

St. John is a birder's paradise, with more than 144 species spotted throughout the year. According to NPS, the best trail for spotting feathered friends is the Francis Bay Salt Pond Trail.

### WORDS TO THE WISE

Driving in the Virgin Islands is different than an American road trip. Why? There, residents drive on the left side of the road! Be sure to follow the correct traffic patterns on your vacation.

There are more than 500 types of fish in the Virgin Islands, but rangers ask that you refrain from feeding any of them. Doing so can disrupt their patterns and make them less friendly to visitors.

We quickly discovered on a drive inland that the residents have adopted many British customs. We also found that picking up hitchhiking locals, especially elders, was not an option—it was mandatory. From that experience we learned about places to see, most of them within the park. Hiking to sugar mills that were abandoned, historical Taino petroglyph rock carvings and subtropical rainforests filled our days.

The Annaberg sugar factory ruins date back to the 1780s, when the island was owned by Denmark, sugar cane was king and more than 300 slaves were used to clear the land, build stone structures and toil in the fields. Terraced hillsides are reminders of plantation farming, but tropical plants that were once cleared for raising cane are now reclaiming the site.

Twenty hiking trails offer short and long ventures to moist high-elevation forests, desert terrain, mangrove swamps and beautiful beaches. The island's highest point and some of the most spectacular views are found on Bordeaux Mountain, which rises to 1,277 feet and plunges dramatically to the sea over a distance of just three-quarters of a mile.

There is much to see in the national park, including more than 50 species of tropical birds and some 800 species of plants like bay rum trees and tropical orchids. But throughout our trek the sea was never far from sight, beckoning to us. A day of sightseeing must be followed by sight-sea-ing along sandy, sun-drenched beaches and pristine, vibrant blue waters.

Larry and I spent most of our time photographing, but at day's end, sunsets were watched, local culinary specialties were consumed and warm breezes lulled us to sleep each night.

EAST

▼
*A soothing sunset silhouettes a teyer palm at Cinnamon Bay on the north coast.*

EAST **THEN AND NOW**

# EVERGLADES NATIONAL PARK

### 1920
Even before it was a national park, the Everglades drew many with its natural beauty. At right, Ezra B. Thompson makes movies in the park.

### 2008
Above, the Everglades still attract creative people who want to preserve the beauty of nature through photography.

THEN: U.S. NATIONAL PARK SERVICE; NOW: PBNJ PRODUCTIONS/GETTY IMAGES

# GREAT AMERICAN ROAD TRIPS
## Scenic Drives

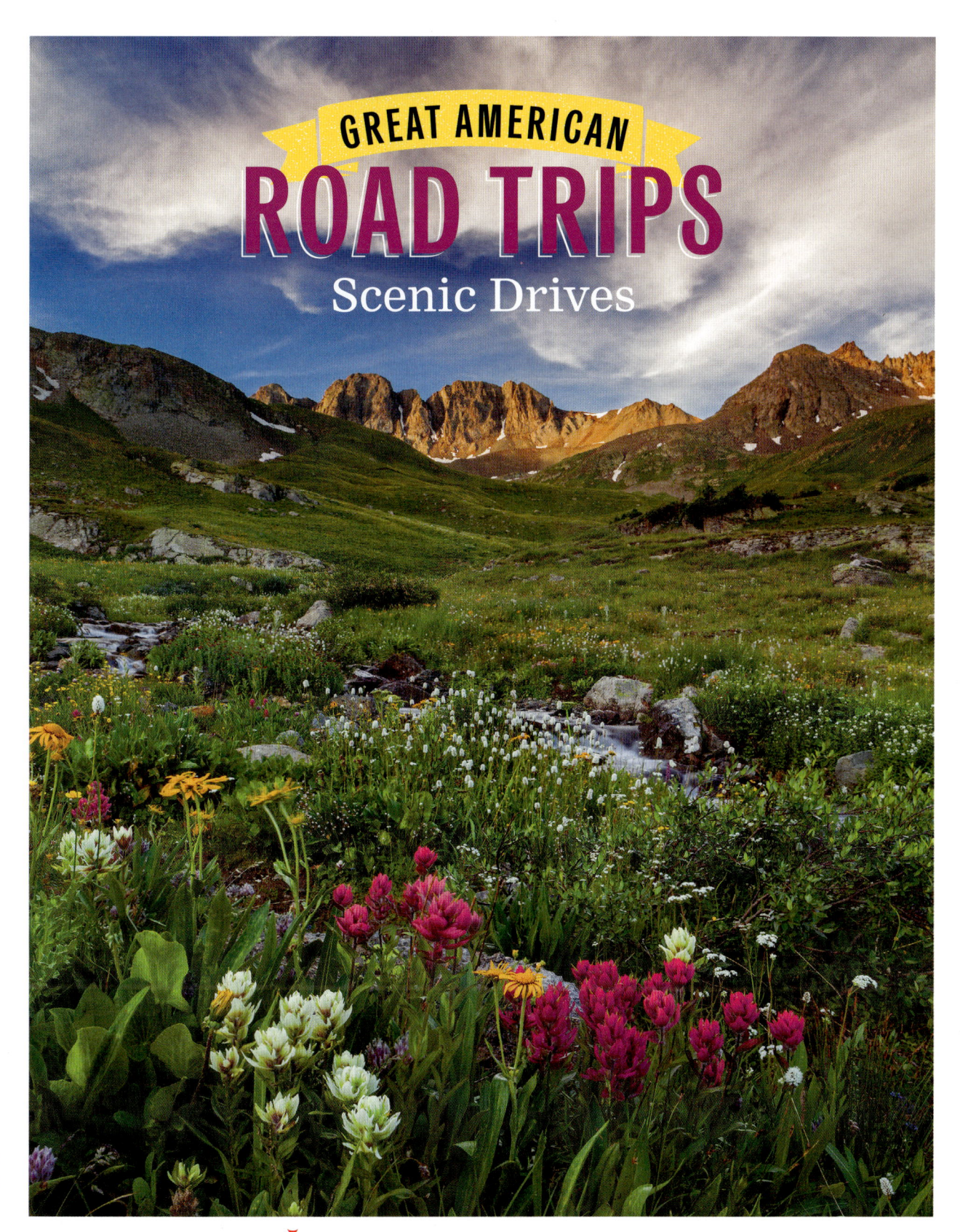

*Morning light approaches beneath Handies Peak in Colorado's San Juan Mountains.*

# CONTENTS

## WEST
**SEWARD HIGHWAY** Alaska • 8
**BIG SUR COAST** California • 12
**CALIFORNIA'S U.S. ROUTE 395** California • 16
**MOUNT EVANS SCENIC BYWAY** Colorado • 22
**SAN JUAN SKYWAY** Colorado • 26
**SALMON RIVER SCENIC BYWAY** Idaho/Montana • 30
**RED SLEEP MOUNTAIN** Montana • 32
**OREGON COAST HIGHWAY** Oregon • 34
**HELLS CANYON** Oregon • 38
**MOUNT HOOD SCENIC BYWAY** Oregon • 42
**JOURNEY THROUGH TIME** Utah • 46
**HEART OF THE PALOUSE** Washington • 50

## SOUTHWEST
**APACHE TRAIL** Arizona • 58
**MONUMENT VALLEY** Arizona/Utah • 60
**OAK CREEK CANYON** Arizona • 64
**NEW MEXICO'S NORTH** New Mexico • 68
**TALIMENA SCENIC BYWAY** Oklahoma/Arkansas • 70
**TEXAS HILL COUNTRY** Texas • 74

## MIDWEST
**ILLINOIS RIVER ROAD** Illinois • 80
**KEWEENAW PENINSULA** Michigan • 84
**LEELANAU PENINSULA** Michigan • 88
**U.S. HIGHWAY 2** Michigan • 92
**NORTH SHORE SCENIC DRIVE** Minnesota • 94
**OHIO'S AMISH COUNTRY** Ohio • 98
**DOOR COUNTY COASTAL BYWAY** Wisconsin • 102
**GREAT RIVER ROAD** Wisconsin/Minnesota/Iowa • 106

## SOUTHEAST
**SCENIC HIGHWAY 7** Arkansas • 112
**BAYOU COUNTRY** Louisiana • 116
**HISTORIC NATIONAL ROAD** Maryland • 118
**NATCHEZ TRACE PARKWAY** Mississippi/Alabama/Tennessee • 122
**OUTER BANKS SCENIC BYWAY** North Carolina • 126
**CHEROKEE FOOTHILLS BYWAY** South Carolina • 130
**BLUE GRASS VALLEY ROAD** Virginia • 132
**BLUE RIDGE PARKWAY** Virginia/North Carolina • 138

## NORTHEAST
**KATAHDIN WOODS** Maine • 146
**RANGELEY LAKES SCENIC BYWAY** Maine • 152
**BERKSHIRE BYWAYS** Massachusetts • 156
**CAPE COD'S ROUTE 6** Massachusetts • 160
**KANCAMAGUS SCENIC BYWAY** New Hampshire • 164
**OLD MINE ROAD** New Jersey • 170
**CENTRAL ADIRONDACK TRAIL** New York • 172
**HIGH PEAKS BYWAY** New York • 176
**PENNSYLVANIA ROUTE 655** Pennsylvania • 178
**SCENIC ROUTE 100 BYWAY** Vermont • 182
**VERMONT ROUTE 108** Vermont • 188

*A pink sky is cast as the sun sets over farmland in Vermont. Mount Mansfield is seen in the distance.*

# COME ALONG FOR THE RIDE!

**LET THE NATURAL BEAUTY** of America's most scenic drives inspire the travel bug within you and get you out exploring wide-open spaces and breathtaking vistas. These trips will take you on an odyssey in your car, van or RV. Whether you're an armchair traveler or ready to pack and roll, this first book in our new *Great American Road Trips* series covering *Scenic Drives* has exactly what you are looking for.

All accounts here are firsthand from the travelers and photographers themselves, with helpful added tips. Some drives are more leisurely, like Cape Cod's Route 6 in Massachusetts (page 160), which will lead you to exquisite sandy beaches and charming shops. Others, like Cathy and Gordon Illg's trip along North America's highest paved road, the Mount Evans Scenic Byway in Colorado (page 22), are for the more adventurous, or as they put it: "…just because you can drive up to this rarefied atmosphere doesn't mean you don't have to earn it."

Just imagine, as you take on these routes, the ingenuity that went in to creating them and how much more difficult it would be to traverse the terrain without these modern wonders of roads.

So meander through the spectacular scenery, and don't forget to take photos along the way! For now, sit back, relax and enjoy the ride!

—FROM THE EDITORS

*Evening clouds roll over Captain Jack's Wharf at Provincetown Harbor in Massachusetts.*

# WEST

ALASKA

WASHINGTON
MONTANA
OREGON
IDAHO
WYOMING
NEVADA
UTAH
COLORADO
CALIFORNIA

HAWAII

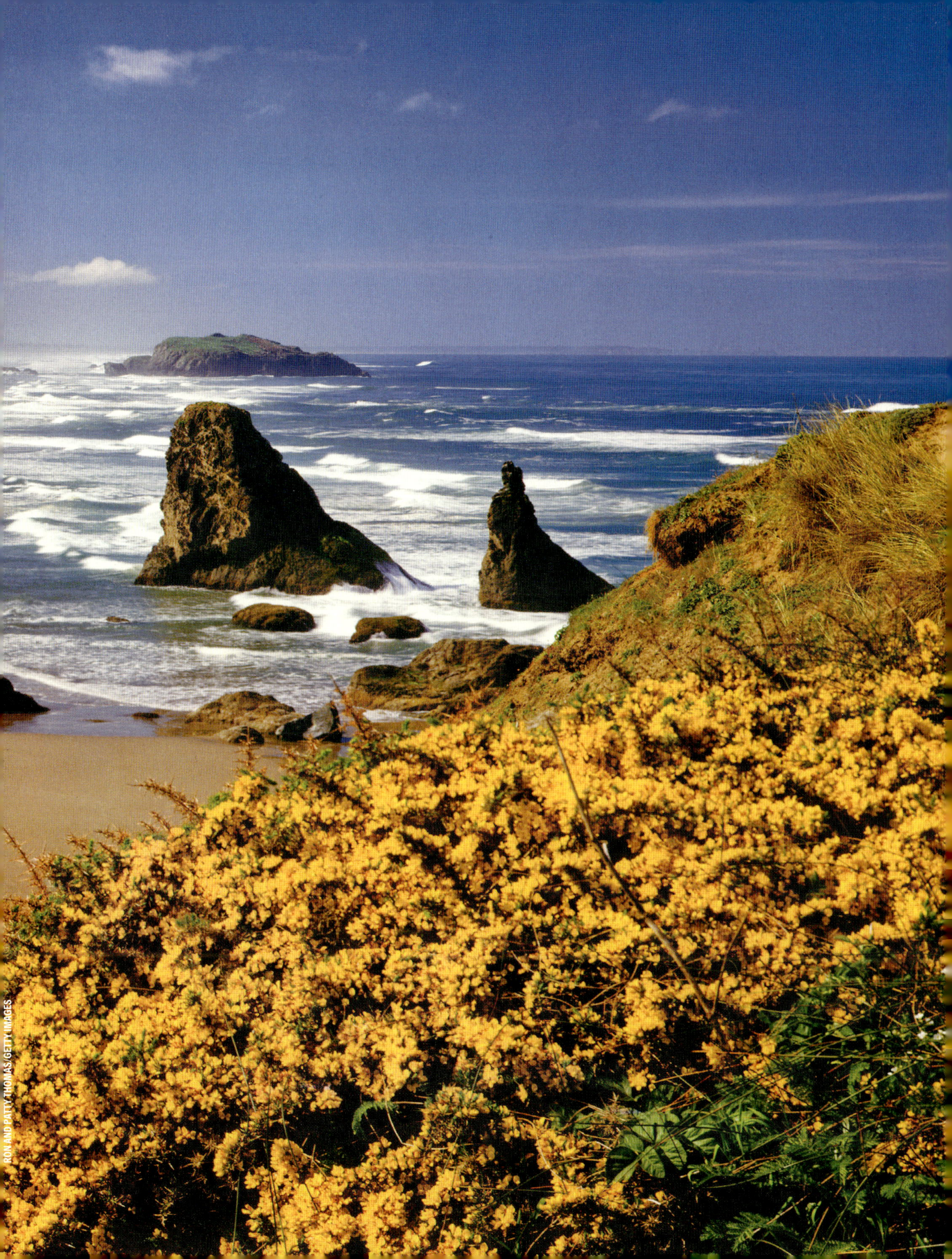
RON AND PATTY THOMAS/GETTY IMAGES

▼ *The Resurrection River curves below Mount Benson.*

WEST

STORY BY **JANINE NIEBRUGGE**
PHOTOS BY **RON NIEBRUGGE**

# SEWARD HIGHWAY

**TRAVEL 127 UNFORGETTABLE MILES THROUGH ONE OF NORTH AMERICA'S MOST PRISTINE WILDERNESSES.**

**DESIGNATED BOTH A** National Forest Scenic Byway and an All-American Road, the Seward Highway takes you through 127 miles of remote wild beauty.

Also known as Alaska Route 9, the highway stretches from Anchorage to the charming coastal community of Seward, the gateway to Kenai Fjords National Park.

The road climbs over mountain passes where you're surrounded by jaw-dropping views of jagged peaks, rainforests, crystal lakes and the Pacific Ocean.

On any given day, you're likely to see Dall sheep, whales, waterfowl, moose and bears. What you won't see are billboards or many other signs of civilization.

The highway is a photographer's dream, with easy access to dramatic scenery. While it's not hard to complete the drive in a few hours, give yourself most of a day, or even two, to explore this stunning road.

To guide you along on your journey, here are a few of the highlights that my husband, Ron, and I enjoy.

As you start out, Potter Marsh, on the outskirts of Anchorage, marks the end of city views and the beginning of wilderness. It's truly a birder's paradise, with views of a rich variety of waterfowl and other birds, including northern pintails, Canada geese, red-necked phalaropes, canvasback ducks, horned and red-necked grebes, and northern harriers. Gulls, arctic terns and yellowlegs can be spotted during spring and fall migration. This is also a good place to see spawning salmon and an occasional moose.

As you continue down the highway, wind your way along the Turnagain Arm, with scenic views of Chugach State Park. Turnagain Arm offers

SCENIC DRIVES  9

WEST

# POINTS of INTEREST

**LENGTH**
127 miles

**FUN FACT**
The five massive glaciers in Portage Valley on Turnagain Arm are remnants of Portage Glacier, which once covered the valley's entire 14-mile length.

**SIDE TRIP**
Two miles north of Seward, turn west onto a gravel road that parallels the Resurrection River for 9 miles. The road ends at the Exit Glacier Ranger Station in Kenai Fjords National Park.

A 3-mile-long river of ice flowing from massive Harding Icefield, Exit Glacier looms like a blue monolith. Visitors can approach the glacier's base by walking about a half-mile on an easy trail from the ranger station. A longer, more strenuous trail leads hikers up the flank of the glacier to a spot overlooking the Harding Icefield.

The mantle of ice measures an imposing 35 miles by 20 miles, and buried within its frigid bulk are all but the tallest peaks to be found in the Kenai Mountains.

*A bull moose crosses the road in Chugach National Forest.*

some of the world's largest bore tides, attracting surfers, paddleboarders and kite boarders.

Ron and I like to stop at Beluga Point or Bird Point to watch for beluga whales and scour the mountainsides along the road for Dall sheep.

Milepost 79 is the turnoff for the skiing community of Girdwood, a quaint mountain town that's worth exploring. If you have time, take a hike on the Winner Creek Trail. Winner Creek is a beautiful, clear-running stream flowing through the rainforest. A little farther up, the creek drops into a steep, narrow, rocky gorge. You'll want to stop and enjoy the view.

This milepost is also your last opportunity for gas and any other supplies you might need until you reach Seward.

As you continue down Turnagain Arm, check out Portage Valley, a 14-mile isthmus that connects the Kenai Peninsula to the mainland.

Going farther, you'll find yourself climbing Turnagain Pass into the heart of the Chugach National Forest. Here you'll be treated to towering snowcapped peaks, lush rainforest, rivers, lakes and ponds.

Traveling through the communities of Moose Pass and Crown Point will make you feel like you've taken a step back in time. Stop to take in the beauty of the turquoise waters of Kenai Lake, and look for nesting trumpeter swans in the lily pad pond at Mile 15.

The drive ends as you enter the charming seaside community of Seward, with views of Resurrection Bay. Take a boat tour to watch for humpback and orca whales, sea otters and sea lions in Kenai Fjords National Park—the perfect way to end a great road trip.

SCENIC DRIVES

WEST

*Autumn glows in Chugach National Forest on the Kenai Peninsula.*

*The picturesque Santa Lucia Mountains line the Big Sur coast.*

WEST

STORY AND PHOTOS BY
**LONDIE GARCIA PADELSKY**

# BIG SUR COAST

SHEER CLIFFS, HAIRPIN TURNS AND MAJESTIC OCEAN VIEWS MAKE THIS COASTAL ROUTE A THRILLING RIDE.

**CALIFORNIA'S STATE ROUTE 1,** also known as the Pacific Coast Highway, stretches along some of the most beautiful coastline in the world. The highway runs virtually the entire length of the state, but my favorite stretch is the Big Sur section from San Simeon to Carmel, which is so stunning that it is a designated National Scenic Byway.

As you drive north from San Simeon, the highway makes its first ascent to Ragged Point Vista, where you come face to face with the ruggedness and steepness of the Santa Lucia Mountains as they rise up along the ocean. For those of us with a fear of heights, there's comfort in driving north, hugging the mountainside.

On the other hand, if you only drive north, you might miss the McWay Falls in Julia Pfeiffer Burns State Park—the only falls in California that empty into the ocean.

I like to camp at Pfeiffer Big Sur State Park, where a walk on the beach leads past the intriguing rock formations known as sea stacks that rise out of the ocean like mysterious towers. The park is also known for its ancient redwoods. Don't miss the chance to hike among some of the world's tallest living trees, soaring 200 to 350 feet into the sky.

Another of my favorite places, just to the north, is Andrew Molera State Park. Here, where the Big Sur River meets the ocean, the mountains flatten out to meadows, and oaks and eucalyptus replace redwoods. I follow the trail along the river to the beach, which is scattered with uniquely crafted beach shelters made of driftwood, rocks and bizarre odds and ends that have washed ashore.

Farther inland, you can spot herds of Holstein dairy cattle grazing in pastures, their familiar black-and-

SCENIC DRIVES 13

WEST

# POINTS of INTEREST

**LENGTH**
About 90 miles

**WORDS TO THE WISE**
Rainstorms will sometimes cause landslides. Morning fogs are frequent in summer. Strong currents, cold water and surf along much of the coast make swimming extremely dangerous.

**SIDE TRIPS**
Point Sur Lighthouse, on the National Register of Historic Places, sits on a volcanic rock 361 feet above the Pacific Ocean. Erected in 1889, the lighthouse has stayed in continuous operation, and is the only complete lighthouse of its era open to the public in California.
pointsur.org

Sunset Drive swings inland after Asilomar State Beach, passes the well-landscaped grounds of a conference center, then intersects with 17-Mile Drive. Monterey cypresses, gnarled by the wind and ocean spray, are highlights along the toll road, which loops through part of the Monterey Peninsula. Tour maps are provided at tollgates.

*Redwood trees along the drive rise to meet the sky.*

white patterns making a striking contrast with the background colors.

Continuing north, if you're starting to get sleepy in the flats, the next couple of cliff turns will wake you up. Then comes Bixby Bridge, one of the world's highest single-span bridges. Fortunately there's a big turnout, so you can relax, check out the bridge and safely enjoy the breathtaking view.

At this point I often turn around and head south on the narrow cliff side of the road. The hairpin turns are worth braving because this is a ride you have to experience; words can't describe it.

Once you reach Ragged Point again there are only two more switchbacks, and then the road mellows out. On one trip I cruised past an unexpected herd of elk and then was lucky enough to spot zebras grazing below Hearst Castle, the legendary home of millionaire publisher William Randolph Hearst and one of the state's prime sightseeing destinations.

I'm lucky to live only about 100 miles from this part of the highway. I've driven it often, and I never get tired of it.

WEST

*Wildflowers bloom on the cliffs above the coastline.*

▼ *A fisherman has Lake Sabrina and autumn majesty all to himself.*

STORY AND PHOTOS BY
**LONDIE GARCIA PADELSKY**

# CALIFORNIA'S U.S. ROUTE 395

VISIT THE EASTERN SIERRA TO EXPLORE GRANITE PEAKS, GOLDEN ASPENS AND ALPINE LAKES.

**"THIRTY-FIVE YEARS OF LIVING** in the eastern Sierra and I'm as mesmerized by its incredible beauty as though it were my first day traveling through!" I said this out loud to my dog, Buddy, who was sitting beside me on a steep hillside.

We had hiked to this spot at dawn right after a light snow dusting. After two hours, the ground beneath us was almost dry even though the air was still frosty cold.

All week I'd been photographing fall colors while scoping out this particular scene. I was watching an aspen grove, hopeful that all the leaves would turn color at the same time. Now I was waiting for the sun to break through the thick clouds to brighten the yellow and orange leaves on the trees.

Finally, the sun did just that! The aspen trees glistened and glowed in the bright spotlight and in the midst of that moment, surrounded by all the quietness, it was as though an orchestra were playing.

As the weather forecast predicted, by midmorning the wind was blowing the leaves off the trees into the pelting snow. Buddy and I left just in time and hiked downhill to the road that brought us here: U.S. Route 395.

Originally known as El Camino Sierra (the mountain range road), U.S. Route 395 is a highway that in California stretches about 600 miles north from Interstate 15 in the Mojave Desert community of Hesperia to the Oregon state line in Modoc County.

U.S. Route 395 is designated as a scenic highway from the Inyo-Mono county line to the town of Walker. This is the area I call my homeland—it's the heart of the El Camino Sierra.

From the highway there are exits upon exits that lead to streams, roadside lakes and high country

WEST

*These two enjoy fly-fishing from a canoe on North Lake.*

## POINTS of INTEREST

**REST STOP**
After hiking, biking or kayaking, visit the cafe at Rock Creek Lakes Resort for barbecue and cobbler. *rockcreeklakesresort.com*

**SIDE TRIPS**
To recharge along the way, take a relaxing soak in one of many natural hot springs in Travertine Hot Springs and Hilltop Hot Springs to enjoy the amazing views!

If you have extra time, Sequoia and Kings Canyon national parks are just a short drive away. The winding Generals Highway neatly connects both parks and travels through Giant Sequoia National Monument, where you can see groves of the massive trees.

---

trails to the John Muir and Ansel Adams wildernesses. With such easy access to nature's extraordinary getaways, you can hike, bike, fish, ride horseback and climb rocks all in one day—or simply enjoy a secluded picnic.

I treasure all seasons in the eastern Sierra, but am especially partial to fall. I love watching the leaves and desert sages come to life with a rainbow of hues. Red, orange and gold add the most brilliant splash of color on a canvas of gray granite rock walls.

Along U.S. Route 395, fall sets the treetops ablaze first at Bishop Creek Canyon. From Bishop, drive about 12 miles west toward the mountains on California Route 168. At an elevation of 9,000 feet and climbing, here you will enter an autumn dream where aspens sparkle in groves and across steep, majestic mountainsides.

South Lake, Lake Sabrina and North Lake are easy to reach and boast spectacular reflections from the surrounding peaks, which rise up to 13,000 feet. Fishing streams, trailheads and horseback riding opportunities are scattered in between. In this canyon you can spend a couple of hours or a couple of days, as Buddy and I did.

Soon after the leaf colors have peaked in Bishop Creek Canyon, areas at higher elevations take off full blast. From Bishop, drive north on U.S. Route 395 toward Mammoth Lakes and follow the road signs to more of my fall favorites: Rock Creek, McGee Creek and Convict Lake canyons. Keep in mind that there are campgrounds and restaurants in most canyons, but often no fuel.

At the Mammoth Lakes exit, drive into town and take the scenic gondola to the top of Mammoth Mountain Ski Area. There are no fall trees at this 11,000-foot vista, but you will certainly spot them looking down on the Sierra

18  SCENIC DRIVES

WEST

▼
*Expect a dusting of snow to cover the mountaintops in McGee Canyon.*

WEST

▼ Londie's dog, Buddy, loves joining her on excursions, and he is well-versed in posing nicely.

*McGee Creek is known for its beautiful fall foliage.*

Nevada landscape. Just beyond the town, there is a loop road along serene, cobalt blue alpine lakes. Fishermen, paddleboarders, walkers, kayakers and bicyclists enjoy the beauty.

There are more pines than aspens surrounding the Mammoth Lakes Basin loop. For the next big blast of fall colors, continue on the highway to California Route 158. Turn west and follow the vibrant aspens along the June Lake Loop. At the start of the loop road is a stunning view of Carson Peak, perfectly mirrored in crystal clear June Lake. It sets the stage for what's ahead. The two-lane road goes through the small, full-service community of June Lake, and passes several quaint cafes and fishing resorts. The lower hillsides and shorelines shimmer with gold and sparkle in all four glacial lakes: June, Gull, Silver and Grant.

Beyond the June Lake Loop, I like to check out Lundy Canyon, Mono Lake and the panoramic aspen grove on Conway Summit. I often continue up to Bridgeport to photograph the golden grasses in the big meadows with the Sawtooth Range in the distance.

Then I stay on U.S. Route 395 and head to Walker River Canyon, where the water flows by cottonwoods and aspens. It's the perfect scene to take gorgeous photos.

Throughout autumn, you will likely run into Buddy and me in one of these canyons. Just when I start to think the fall color season is over, I drive south on Route 395 to Owens Valley and start taking photos all over again.

A friend once said that from Inyo to Mono County, the fall season on Route 395 is like the staircase to heaven. I wholeheartedly agree.

*Another perfect day dawns on Mount Evans.*

WEST

STORY AND PHOTOS BY
**CATHY & GORDON ILLG**

# MOUNT EVANS SCENIC BYWAY

TAKE A DEEP BREATH AND ENJOY THE UNMATCHED VISTAS ALONG AMERICA'S HIGHEST PAVED ROAD.

**THE ANIMALS WE WERE TRYING TO PHOTOGRAPH** didn't appear to be moving quickly, but they were white dots in the distance within minutes. There was no way we could keep up with them.

Of course, it didn't help that the landscape was straight up and straight down, and that we gasped for breath whenever we tried to walk faster than a stroll. But we weren't complaining.

At 14,000 feet above sea level, we were near the summit of Mount Evans, one of Colorado's fourteeners. We could see the snow-dappled Rockies stretching north, south and west to the horizon. To the east, foothills glowed in the sunrise as they tumbled down toward Denver and the Great Plains beyond.

Spectacular surroundings like these are typically reserved for mountain climbers and long-distance hikers, but the Mount Evans Scenic Byway lets anyone with a car and a reasonable cardiovascular system enjoy the high alpine scenery and the creatures that call it home. The byway, which includes sections of Clear Creek County Road 103 and State Highway 5, climbs more than 7,000 feet.

Construction on the road began in the summer of 1923; eight years later it was open to the public. Workers trudged up the mountain with shovels, hammers, drills and dynamite to blow a path through the rocks. In an area notorious for its heavy weather, they worked through rain, snow and hail. One contractor noted in a report that they "literally forced the work through by hand in spite of every obstacle."

But just because you can drive up to this rarefied atmosphere doesn't mean you don't have to earn it. Highway 5 from Echo Lake to the summit is not for the faint of heart. (Imagine what it must have been like for those early

SCENIC DRIVES 23

WEST

# POINTS of INTEREST

**LENGTH**
28 miles

**FUN FACTS**
The road in the sky, Mount Evans highway is the highest paved road in the nation. At more than 14,000 feet up, you'll literally be driving close to the clouds!

Mountain goats are not native to Colorado. The first goats were released in the Mount Evans area in the late 1950s and early '60s. The goats' natural southern range was northern Wyoming.

**SIDE TRIP**
Estes Park is the eastern gateway to Rocky Mountain National Park and a popular year-round recreational center. The historic Stanley Hotel, a sugar-white grande dame with a red roof, is a popular spot for visitors. It was not only built by F.O. Stanley of Stanley Steamer, it was also the setting that inspired *The Shining*, written by Stephen King.

*A mountain goat kid and its mother share a tender moment.*

road workers.) The highest paved road in North America, it's also one of the loftiest in the world. There isn't a single section of guardrail along its twisting 14-mile ascent, and it skirts some impressive precipices. For the last 5 miles there's no centerline, and drivers unused to the exposure do tend to hog the middle of the road.

At the edge of the timberline, the road passes through a grove of bristlecone pines. They are the oldest living things in the state. One of the patriarchs of the grove sprouted as the Roman Empire was falling into decline, and their gnarled branches seem to wave goodbye as you leave the trees behind.

The road climbs for 11 more miles without a single tree blocking the view—or the wind. It may be 90 degrees on the prairie below, but it can be below freezing at the top at any time. In fact, the annual mean temperature on the summit of Mount Evans is 18 degrees, and it's never been warmer than 65. The byway is typically open only from Memorial Day weekend to early October, and sometimes not even that long. Conditions can change at a moment's notice on the mountain. One year early snows closed it down Sept. 3.

The usual assortment of Rocky Mountain critters—marmots, pikas, ptarmigan, mule deer and elk—call Mount Evans home. But it's the bighorn sheep and mountain goats that attract wildlife watchers from around the world. Mountain goats weren't brought to Colorado until the late 1950s, but they have adapted to their new home so well that this is perhaps the best place in the world accessible by car to see them at close range.

If expansive views of alpine wonders or the sight of baby goats playing get your juices flowing, this is the scenic road for you.

WEST

*Yellow flowers and a blue sky frame this photo of Summit Lake terrifically.*

*Sunlight paints Mount Sneffels Wilderness Area in the San Juan Mountains.*

WEST

STORY AND PHOTOS BY
**TIM FITZHARRIS**

# SAN JUAN SKYWAY

ADVENTURE AND FRAGRANT ALPINE WILDFLOWER MEADOWS AWAIT IN COLORADO'S SAN JUAN MOUNTAINS.

**FEW ROADS IN THE WORLD** offer more beauty and adventure per mile than the San Juan Skyway in southwest Colorado. Along with fabulous alpine views, you'll find historical sites, river rafting, rock climbing, camping, hiking, fishing, horseback riding, mountain biking, high country four-wheeling, spas, hot springs, fine dining, ghost towns and abandoned mines.

The skyway is a 232-mile loop in the shape of a rough triangle, with Cortez, Durango and Ridgway at the corners. While I highly recommend the entire drive, my very favorite section runs along U.S. Route 550 from the iconic cowboy town of Durango to Ouray.

Much of Durango's well-preserved downtown dates back to the region's high-rolling gold mining days in the late 1800s. It's a great place to soak up some atmosphere and gather supplies before heading north into the San Juan Mountains. The fun starts almost as soon as you leave town. Depending on the season, brilliant wildflowers or golden aspens vie with the road for your attention as the drive steadily climbs into the scented wilderness stands of pine and fir of the San Juan National Forest.

Before you know it, you find yourself in open subalpine terrain, winding through one switchback after the next, each offering a new view of the craggy, snow-capped peaks looming above the road and far into the distance. The road climbs through two high mountain passes, Coal Bank and Molas, before arriving in the historic little mining town of Silverton.

Heading north out of Silverton toward Ouray, the road climbs up 11,008-foot-high Red Mountain Pass, then plummets into a heart-in-your-mouth run through Uncompahgre Gorge on the Million Dollar Highway. Built over the course of three years in the 1880s, this monument to human ingenuity hugs sheer rock walls 500 feet above the river. The narrow lanes and lack of guardrails make it one of the most memorable and adventurous drives anywhere.

WEST

## POINTS of INTEREST

**LENGTH**
232 miles

**FUN FACT**
A portion of the road between Silverton and Ouray is known as the Million Dollar Highway. Depending on whom you ask, the highway was named for the amount of gold and silver mined in the area, the value of the low-grade ore tailings used to pave the road, the cost of the construction or the rewarding views.

**SIDE TRIP**
Grander vistas await beyond the highway. Go off-road and rent a 4x4 or take a Jeep tour in Ouray. *ouraycolorado.com*

**NEARBY ATTRACTIONS**
Chimney Rock National Monument, west of Pagosa Springs; Lowry Pueblo Ruins, west of Pleasant View; Ute Indian Museum, Montrose; Southern Ute Cultural Center, Ignacio

▼
*The appropriately named Red Mountain in Gray Copper Gulch.*

While the Million Dollar Highway is perhaps the most exciting section of the skyway, virtually every mile of this high-mountain drive offers great opportunities for photos, sightseeing and daydreaming. Alpine lakes, tarns and streams jeweled with wildflowers flank the road. Distant slopes are spread with aspen and braided with waterfalls; cloud-wreathed pinnacles frame the sky above.

The road also offers access to some of the planet's finest alpine wilderness, easily accessible by foot, horseback or Jeep via a network of trails and mining roads carved through forest and granite mountainside. My favorite off-road destinations are the alpine wildflower meadows that overwhelm the senses in July and August, particularly those at Yankee Boy, American and Governor basins.

Four-wheel it into the backcountry on your own (off-road rentals are available in Silverton and Ouray) or play it safe and join a tour. However you choose to explore this route, you'll have the time of your life. ♣

28  SCENIC DRIVES

WEST

*The West Needle Mountains loom in the distance of the Weminuche Wilderness in the San Juan National Forest.*

WEST

STORY AND PHOTO BY
**LELAND HOWARD**

# SALMON RIVER SCENIC BYWAY

**BLAZE A TRAIL OF PIONEER SPIRIT WITH AMAZING SIGHTS ON THE LEWIS AND CLARK NATIONAL HISTORIC TRAIL.**

**IDAHO'S SALMON RIVER SCENIC BYWAY** begins as Highway 93, crosses the state line from Montana and descends in winding curves through mountain canyons flanked by pines, firs, spruce and cedars. For most of the 161-mile route, the two-lane road follows the main fork of the Salmon River, one of the longest free-flowing rivers in the lower 48 states. A little more than two-thirds of the way down the byway, at Challis, the route veers to the southwest along Highway 75 and ends in Stanley.

It's a 3½-hour drive, but carve out a full day for exploring all the historical sights along the way. In fact, this byway begins at a place called Lost Trail Pass—take it as a sign to lose yourself while you're exploring. The Lewis and Clark exploration party allegedly got disoriented here during its journey from the Mississippi River to the Pacific Ocean in 1804-'06. Much of this scenic drive follows part of the Lewis and Clark National Historic Trail, and many of the views haven't changed.

Salmon's Sacajawea Interpretive, Cultural and Educational Center offers rich insight into the area's natural and native history. Ghost towns like Custer, Bonanza and Bayhorse testify to the gold mining history stemming from the mid-1800s.

After you take the self-guided tour of Bayhorse, I recommend continuing up the canyon. Drive slowly on this steep road and you'll spy a deteriorating cemetery on the hillside. Farther up are structures that once transported ore down and supplies up the extreme incline of the rocky talus slopes.

With views of the Bitterroot Range's White Cloud, Lemhi and Beaverhead mountains, and with glimpses of the Sawtooth peaks between them, plus all the wildlife the Salmon River attracts, you'll find that blazing this pioneer trail will reinvigorate soul and spirit.

WEST

## POINTS of INTEREST

**LENGTH**
161 miles

**FUN FACT**
Hemmed in by sheer cliffs, the dangerous, churning rapids of the Salmon River—a powerful torrent that the Shoshone tribe believed no human could even survive—have earned the waterway the nickname River of No Return. Eventually, however, boatmen learned to master its white water, and today thrilling raft trips and jet-boat tours are available.

**SIDE TRIP**
Ski the slopes at Lost Trail Ski Area, a family-owned hidden gem with breathtaking views atop the Continental Divide. *losttrail.com*

**NEARBY ATTRACTIONS**
Painted Rocks State Park, on Route 473 southwest of Hamilton, Montana; Lake Como, nestled in a valley on Como Road northwest of Darby, Montana

*As it sinks to the horizon, the sun casts soothing light over the wild Salmon River.*

SCENIC DRIVES

WEST

STORY AND PHOTOS BY
**CHUCK HANEY**

# RED SLEEP MOUNTAIN

**SUPERB SCENERY, ABUNDANT WILDLIFE AND A BISON HERD MAKE THIS ROUTE ONE OF THE BEST TREKS IN THE WEST.**

**RED SLEEP MOUNTAIN DRIVE** in the National Bison Range winds past some amazing vistas in Big Sky Country. As the 19-mile, one-way gravel road climbs and descends Red Sleep Mountain, every mile reveals a panoramic view.

I often need three or four hours to complete the loop as I like to stop the car and shut off the engine to listen to the melodic songs of the colorful lazuli bunting or the western meadowlark, Montana's state bird.

A series of switchbacks in the road near its 4,885-foot-high point lead to several short hiking trails. At this lofty altitude, Douglas firs and ponderosa pines replace native grasses. It's a good place to see a rambling black bear, whitetail deer or bighorn sheep.

National Bison Range, located between the Bitterroot and Mission mountains, is home to about 350 bison. These 18,500 untamed acres pack in a lot of diverse wildlife including elk, pronghorn antelope, mountain lions, badgers and muskrats, to name a few. And, with about 200 bird species, it's a birding paradise.

The upper stretches of the road are closed from early October to late spring. Prairie Drive, an out-and-back option through the lower "flats," is open all year.

My favorite time to visit is in May, when the road is fully open, the native prairie grasses have greened up and bison calves can be seen following their mothers about.

Traveling Red Sleep Mountain Drive is an adventure that embodies the spirit of the West—independent, rugged and awe-inspiring.

WEST

*Top: Green grasses make a lovely canvas for bright yellow arrowleaf balsamroot wildflowers. Bottom: Diverse wildlife, including bison herds, is a fixture along the drive.*

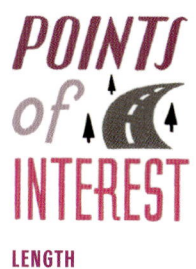

# POINTS of INTEREST

### LENGTH
19 miles

### REST STOPS
Book the lakefront cabin at Swan Hill Bed & Breakfast and start the day with a meal made using fresh local ingredients. *swanhillbedandbreakfast.com*

Look for the windmill in the town of Ravalli. There you'll find the best doughnuts around at the Windmill Village Bakery. *windmillvillagebakery.com*

### NOT TO BE MISSED
Open on Fridays from May to October, the Polson Farmers Market is the place to find local produce, art, baked goods, jams, jellies and more. *polsonfarmersmarket.com*

### SIDE TRIP
Grab your binoculars and be on the lookout for great blue herons, double-crested cormorants and about 200 other bird species at Ninepipe National Wildlife Refuge.

SCENIC DRIVES

*The rays of a sunset illuminate Haystack Rock at Cannon Beach.*

WEST

STORY BY
**DONNA B. ULRICH**

# OREGON COAST HIGHWAY

NATURAL BEAUTY AND CULINARY ADVENTURES ABOUND WHEN TRAVELING "THE PEOPLE'S COAST."

**THE BREATHTAKING VIEWS,** forested headlands, sublime sandy beaches and, best of all, accessibility of the Oregon coast make for a scenic drive unlike any other in the country. The ocean is often within sight of the road, which offers easy access to more than 80 state parks and recreation areas.

The Oregon shore truly is "the people's coast," as it's been dubbed. More than 100 years ago, Gov. Oswald West went before the state legislature and successfully argued that the state's entire 363-mile coastline should be established as a public thoroughfare. Construction of what is now Highway 101 soon followed.

In conjunction with this plan, the state's parks department bought land for 36 state parks along the coastal road, an average of one every 10 miles. Tourists soon took advantage of the improved roadways, putting little towns like Depoe Bay and Yachats on the map. In 1967 the legislature passed the Oregon Beach Bill, preserving free beach access for all.

The late Ray Atkeson wrote in his book, *Oregon Coast*, "I realiz(ed) that I was enjoying the privilege of seeing one of the most magnificent stretches of coastline in the world." We met Ray early in our photographic career; his photos influenced my husband, Larry, and me to share his love for the shore.

We are lucky to live only 80 miles from the Oregon border. When we first started traveling and photographing for calendars, magazines and books, images of crashing waves on rugged coastlines sold well, as did lighthouses and sunsets over sandy beaches.

We still like to take off for a few days, camp in the state parks, hike the rugged trails and eat our way up the coast. Try breakfast at the Crazy

SCENIC DRIVES 35

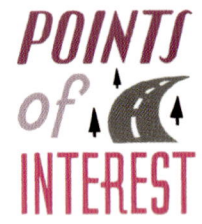

WEST

*A gate stands open at Fort Clatsop National Memorial.*

## POINTS of INTEREST

**LENGTH**
363 miles

**WORDS TO THE WISE**
In summer allow plenty of time, since traffic can be heavy and the road is narrow and winding.

**SIDE TRIP**
For a look at inland scenery, turn east at Gold Beach (29 miles north of Brookings) and follow the 140-mile loop along the Rogue and Coquille rivers. Take Routes 595, 33 and 219 north, then continue on Route 42 from Myrtle Point to Coos Bay. The drive, which passes through a forest containing rare myrtlewood trees, treats travelers to splendid views of cliffs, canyons and the deep blue waters of the rivers.

**NEARBY ATTRACTIONS**
Tillamook Air Museum; Tillamook County Pioneer Museum; Latimer Quilt & Textile Center, Tillamook; Columbia River Maritime Museum, Astoria

Norwegians Fish & Chips in Port Orford, a scoop of mudslide ice cream from the Tillamook Cheese Factory, and then a feast of Oregon's only native oysters, the Olympia, in Netarts Bay. These tiny oysters were harvested to near extinction but are now making a very tasty comeback.

After all that eating, we usually need to take a hike. I recommend the trail up to the top of Humbug Mountain near Port Orford. Or head to the Oregon Dunes National Recreation Area, where more than 40 miles of coastline are waiting for your footprints.

Whale-watching is a year-round activity here. Gray whales make their way up the Oregon coast from late March to June and down from mid-December through January. For a week during each peak season, volunteers at 24 sites will help you spot the giant mammals. Larry and I also enjoy bird-watching; when the whales are playing hard-to-get, we'll watch brown pelicans diving for fish or osprey soaring above.

In any season, we like to travel the coast to shoot stunning offshore rock formations called sea stacks. Cannon Beach features the famous Haystack Rock, and the area around the town of Bandon is full of these rock formations. They are especially gorgeous during low tide, when the sunset is reflected in the sand.

Waves crashing on the headlands at Shore Acres State Park, near Charleston, also make for a spectacle—especially from November through January. And near the city of Astoria, the first permanent settlement on the Pacific, you'll find the reconstructed Fort Clatsop, where the Lewis and Clark expedition spent a winter.

Whether you're taking pictures, fishing or watching whales, the Oregon Coast Highway offers an accessible adventure, free of freeways and full of enough beauty to stop traffic.

36  SCENIC DRIVES

WEST

*Humbug Mountain State Park offers a stunning seaside view.*

▼ *Rushing waters carved the Minam River Canyon, accessible from the western side of the Hells Canyon Scenic Byway.*

WEST

STORY AND PHOTOS BY
**DAVID JENSEN**

# HELLS CANYON

RUGGED LANDSCAPE, ROLLING HILLS AND IDYLLIC FARMS—THIS OREGON ROUTE HAS IT ALL.

**BEFORE HELLS CANYON SCENIC BYWAY** existed even as an idea, I made several painful, frustrating attempts over the years to follow some of its most primitive segments. The journey never went well, and I often returned home in a vehicle prematurely aged by battles with the rocky, rough track. I always carried two spare tires, and sometimes I needed them both and regretted not having a third. The wonders of Oregon's Hells Canyon, the deepest river gorge in North America, were tantalizingly close and yet so far away.

Then, in 1992, the Wallowa-Whitman National Forest finished paving the 45 miles of primitive track linking the Wallowa Valley with the paved Highway 86 in Baker County. The loop was soon designated as the Hells Canyon Scenic Byway by the U.S. Forest Service. The route I had struggled with was finally on the map in a really big way, eventually becoming an All-American Road and a scenic travel destination.

The byway is at its very best in October, providing access to achingly beautiful autumn vistas along a winding road through coniferous forests, snowy mountains, deep river canyons, and valleys dotted with farms and small towns.

Along the way you will peer right into the plunging depths of Hells Canyon, which was carved over time by the rushing waters of the Snake River. Driving it so late in the season increases the beauty but also the adventure, because you never know when the first big snowstorm will close the high-elevation segment of the route on the east side of the Wallowa Mountains. The forest service cautions that the byway is usually closed due to snow from late October through late May or early June. Timing is important when chasing fall beauty here.

The foliage color intensifies as October advances, reaching its peak late in the month when the reds of huckleberry and hawthorn and the yellows and oranges of cottonwood and larch are at their best, standing out dramatically against the fresh, pristine snow accumulating on the high peaks.

SCENIC DRIVES 39

WEST

# POINTS of INTEREST

**LENGTH**
213 miles

**NOT TO BE MISSED**
Mules get the recognition they deserve for carrying loads out west during Hells Canyon Mule Days. Held the weekend after Labor Day in Enterprise, the event promises a Dutch oven cook-off, a parade and more. hellscanyon muledays.com

**SIDE TRIPS**
Follow Highway 86 to the northeast at Pine Creek for an optional side trip to the Snake River at the bottom of Hells Canyon. Carved by the waters of the Snake River, the canyon is deeper than Arizona's Grand Canyon. The road into the canyon and then downstream along the Idaho side of the river is paved to the Hells Canyon Creek Visitor Center. You'll see stunning views of the river winding through stupendous cliffs. This 48-mile round-trip diversion adds two to three hours to the trip.

Hike the trails at the Nez Perce Wallowa Homeland and tour the visitor center to learn about the tribe's history.

*Farms with vibrantly colored barns add a peaceful touch to the drive.*

Although doing it in eight hours is quite possible, you would get just a sampling of what there is to see. At the start, Highway 84 out of La Grande heads north through farmland along the Grande Ronde River and swings east over Minam Summit, dropping then into the rocky, cottonwood-lined canyons of the Minam and Wallowa rivers. From there, the route follows the Wallowa to its broad upper valley, where snowy mountains stand over a foreground of red barns and where the cottonwoods are brilliant in late October. Fall color also peaks late in the month at Wallowa Lake, a highlight of the drive for many travelers.

Gas up in the tourist town of Joseph, because if you opt for a side trip into the depths of Hells Canyon, your next chance won't come until about 120 miles later at the town of Halfway on Highway 86. From Joseph, a succession of mountain passes through stands of colorful western larch leads to the Imnaha River and then to a final pass where a 2-mile diversion leads to the Hells Canyon Overlook. Then descend south along Pine Creek to Highway 86. Here you will have two options: Turn northeast for the very depths of Hells Canyon (see the side trip at left) or turn southwest toward the town of Halfway.

At Halfway, the byway continues on 86 to the historic Powder River, which led early explorers to the route that came to be known as the Oregon Trail. Flagstaff Hill is the next stop, and there you will find the National Historic Oregon Trail Interpretive Center near I-84 where the byway officially ends.

At the center, reflect on this: From the days of covered wagons until the byway's recent creation, your effortless excursion had been beyond the reach of all but the boldest of adventurers.

40  SCENIC DRIVES

WEST

*Mountain peaks dominate the skyline along the road near Enterprise.*

▼ *Eleven active glaciers comprise Mount Hood's icy coat.*

WEST

STORY AND PHOTOS BY
**STEVE TERRILL**

# MOUNT HOOD SCENIC BYWAY

DELVE INTO FARMLAND AS FAR AS THE EYE CAN SEE, FLOWING WATERS AND ALPINE VISTAS.

**HEADING JUST EAST OF PORTLAND,** where the Columbia River divides Washington from Oregon, the Mount Hood Scenic Byway offers a breathtaking drive. This nearly triangular loop, roughly 130 miles long, first follows along the Columbia River Gorge, then arcs down and around magnificent Mount Hood.

I start with a piping hot coffee and mouthwatering cinnamon roll from the Troutdale General Store, a homespun gift shop with a nostalgic soda fountain and fun 1950s decor. Merging onto eastbound I-84, I follow the rolling Columbia River. Undulating forested hills, jutting basalt cliffs and rolling grasslands color my view. Union Pacific Railroad tracks snake in and out of sight, promising the sudden excitement of spying a bright yellow locomotive.

So many incredible places branch out along this 50-mile or so stretch, it's hard to pick just one to investigate. In less than an hour's drive, I'll pass 11 state parks and at least as many waterfalls. Between the Sandy River and the Hood River, the highway passes little lakes and crosses many tributaries. There are recreation areas and islands, wildlife refuges and state trails, plus the Bridge of the Gods, Cascade Locks and Bonneville Dam.

But Multnomah Falls, one of the tallest waterfalls in the country, simply cannot be bypassed. Whether you make the short hike to the Benson Bridge or trek the steep 1.2 miles to the top, the view will send your soul soaring.

Onward and eastward, I turn south at the city of Hood River and head into the upper section of the Hood River County Fruit Loop. Here, volcanic soil and moderate climate make this one of the major fruit-producing regions of the world. Roadside stands offer a bounty of local wares: fresh fruits and

SCENIC DRIVES 43

WEST

# POINTS of INTEREST

**LENGTH**
About 130 miles

**FUN FACTS**
Steam rising from volcanic vents hint at the magma lurking deep inside the dormant behemoth. National Science Foundation research indicates Mount Hood isn't an explosive eruptor, but more of an oozer.

The volcanic slopes of Mount Hood enrich the rainwater runoff and make the Hood River Valley one of the largest fruit-growing regions in Oregon. Apricots, blueberries, pears, apples and grapes flourish there.

**WORDS TO THE WISE**
If you are new to mountain climbing, licensed groups like Timberline Mountain Guides and the Northwest School of Survival can teach and guide you.

**NEARBY ATTRACTIONS**
Hood River and Flerchinger vineyards and Pheasant Valley Winery, Hood River

*Cows graze in the pastoral setting of Metzger Prairie.*

vegetables, jams, jellies, syrups, wine, baked goods, crafts, antiques and more. Mount Hood looms over this valley of vast orchards, urging me forward, while the reflection of Mount Adams fills my rearview mirror.

Heading south, the road rises and deciduous trees give way to an evergreen forest of Douglas fir. While I follow the Hood River, crisscrossing bridges, the mountain plays peek-a-boo through these trees. Campgrounds dot the forest, with enchanting medieval names like Nottingham and Sherwood Campground. Trails like the Robin Hood Loop lead to wildflower-speckled meadows, waterfall-dotted creeks and other riches.

After rounding the foot of Mount Hood, I detour slightly to the historic 1930s-built Timberline Lodge, a WPA project crafted almost entirely by hand. This National Historic Landmark features fine dining, snack bars, gift stores, overnight lodging and year-round skiing. The U.S. Forest Service gives an engaging free tour of the lodge and surrounding area.

Finally, I head northwest on Highway 26 back toward Troutdale, winding down the foothills. A pastoral landscape greets me as I emerge from the forest. Small villages here cater to outdoor recreation enthusiasts.

I make one more stop, this time at the Wildwood Recreation Site. After an easy hike along the boardwalk trail, I gaze through a fish-viewing window built into the streambed, amazed by the perspective into underwater life. I'll return to my starting point by nightfall—having spent a full day driving what would take less than three hours without stops. Yet even now, I feel like I could explore so much more!

WEST

*Multnomah Falls is a popular spot to visit and photograph.*

*The blue sky here makes a sharp contrast to the Castle, a formation of Navajo and Wingate sandstone.*

WEST

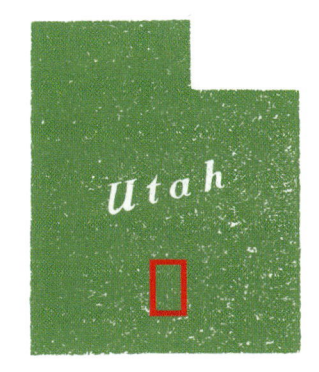

STORY BY
**CATHY & GORDON ILLG**

# JOURNEY THROUGH TIME

AN ETHEREAL WORLD GLOWS IN GOLD AS FALL ARRIVES IN UTAH'S RED ROCK COUNTRY.

**THE FALL COLOR WAS** some of the most intense we'd ever seen, and it was in a place few people consider for leaf peeping. It wasn't that the variety of colors was so spectacular, for the leaves were all the same vibrant gold; it was the setting. We were traveling through the desert on the Colorado Plateau in southern Utah.

Our five days without a stoplight, along the 123-mile stretch of state Highway 12 known as the Journey Through Time Scenic Byway, began the last week of October, outside the small community of Escalante.

If you are an intrepid explorer, willing to hike and get your feet wet (and if you can negotiate slick rock and sandy washes), countless hidden patches of autumn are waiting for you. However, if you find easy walks and roadside viewing enough to satisfy your desire for adventure, as we do, Highway 12 itself and the Burr Trail Road—and for a side trip, the Hole-in-the-Rock Road—will fill the bill nicely.

Lower Calf Creek Falls is a popular attraction. This impressive 126-foot waterfall drops down a colorful sandstone rock face. The trailhead to the falls is about halfway between the towns of Boulder and Escalante. The nearly 6-mile round-trip hike is a bit more than an easy walk, but the steep sections are short and without technical difficulty. The entire bottom of the canyon is filled with amber hues at this time of year. Cascading water in the desert is always a miracle.

From pullouts on the ridge high above the canyons of the Escalante River drainage, visitors can look down on these ribbons of fall color slicing their way through sheer rock. Just eight minutes by car from the waterfall, the Escalante River Trailhead leads to

SCENIC DRIVES   47

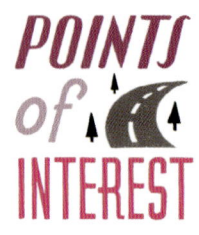

WEST

# POINTS of INTEREST

**LENGTH**
123 miles

**REST STOP**
Just off Highway 12, Boulder Mountain Lodge is a convenient place to stay. Plus, an 11-acre bird sanctuary surrounds the lodge.
*boulder-utah.com*

**SIDE TRIPS**
Spot the Milky Way as it twinkles in the dark skies over Capitol Reef National Park.
*nps.gov/care*

Hole-in-the-Rock Road is a 62-mile one-way route that follows a path taken by Mormon pioneers on their way to a new settlement in 1879. If you have a high-clearance vehicle with four-wheel drive, this is the place for off-roading.

When the settlers reached a thin crack in the canyon rim, they camped and worked all winter to widen the opening so 250 people, over 1,000 animals and 83 wagons could pass. The actual Hole in the Rock is at mile 55.

Devils Garden, about 12 miles down the road, is popular for its oddly shaped rock formations.

*Witness wildlife such as mule deer in Capitol Reef National Park.*

a short, easy walk through lovely cottonwoods, and there is an overlook above the river on the south side.

Heading north from Escalante toward Capitol Reef National Park, we took a side trip along the Burr Trail Road outside the town of Boulder. The western part of the road is paved, and this 17-mile section of the Burr Trail is among our favorites in fall for two reasons: Long Canyon and the Gulch. Above both gorges, pullouts look out on phenomenal views of golden trees dwarfed by red canyon walls.

We ended our Highway 12 road trip with two nights in Torrey, on the edge of Capitol Reef National Park. Fall color is so close to park roads, it almost demands you to stop and admire it.

One of the best places for leaf peeping is just across the highway from the Capitol Reef National Park Visitor Center. Fantastic monumental natural sculptures of Navajo and Wingate sandstone rise up all around, dominated by one that's called the Castle. Cottonwoods in twos and threes follow the course of Sulphur Creek at the base of the formations as its waters flow to the junction with the Fremont River, carving a narrow route through the Waterpocket Fold, a 100-mile-long buckle in Earth's surface.

Autumn in this arid part of the West is unique. Here, unlike many places, you can see a handful of glowing cottonwoods softening the outlines of towering red rock formations.

WEST

*Highway 12 leads to many wonders, including the rock arches of Devils Garden.*

▼ *Lupine blossom across the side of Steptoe Butte.*

WEST

STORY BY **MARY LIZ AUSTIN**
PHOTOS BY **MARY LIZ AUSTIN & TERRY DONNELLY**

# HEART OF THE PALOUSE

**WASHINGTON'S U.S. HIGHWAY 195 SERVES UP SOME OF THE WORLD'S MOST FERTILE AND UNIQUELY SCENIC FARMLAND.**

**IT'S A LATE AFTERNOON IN JUNE** as Terry and I make a beeline down U.S. Highway 195 in the heart of Washington's Palouse country. Heavy rain clouds have accompanied us on our drive to the southeastern corner of our state, and it appears they might clear.

When you say "clearing storm" to photographers on the way to a shoot, watch them step on the gas.

The Palouse, one of the most productive agricultural regions in the world, encompasses thousands of square miles of undulating hills formed by wind-borne silt. As you drive through, you can't help but imagine you're at sea, with clusters of grain elevators and isolated barns resembling ships' hulls breaking against the sky.

Rivers and streams did not create these rolling hills; there are no continuous valleys in the area, and the hills don't connect. Rather, a series of geologic events forged the Palouse—massive floods, volcanic eruptions, lava flows and dust storms that blew silt from the South. Some say that at today's wind speeds it would take 25,000 years to re-create one 80-foot hill of silt.

U.S. Highway 195 runs from Spokane, Washington, to Lewiston, Idaho, just across the border. Along the way it passes through a number of friendly farm towns, as well as Pullman, home of Washington State University. My favorite section of the road spans Whitman County, a 55-mile stretch from Rosalia to Uniontown. I love to stay in the bustling town of Colfax. With roads radiating in all directions, it's a wonderful base camp for exploring the Palouse.

Head to Steptoe Butte State Park in the small town of Steptoe for the region's most dramatic view. The butte,

SCENIC DRIVES

WEST

*The iron-wheel fence of Dahmen Barn.*

## POINTS of INTEREST

**LENGTH**
105 miles

**FUN FACT**
Frank Smith discovered a giant earthworm in the soil near Pullman in 1897. *Driloleirus americanus* can grow to be 3 feet long; it was last spotted in 2010.

**SIDE TRIP**
Palouse Falls is a must-see for anyone traveling through the area. The Palouse River drops 198 feet into a rocky canyon, making for one of the most beautiful landmarks in the state of Washington. *parks.wa.gov*

a towering thimble-shaped remnant of an ancient mountaintop, is easy to spot in this sea of green. A spiraling road leads to the 3,612-foot summit, and panoramic views of the outlying farmlands and towns appear as soon as you start the ascent. On a clear day you can see for 200 miles from the top. It's a perfect place to watch raptors ride the wind currents while sunlight rakes the patchwork fields—and on this day, to photograph a clearing storm!

There are also plenty of handsome barns in this region, built by early settlers to store hay, shelter farm animals and serve as workshops. Today, many have been remodeled to fill new roles. One of our favorites, the Dahmen Barn in Uniontown, once housed a commercial dairy operation. Now it's a thriving art center with studio space for 20 local artists and a very distinctive fence constructed from a thousand antique iron farm-machinery wheels. Resident artists teach classes in painting and other media to visitors of all ages.

I especially love this area in June, with its colorful mix of greens ranging from maturing wheat fields to the new fuzz of germinating legumes. In July, you will see golden waves of ripe wheat and bright yellow canola flowering against a blue sky as red barns peek out of the folds of the hills.

Of course, you can enjoy the view from 195 any time of year. The seasons transform the Palouse. In autumn, the changing leaves of deciduous trees add vibrant oranges, reds and yellows to the horizon. Farmers bring out their machinery to harvest crops, adding another layer of depth to the surrounding landscape. In winter, light snow drapes these rolling hills in serenity and stillness. Come spring, the cycle begins again, and beautifully blossoming wildflowers emerge on hillsides and buttes. Spring weather is unpredictable, with storms as sudden as they are intense.

You might even catch that clearing storm and see a cloud sailing across the sky with a rainbow for its tail! ❧

SCENIC DRIVES

WEST

*A weathered barn stands before a carpet of ripe canola.*

WEST

*Isolated farms look like ships in a sea of wheat throughout the Palouse.*

WEST

> **"Another glorious day, the air as delicious to the lungs as nectar to the tongue."**
>
> —JOHN MUIR

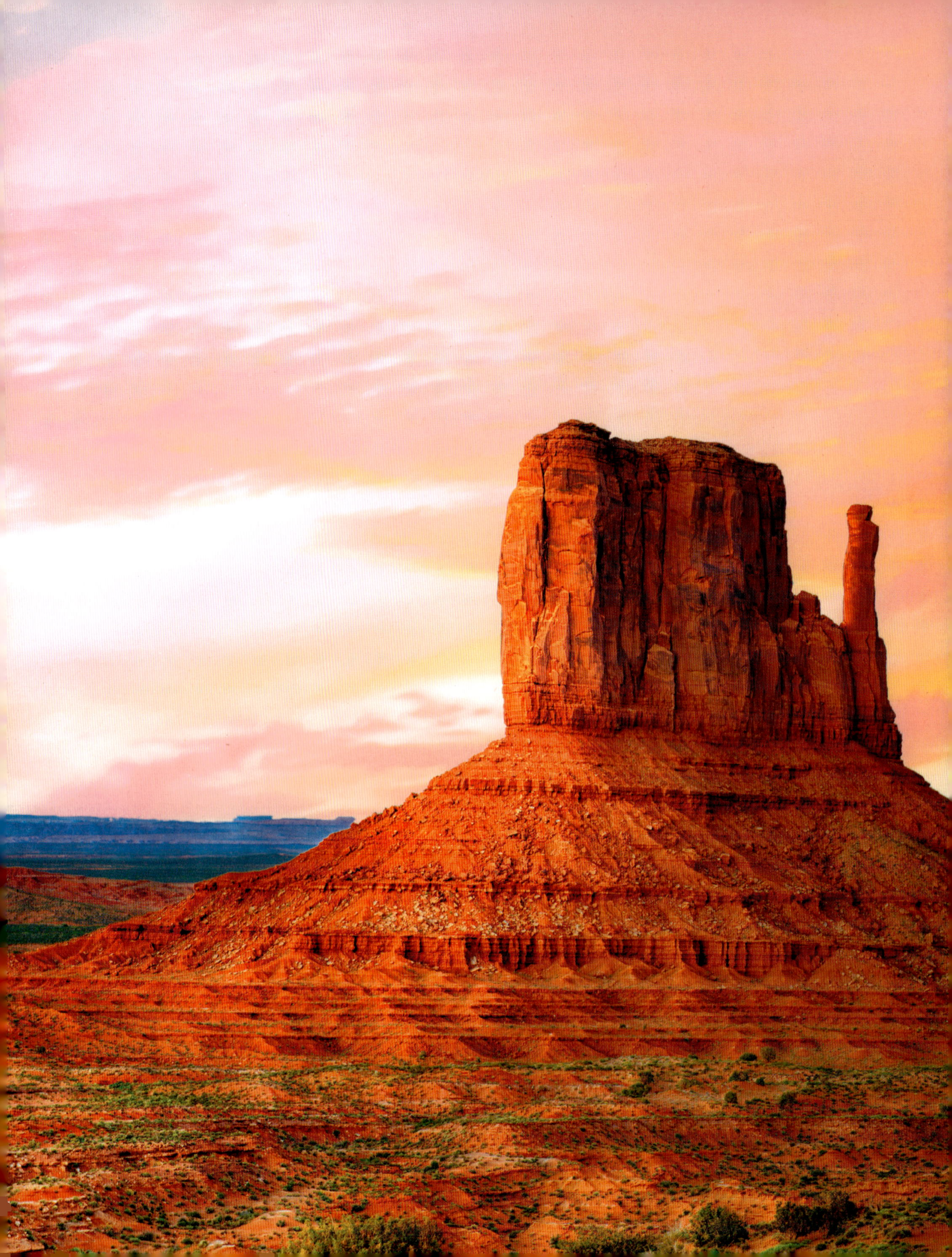

# SOUTHWEST

ARIZONA · NEW MEXICO · OKLAHOMA · TEXAS

SOUTHWEST

STORY BY **DONNA B. ULRICH**
PHOTOS BY **LARRY ULRICH**

# APACHE TRAIL

MEET THE ROAD THAT MAKES RENTAL CAR DRIVERS WEEP.

**THE APACHE TRAIL** is not for the faint of heart who prefer their roads paved and with guardrails. Though the 41.5-mile drive snakes through some of the most beautiful and rugged terrain in the Sonoran Desert, it's a challenge for drivers unaccustomed to one-lane dirt roads with turnouts, precipitous drop-offs and nothing between you and the canyon below.

The first time we drove it, in the early '80s, it was as rough as any regularly maintained road can be. One of Larry's favorite sayings (and one that has gotten us in trouble more than I care to reveal) is, "The road is on the AAA map; it must be good."

Larry studies maps constantly (that's why we get in trouble so often) and wants to go somewhere because it sounds cool. I have to admit, he was right about the Apache Trail.

The road has threads of history running through it. Also known as State Route 88, it follows a path first used by the Salado Indians to traverse the Superstition Mountains. Later it became a stagecoach route connecting Phoenix to Globe, and finally a roadway to construct dams along the Salt River.

Be there at dawn to capture an iconic image of the Arizona landscape. The road runs east to west, perfect for taking photos in early-morning and late-afternoon light.

The Apache Trail begins in Apache Junction and heads east into the Old West. You'll pass places with names like Goldfield Ghost Town, Sweetheart Peak, Lost Dutchman State Park and Tortilla Flat. Prehistoric cultural sites are scattered throughout the area, but our favorite at the east end of the trail is Tonto National Monument, well-preserved cliff dwellings inhabited by the Salado people in the 13th, 14th and 15th centuries.

Fish Creek Hill starts the second half of the drive; this is the stretch that can make the city driver in a rental car nervous. The pavement ends and the dusty road becomes a steep series of twists and turns. The road hangs on the side of Fish Creek Canyon, which drains the Superstition Mountains.

If you're looking for grand views, great geology, reservoirs full of fish, lots of hiking trails and a year-round creek, head out of the city and take a day to explore this historic trail.

SOUTHWEST

# POINTS of INTEREST

**LENGTH**
41.5 miles

**WORDS TO THE WISE**
Start with a full tank of gas and plenty of water. The speed limits are low, so the drive may take you longer than expected.

**SIDE TRIPS**
Lost Dutchman State Park offers campsites and nature trails. The 300-acre park derives its name from Jacob Waltz, a shadowy figure who—according to legend—discovered a rich gold mine during the late 1800s but never revealed its exact whereabouts. Over the years, at least 36 treasure seekers have died or disappeared seeking the elusive lode.

Tortilla Flat was once a stagecoach stop. This resurrected ghost town has a cafe, country store and a permanent population of six. But its weekend visitors, lured by souvenir shops, prickly-pear ice cream and the cool waters of Tortilla Creek, are far greater in number.

**NEARBY ATTRACTION**
Superstition Mountain Museum, Apache Junction

*Top: The storied Superstition Mountains loom over saguaro cactuses and wildflowers. Bottom: A creek trickles through West Boulder Canyon, Tonto National Forest.*

SCENIC DRIVES  59

*The view from Monument Valley's North Window presents an otherworldly landscape.*

SOUTHWEST

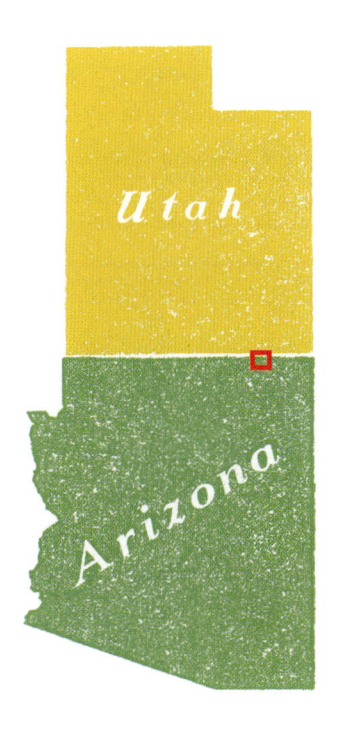

STORY AND PHOTOS BY
**TIM FITZHARRIS**

# MONUMENT VALLEY

MEANDER AMONG ARIZONA AND UTAH'S FAMOUS SPIRES, PINNACLES AND BUTTES, WHICH ARE EVEN MORE AMAZING IN REAL LIFE THAN THEY ARE IN THE MOVIES.

**YOU'VE PROBABLY SEEN THIS PLACE** before in a zillion cowboy movies, not to mention *Thelma & Louise*, *Forrest Gump* and Road Runner cartoons. Monument Valley, mostly in Arizona and partly in Utah, is every bit as impressive in real life.

For starters, it generates a feeling of the surreal, a combination of film deja vu and otherworldly landforms. I ask myself, *Am I really seeing this without a remote in my hand?* Well, it's there for sure, and you can drive among the soaring 400- to 1,000-foot red monoliths and scamper about jumbled boulders.

For photographers like me, it's an abundance of powerful graphic elements just waiting to be wrestled into a composition. The giant towers of rock, glowing red against a blue sky, have names to match their extravagant shapes: Totem Pole, Bear and Rabbit, Elephant Butte, the Mittens, Gray Whiskers and Rain God Mesa.

Monument Valley is Navajo Nation tribal land, and occasionally you'll see their herdsmen, wild ponies and livestock wandering through the mesas. I also look for these when I'm shooting photos, as they make great perspective

SCENIC DRIVES **61**

SOUTHWEST

# Points of Interest

**LENGTH**
17 miles

**FUN FACT**
In the mid-1500s, when Spanish explorers first encountered the southwestern Native American tribes, there were three major cultures in the Southwest: the Hohokam, an agricultural group located in the river valleys of the desert; the Mogollon, who were hunters and gatherers; and the Anasazi, who were cliff dwellers.

**WORDS TO THE WISE**
When on Indian reservations, abide by local customs. Ask permission before taking photos; never disturb artifacts.

**SIDE TRIP**
Directly east of Monument Valley find Four Corners Navajo Tribal Park. Here you can stand in the spot where Arizona, Utah, Colorado and New Mexico meet.

**NEARBY ATTRACTIONS**
Grand Canyon National Park, Arizona; Petrified Forest National Park, near Holbrook, Arizona; Zion National Park, Springdale, Utah

*This aptly named oddity is Mushroom Rock.*

references that show the grand scale of this place.

The 17-mile scenic drive through the valley features 11 numbered stops, each with a special view of rock formations. If you want to photograph the sand dunes like I did, you need to hire a Navajo guide to escort you into these areas. It's worth the extra fee. You don't need four-wheel drive, but a high-clearance vehicle saves wear and tear on your car.

The photographic challenge is timing the sun's route to spotlight rock faces and sandstone summits. I accomplish this by rising before dawn, and driving, hiking, rock-scrambling and chasing the perfect light and shadows by car during the day.

A spiritual place for the Navajo people, Monument Valley's exotic desert wilderness works its magic on most anyone.

SOUTHWEST

*As the sun rises behind East Mitten rock, it's clear how it received its name.*

▼
*In autumn, sumacs, oaks and maples paint Oak Creek Canyon in gold and crimson.*

SOUTHWEST

STORY BY
**MARIJA ANDRIC**

# OAK CREEK CANYON

RED ROCKS, STEEP SWITCHBACKS AND DRAMATIC VIEWS MAKE THIS ARIZONA DRIVE A NAIL-BITER.

**GROWING UP IN ARIZONA,** I loved the biodiversity of the state. Minutes from my home, I could hike the best trails in the Sonoran Desert, and after a few hours of driving, I could breathe fresh alpine air and marvel at fall foliage. And there's one scenic drive in Arizona that has it all: Oak Creek Canyon.

This 15-mile state-designated scenic road along Route 89A begins in Sedona (if you're coming from Phoenix) and winds its way north to Flagstaff. It curves up the Colorado Plateau from the high desert to a landscape of ponderosa pines.

Getting to the start of the drive is a treat for the senses. Route 89A rolls through Oak Creek Village, passing iconic red rocks that are named for their shapes. The landscape has an unearthly feel, and its singular beauty is unforgettable. Bell Rock, which is just off the road, is a popular spot to pull over for pictures or go on a hike along the lower, easier trail.

My family and I took this drive in the summer to escape the dry desert heat and in the fall to see the foliage, which begins to turn in November. After crossing the Midgley Bridge, our first stop was Slide Rock State Park, a 43-acre historic apple farm that was at one time the Pendley homestead. Growing apples in the high desert sounds far-fetched, but Frank Pendley mastered an innovative irrigation technique in 1912 that allowed his orchards to thrive. In fact, today park officials still use the same technique to water the remaining heirloom trees.

Though the apple orchard is amazing, the main attraction is the park's namesake natural slide, which is a slippery chute of worn sandstone about 80 feet long and up to 4 feet wide. The waters of Oak Creek, which carved this canyon, are icy cold and refreshing. Children and adults alike squeal in delight as the water carries them down the slide into a pool.

Algae makes the rocks especially slippery, so it's important to wear water shoes. It's also important to look up and appreciate the canyon walls and

SCENIC DRIVES **65**

SOUTHWEST

# POINTS of INTEREST

**LENGTH**
15 miles

**FUN FACT**
The dramatic reds and oranges in the rocks of Sedona come from iron oxide, left from a post-glacial ocean that filled the Verde Valley.

**WORDS TO THE WISE**
A Red Rock Pass is required if you want to stop and park your car along the drive.

**SIDE TRIP**
Thousands of years before Hollywood discovered the red rocks of Sedona and the beauty of Oak Creek Canyon, the Sinagua called this place home. Though they moved on centuries ago, they left behind the Palatki and Honanki cliff dwellings. The sites are open to the public and overseen by Coconino National Forest staff. Call 928-282-3854 to reserve a tour spot.

**NEARBY ATTRACTIONS**
Lowell Observatory, Flagstaff; Tlaquepaque district, Sedona; Fort Verde State Historic Park, Camp Verde; Sharlot Hall Museum, Prescott; Smoki Museum, Prescott

▼
*Red Rock Crossing, with its view of Cathedral Rock, is a must-see.*

cliffs that surround the park. I've never been disappointed by that view.

Back on the highway, you could easily stay in your car to take in the sights, but along the road, a few picnic sites, campgrounds and overlooks, such as Banjo Bill and Halfway, are well worth exploring.

The farther you drive, the higher you climb. The air cools, and by the time you reach the West Fork Trail, ponderosa pines appear alongside oaks and junipers. The trail, one of the most popular in the area, follows the west fork of Oak Creek.

In fall, the trees are ablaze with reds, oranges and yellows. The canyon walls soar, and the sound of the moving water soothes. You'll step onto a paved trail that leads to a footbridge over the creek and Mayhew's Lodge, the ruins of an old guesthouse that burned down in 1980. At that point, your West Fork Trail adventure begins. The in-and-out hike is about 6 miles round trip.

The thrilling part of the drive begins at Pumphouse Wash. For the following 2 miles, the road curves into a series of switchbacks, each steeper than the last.

If you're lucky enough to be the passenger, you'll see some gorgeous views of the canyon. (My mother always kept her head down during this part of the drive.) If you're the driver, well, you're probably looking at your knuckles and the road ahead.

Years ago, my husband-to-be and I went on this curvy drive. Though I knew where we were going, he insisted on using GPS. As the GPS attempted to chart the switchbacks, the fine pink line of the road turned into a blob.

It's a slow drive to the top, but when you get there, be sure to stop at the Oak Creek Vista. Take a look back at where you've been, and marvel at the wonder of it all. The elevation changes and the diverse ecosystems of the drive are laid out before you. It's a popular stop with visitors. The overlook is also home to a market offering Native American arts and crafts.

At this point, you're on the Colorado Plateau's southwestern edge. This is commonly referred to as the Mogollon Rim. The air up here is cooler and the forest is thick with pine trees.

The old lumber town of Flagstaff (home to the San Francisco Peaks, Northern Arizona University and Route 66) lies ahead. But that's a scenic drive for another day. ✤

SCENIC DRIVES

SOUTHWEST

*Slide Rock State Park's natural slide is an oasis of fun.*

SOUTHWEST

STORY AND PHOTO BY
**ADAM SCHALLAU**

# NEW MEXICO'S NORTH

TRAVEL HIGHWAY 64, AND YOU'LL SEE WHY THIS STATE IS DUBBED THE LAND OF ENCHANTMENT.

**WHEN YOU PLAN A TRIP** across New Mexico, you may have visions of arid desert and long stretches of flat, desolate roads. But if you're driving on Highway 64 in the northern reaches of the state, what you find will surprise you.

From the town of Cimarron in the northeast, you leave the grasslands of the high plains behind and head west toward the Sangre de Cristo Mountains. Along the way, you'll follow the Cimarron River as it flows through Cimarron Canyon State Park, where tall cliffs known as the Palisades dominate the landscape.

As the road climbs up out of the canyon, you are rewarded with a view of the Moreno Valley. The valley is home to the towns of Eagle Nest and Angel Fire, which is where parts of the TV miniseries *Lonesome Dove* were filmed. This area is also part of the Enchanted Circle Scenic Byway, a great detour from Highway 64. The Sangres surround Moreno Valley. Wheeler Peak, the tallest in the state and part of the Sangres, sits at the northern end of the valley.

Continuing west, you will come to the historic town of Taos, which is known for its countless artists, adobe architecture, great northern New Mexican cuisine and the Taos Pueblo community. Be sure to give yourself plenty of time to explore the area as well as the many galleries and museums in Taos.

About 10 miles northwest of Taos, you'll cross Rio Grande Gorge Bridge 650 feet above the Rio Grande Gorge. The gorge, which is part of the Rio Grande del Norte National Monument, is the result of a separation in the Earth's crust as tectonic plates scraped against each other. A walk across the bridge is not for the faint of heart, but the view is stunning.

Next pass through the village of Tres Piedras. Here you'll discover that the forest is a mix of pines in the lower elevations, transitioning to aspens as you reach the high point on the journey at over 10,000 feet at Brazos Cliffs. When you look back on the experience, you can see why New Mexicans call their state The Land of Enchantment.

SOUTHWEST

# POINTS of INTEREST

### NOT TO BE MISSED
Every July, Native American dancers from across the country perform traditional dances at the Taos Pueblo Pow Wow. taos.org/events/taos-pueblo-pow-wow

### WORDS TO THE WISE
Roads can be icy and snowpacked in winter and early spring.

### NEARBY ATTRACTIONS
Aztec Ruins National Monument, Aztec; Bisti Wilderness and Chaco Culture National Historical Park, south of Farmington; Heron Lake State Park, near Rutheron; Kit Carson Home and Museum, Taos

▼ *Rio Grande River Gorge must have startled early explorers who happened upon it.*

SCENIC DRIVES **69**

▼
*The Talimena Scenic Byway cuts through the Ouachita National Forest.*

SOUTHWEST

STORY AND PHOTOS BY
**INGE JOHNSSON**

# TALIMENA SCENIC BYWAY

GORGEOUS SCENERY GREETS YOU AT EVERY TURN ON THIS SURPRISING TRIP IN SEARCH OF FALL COLOR IN OKLAHOMA.

**YOU MAY NOT THINK OF OKLAHOMA** as a place of natural splendor—especially not one with blazing fall colors. Yet the Sooner State has plenty of beautiful scenery. For the best fall leaf-peeping, grab the car keys and head to the Talimena Scenic Byway. The route is located in the large, dense Ouachita National Forest (pronounced WASH-i-tah), which crosses the state line between Oklahoma and Arkansas. Named after the towns on each end of the drive, the 54-mile byway stretches from Talihina, Oklahoma, to Mena, Arkansas.

Curving roads on the mountain ridge follow some of the highest peaks in the area, including Rich Mountain and Winding Stair Mountain. If you can resist stopping to marvel at the many vistas and attractions along the way, the route takes 1 ½ to two hours to drive. A leisurely trip can take all day

SCENIC DRIVES 71

SOUTHWEST

## POINTS of INTEREST

**LENGTH**
54 miles

**REST STOPS**
Stay atop Rich Mountain, Arkansas' second-highest peak, at Queen Wilhelmina State Park Lodge, and relax on one of the inviting porches with panoramic views, or hike the nearby trails. *arkansasstateparks.com*

Step back in time to experience an old-fashioned home-style breakfast or lunch at the Skyline Cafe in Mena.

**WORDS TO THE WISE**
Bring your hiking boots, bicycle, ATV or horse to view the spectacular fall foliage from the trails in Talimena State Park, Oklahoma's entrance to the Talimena Scenic Byway. *travelok.com/talimena*

**SIDE TRIP**
Drive about an hour south of the byway to Beavers Bend State Park, where you can canoe on Broken Bow Lake, trout fish on Mountain Fork River, go biking, play a round of golf and more. *travelok.com/beaversbend*

*Vibrant foliage lines the banks of Big Creek.*

or more, but I recommend spending two to three days in the area to really take it all in.

There are many options for overnight accommodations, including camping, cabins, hotels and lodges. Pitch a tent at Winding Stair Campground, which has drive-up camping sites and a walk-in camp area for backpackers.

Talimena Scenic Byway is also a photographer's paradise. Twenty-two panoramic lookouts invite you to stop, explore and photograph the incredible views, steep inclines, fall foliage and abundant wildlife. The fiery red and gold fall colors in this area peak from mid-October to early November, depending on the weather, so let's go!

SOUTHWEST

*Evening settles over Holson Valley Vista.*

SOUTHWEST

STORY AND PHOTO BY
**LAURENCE PARENT**

# TEXAS HILL COUNTRY

RIVERS FLOW THROUGH CANYONS COVERED IN SEASONAL GLORY ON THIS LONE STAR DRIVE.

**I START MY 70-MILE DRIVE** across the most rugged part of Texas Hill Country at the Medina River in Bandera. Tall bald cypresses arch over the clear water, their needles starting to show a rusty orange autumn hue.

Known for its rolling hills, rivers, lakes and spring wildflowers, Hill Country has plenty of scenic drives. But the route that starts in Bandera, the "cowboy capital of the world," is one of my favorites.

Texas Highway 16 moves past Bandera's quaint downtown. I follow the river upstream and soon arrive in the small town of Medina, known for its surrounding apple orchards.

Going west on RM 337 (the RM stands for ranch-to-market road), I climb out of the Medina River Valley, over a steep divide, and down to a junction with RM 187, which leads to a side trip to the Lost Maples State Natural Area in the town of Vanderpool.

Established to preserve the area's trees, rare plants and animals, Lost Maples is home to deeply incised canyons at the headwaters of the Sabinal River that offer shelter from the sun and wind, and a rare, isolated stand of bigtooth maples.

I admire splashes of gold and scarlet along the Maple Trail, one of several in the park. Heading up the East Trail to Hale Hollow, a narrow, rocky passage with ferns growing from the canyon wall and flaming maples spreading overhead, I breathe in the scent of turning leaves and then hike out over a ridge and head to my car.

Back on RM 337, views of multiple canyons open up from the highway. After only a few miles, the narrow road snakes its way down into another valley, this one cut by the bald cypress-lined West Sabinal River. Here, the vistas are never-ending, popping up with each bend in the road.

Soon the highway drops again into yet another valley and continues to Leakey, crossing the Frio River on the east side of the small town. I go south on U.S. 83 and end my drive at Garner State Park. The Frio River tumbles over boulders as it flows through the park. I park my car; the clear water beckons.

SOUTHWEST

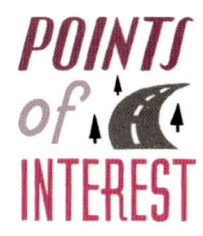

# POINTS of INTEREST

**LENGTH**
70 miles

**NOT TO BE MISSED**
Fiesta San Antonio, San Antonio; Rodeo (summer), Bandera; Texas State Arts and Crafts Fair, Kerrville

**FUN FACT**
One of Texas's most enjoyable spectacles are the wildflowers that carpet its roadsides—the result of decades of planning. Beginning in the 1930s, the state harvested tons of seeds from donors and planted them along the highways (thus eliminating mowing expenses). In 1982 one of the program's most ardent champions, Lady Bird Johnson, founded a national wildflower research center in Austin.

**SIDE TRIP**
Medina earned its nickname as Texas' apple capital thanks to an abundance of orchards. Pick your own or find delicious apple products at Love Creek Orchards. *lovecreek orchards.com*

▼
*The Sabinal River rolls past bigtooth maples and black cherry trees.*

SCENIC DRIVES 75

SOUTHWEST

*Dawn breaks over a field of bluebonnets and Indian paintbrushes near Fredericksburg, Texas.*

SOUTHWEST

"*Where flowers bloom, so does hope.*"

—LADY BIRD JOHNSON

SCENIC DRIVES 77

# MidWEST

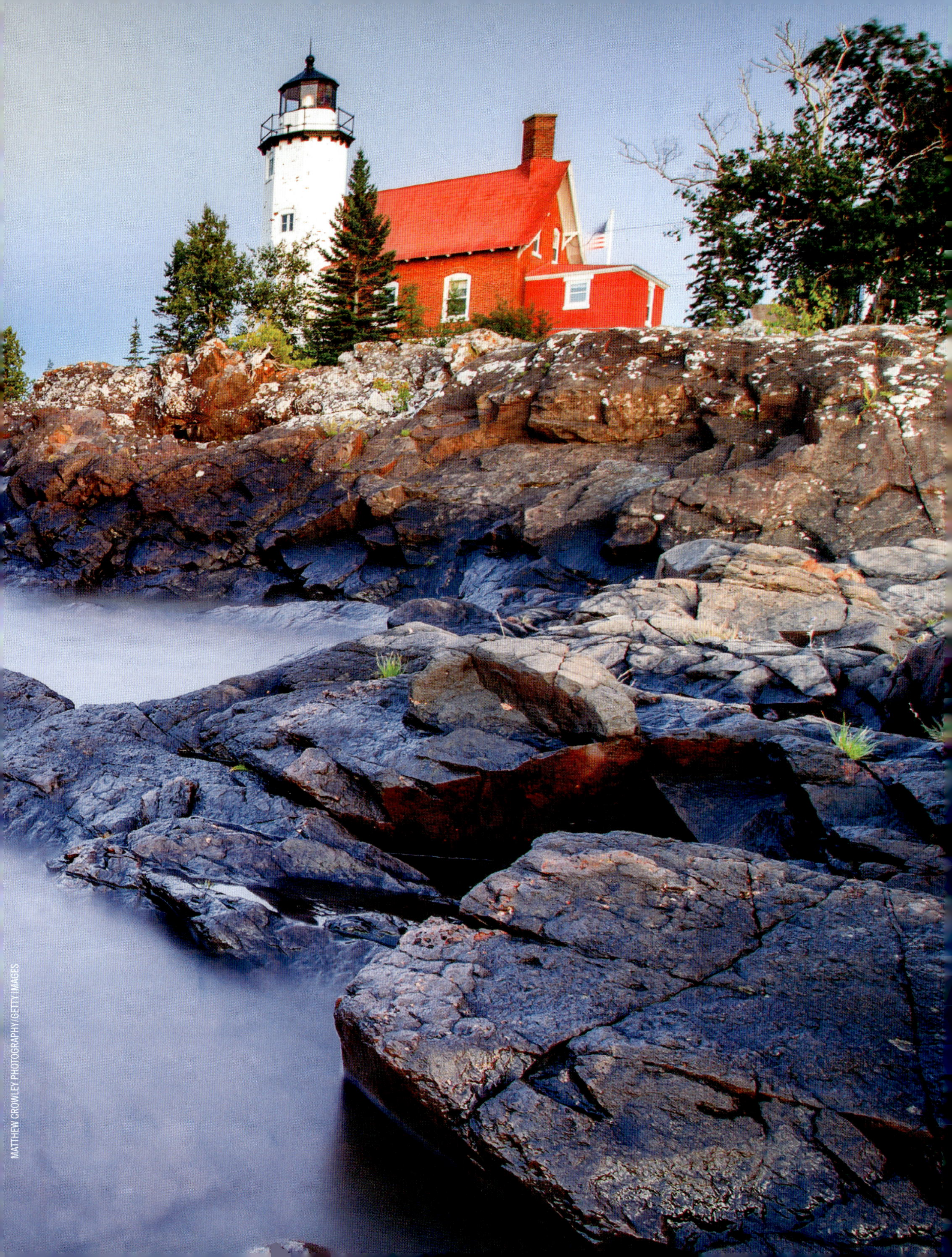
MATTHEW CROWLEY PHOTOGRAPHY/GETTY IMAGES

▼ *Maple leaves frame a gorgeous waterfall at Matthiessen State Park.*

MIDWEST

STORY AND PHOTOS BY
**TERRY DONNELLY**

# ILLINOIS RIVER ROAD

SMALL TOWNS, PRETTY FARMS AND SURPRISING CLIFFS
AND CANYONS DOT THIS SCENIC VALLEY.

**OVER THE YEARS I'VE HEARD** north-central Illinois—the place where I was born and raised—referred to in various ways. Flat as a pancake. America's heartland. A great place to raise a family. And, in fact, all of these observations are true.

The Illinois River Road National Scenic Byway provides a fine chance to come up with your own conclusions about this land, which is full of beautiful farms, hardwood forests, tallgrass prairies and unexpected geological surprises.

The reason I love to drive along this route today is not to engage the Illinois River itself as I once did, but to experience the profound and fascinating things the river has created.

You might be surprised by how flat the region actually is. Blame the glaciers; they scraped the Midwest smooth. But as the glaciers receded, they shed vast amounts of meltwater, which carved some of the world's most bucolic river valleys and dramatic sandstone canyons. The Illinois River is one such watershed: it drains waters from the Lake Michigan region into the Mississippi River.

Ottawa, the seat of LaSalle County, is a great place to start this drive. It is less than two hours southwest of Chicago and the site of the first Lincoln-Douglas debate in 1858. Check out the seasonal Saturday farmers market and the Old Town District.

From Ottawa, drive south across the river and follow its southern banks along Illinois Route 71 to Starved Rock, the gemstone of Illinois' state parks. The park's name is a homage to a tragic legend about a vengeful war between the Illini tribe on one side, and the Ottawa and Potawatomi on the other.

The besieged Illini took their final refuge by climbing the cliffs of a butte on the river. And with their enemies blocking access to food and water, the Illini starved there. Today Starved Rock draws outdoor enthusiasts with miles of hiking trails woven along scenic sandstone cliffs, wooded canyons with spring wildflowers, quiet streams, and waterfalls that flow heavily in spring and freeze over in winter for ice

SCENIC DRIVES

MIDWEST

*Native wildflowers bloom in a prairie at Starved Rock State Park.*

## POINTS of INTEREST

**LENGTH**
291 miles

**FUN FACTS**
Traveling the country roads will surprise you with a village every 8 or 10 miles. These spots may support a gas station, grocery store or a restaurant. Places like Ladd, Cherry, Tiskilwa, Neponset, Bureau Junction, Zearing and Troy Grove have a fascinating history—usually of coal mining, or maybe a grain elevator on the railroad tracks.

**NEARBY ATTRACTIONS**
Owen Lovejoy Homestead, Princeton; Hegeler Carus Mansion, LaSalle

climbing. There are open tallgrass prairies that bloom in August and, of course, there's the river.

Adjacent to Starved Rock, west on Route 71, is smaller but equally engaging Matthiessen State Park. A quiet place of natural beauty, its features include deep sandstone dells, streams and waterfalls carved into the wooded terrain. It was once a private estate that was donated to the state.

To the north, and across the river from both of these parks, is the hamlet of North Utica with an assortment of family-owned shops and restaurants.

Westward along U.S. Route 6 from North Utica, the next cities to see are individual but are collectively known as LaSalle-Peru. These closely linked communities also encompass the cities of Oglesby and Spring Valley. These towns are known for classic architecture and brick downtowns.

LaSalle's commercial district is on the National Register of Historic Places. This is small-town America at its best. Many restaurants here are inspired by the culture of supper clubs.

Back on the road, a perfectly good interstate highway, I-80, goes straight through the Illinois Valley. Avoid it.

The countryside in LaSalle, Bureau and Putnam counties is the reason you are on this drive. These rural blacktop roads take you on a tour through some of the best farmland in America: corn and soybean country.

Winding westward along U.S. Route 6, you get to Princeton, the county seat of Bureau County and hub of agricultural commerce. It's steeped in history.

Here brick streets crisscross neighborhoods with elegant homes claiming carriage houses and barns. The city is also home to one of Illinois' five remaining covered bridges. From Princeton, heading south along Illinois Route 29 brings you once again beside the Illinois River and its wildlife.

There's quite a bit to explore, much to see and do, and great people to meet along the Illinois River Road.

MIDWEST

*Autumn means pumpkin season at Miller's Market in Neponset.*

▼ Colorful leaves drape over the winding road into Copper Harbor.

MIDWEST

STORY AND PHOTOS BY
**CHUCK HANEY**

# KEWEENAW PENINSULA

MAKE YOUR WAY THROUGH LUSH FORESTS, GHOST TOWNS AND COPPER MINES ON MICHIGAN'S HIGHWAY 41.

**EXPLORING THE SCENIC KEWEENAW** located in Michigan's Upper Peninsula is especially glorious in autumn, when the hardwood forests of sugar maples, birch, basswood and ash turn vibrant shades of red, yellow and gold along meandering U.S. Highway 41.

My favorite section of the enchanting highway is the 46-mile stretch from the twin cities of Houghton and Hancock northeast to Copper Harbor, where the mighty blue waters of Lake Superior lap against the coastal village. On the last few miles into Copper Harbor, a spectacular canopy of hardwood trees forms a tunnel along the Keweenaw's twists and turns. It's sheer driving bliss for leaf peepers!

The journey begins on the Portage Lake Lift Bridge, which connects Houghton and Hancock. It's the world's heaviest and widest double-decked lift bridge, with its center section designed to rise 100 feet to permit ships to pass through the canal. Here the Keweenaw Peninsula becomes a narrow island.

Nearby are remnants of the once-thriving copper mining industry. You can even take an underground tour of the huge Quincy Mine just north of Hancock from May to October. A cogwheel tram takes visitors to an area where they can explore the 2,400-foot section of the seventh level.

My next stop along the route is my favorite, the town of Calumet. I love wandering the brick streets to check out the architecture in the Old Red Jacket Downtown Historic District (the town was originally called Red Jacket). Especially endearing is the Calumet Theatre, which first opened its doors in 1900 and is still in use, with more than 60 shows booked annually and 700 seats for its patrons.

Visitors can learn about the peninsula's history at Coppertown USA, a mining museum on Calumet's Red Jacket Road. Railroad items include a four-man, gas-driven rail car and a Russell locomotive with a snowplow nearly as tall as a house.

You can then cross Highway 41 to the small town of Laurium to tour the Laurium Manor Inn (tour times are limited, so call ahead). The stately

SCENIC DRIVES

MIDWEST

*Historic Eagle Harbor Lighthouse looks out over Lake Superior.*

## POINTS of INTEREST

**LENGTH**
46 miles

**FUN FACTS**
In the ghost town of Gay, half an hour east of Laurium, are ruins of the Mohawk Mining Co., opened in 1898. By 1932, residual sand from the method of separating copper and ore went a mile beyond the original shore. Boaters still use a 265-foot smokestack as a landmark.

Upper Michigan mines produced a majority of the United States' copper from 1845 to '77.

At least 27 scenic waterfalls can be enjoyed on the Keweenaw Peninsula.

**NEARBY ATTRACTIONS**
Eagle Harbor Lighthouse, Eagle Harbor; Eagle Harbor Lifesaving Station and Museum, Eagle Harbor

---

13,000-square-foot mansion is the largest and likely the most opulent of the homes built on the peninsula by wealthy copper mine owners. For those who want to stay in the 45-room mansion, now a bed-and-breakfast, there are 10 guest rooms, all with private baths.

Scattered along Highway 41 are small ghost towns that thrived during the copper mining heyday as well as country churches and general stores. Shops offer a local favorite called a pasty, a baked pastry filled with vegetables and meat and topped with gravy. You'll become an honorary "Yooper" (UP-er) after a few of these meat pies, which filled the immigrant Cornish and Finnish miners' bellies after a long day of scraping for copper.

Among the ghost towns is Delaware, where you can take a self-guided tour through the Delaware Mine, one of the oldest on the peninsula.

I like to take a walk along a lovely forested trail leading to the ghost town of Mandan, where 300 residents once thrived in the mining days.

The ghost town of Phoenix has the restored historic Church of the Assumption, which features a white steeple that has been stoically pointing toward the heavens since 1899.

Once in Copper Harbor, I shake off the road weariness by mountain biking along the superb trail system built by the town's adventure-seeking residents or by paddling away in a sea kayak in Lake Medora.

For grander adventure, I can strike out with friends on Lake Superior and take in rocky sea stacks and stately lighthouses. History buffs may want to explore the well-preserved buildings and equipment at Fort Wilkins Historic Complex and State Park.

One jaunt that is immensely worthwhile is the picturesque drive to scenic Brockway Mountain, where the gorgeous views of vast Lake Superior from the northern tip of the peninsula are always awe-inspiring.

To end your Keweenaw exploration, take in the sunset and enjoy a dinner of locally caught whitefish while reflecting on the day's adventure.

MIDWEST

*Portage Lake Lift Bridge connects the cities of Hancock and Houghton.*

▼ *Sleeping Bear Dunes National Lakeshore hugs the northeast shore of Lake Michigan.*

MIDWEST

STORY AND PHOTOS BY
**MARY LIZ AUSTIN**

# LEELANAU PENINSULA

MICHIGAN'S M-22 TRAVELS THROUGH GREAT LAKES SCENERY WITH LIGHTHOUSES, QUAINT VILLAGES AND HISTORIC FARMS.

**IT'S SHORTLY AFTER SUNRISE** when I settle into a cafe booth in the tiny town of Empire, Michigan. The waitress pours coffee with one hand as she points to the menu board with the other.

After a quick scan, I'm stumped on one of the items: two eggs with scrapple and hash browns. "What's scrapple?" I ask.

"Oh," the waitress replies, "it has a variety of things, but you probably don't want to know what they are. Let's just say it's similar to hash. It's good, and very popular. Trust me."

The crisp October air has given me the appetite of a lumberjack, so I decide to trust her and give it a try.

I am working my way along M-22, a Michigan Heritage Route that follows about 100 miles of Lake Michigan shoreline on the scenic Leelanau Peninsula. (On a map of lower Michigan, it's where your left little finger would be in the mitten.)

Like scrapple, this drive also has a variety of things, but these are things you really do want to know about. A rich and varied history and landscape make this a something-for-everyone type of place. You can find an abundance of beaches, lakes and rivers, in addition to historic farming communities and quaint villages from the area's lumbering days.

Lighthouse hunters will enjoy two favorites anchoring each end of M-22. On the southern end, a complete rehab has restored Point Betsie Lighthouse to its historic World War II state. The Grand Traverse Lighthouse in Leelanau State Park guards the peninsula's northern tip.

In between, Sleeping Bear Dunes National Lakeshore offers a vast number of interesting things to explore. For dramatic vistas, Pierce Stocking Scenic Drive is a 7.4-mile loop with spectacular overlooks of the Glen Lakes, Lake Michigan and the extensive Sleeping Bear dune system.

The National Park Service, private organizations and individual owners have preserved more than 300 historic rural structures in this area. One of my

SCENIC DRIVES  89

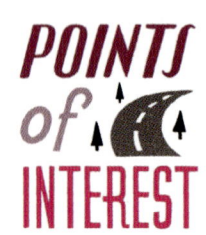

MIDWEST

*A maple tree in fall splendor in the Port Oneida Rural Historic District.*

# POINTS of INTEREST

**LENGTH**
About 100 miles

**NOT TO BE MISSED**
The National Cherry Festival, Traverse City

**FUN FACT**
With its abundant orchards, award-winning wineries and fine swimming beaches, Leelanau lives up to its name, a Chippewa word meaning "delight of life."

**NEARBY ATTRACTIONS**
Colonial Michilimackinac, a reconstructed fur-trading village, Mackinaw City; Mackinac Island, "the Bermuda of the North," accessible by ferry from St. Ignace and Mackinaw City

favorites is the D.H. Day farmstead, which includes one of the nation's most-photographed barns. This magnificent white structure, with towering twin silos flanking its main door, dates back to the late 1800s.

North of Sleeping Bear Dunes is the port town of Leland, home to historic Fishtown and the ferry terminal for the Manitou Islands. Fishtown is a charming collection of weathered fishing shanties, smokehouses and shops along the Leland River. Working fish tugs and charter fishing boats that maintain the long tradition of Great Lakes maritime industry and culture are moored along this rustic quay.

Past Leland, the landscape unfolds in rolling hills with orchards, vineyards and wineries. The seasonal bounty of a produce stand lures me in. I'm greeted by roving hens and friendly golden retrievers and rewarded with apples, pumpkins, homemade preserves and pickled vegetables.

Continuing on past the village of Northport, the scenic route bends back to the southeast along the Grand Traverse Bay and ultimately reaches its end in Traverse City.

If you have an appetite for adventure, I recommend both the scrapple and M-22. Each you can sink your teeth into and come away satisfied.

SCENIC DRIVES

MIDWEST

▼
*The charming Point Betsie Lighthouse at dusk in Frankfort.*

MIDWEST

STORY BY
**DARRYL R. BEERS**

# U.S. HIGHWAY 2

SANDY BEACHES AND AUTUMN BEAUTY AWAIT IN MICHIGAN'S UPPER PENINSULA.

**LIKE A KID CELEBRATING BIRTHDAYS,** I never tire of traveling U.S. Highway 2 across Michigan's Upper Peninsula. For about 300 miles, the drive reveals a stunning array of landscapes—both natural and man-made. I always look forward to it.

Going from west to east, this drive starts in Ironwood and ends in my hometown of St. Ignace. Six hours of drive time will get you from one end to the other, but I highly recommend taking it slowly and breaking up the drive into two days.

The journey from Ironwood to Escanaba goes through a mostly forested stretch famous for its outstanding fall colors. The road winds through a large segment of Ottawa National Forest. Long stretches of highway have few man-made intrusions, and your eyes can feast on the brilliant hues of autumn.

About an hour into the drive, I take a 20-mile detour north to Bond Falls. Bond is one of the most spectacular falls in all of Michigan. The middle branch of the Ontonagon River flows through a series of small drops before reaching the grand finale—a stunning 50-foot waterfall. A boardwalk allows visitors access to views from any angle.

After the detour, pick up the route again in Watersmeet. A few miles south of the town of Crystal Falls, the highway dips into Wisconsin for about 15 miles and twice crosses the Menominee River. On this stretch I once had to stop my car as a black bear sow and her two cubs ambled across the roadway—not an unusual sight.

Upon reaching Escanaba, explore Sand Point Lighthouse, faithfully restored to its original 1867 design, on the shore of Little Bay de Noc.

Much of the drive from Escanaba to St. Ignace borders Lake Michigan. Stretches of highway afford views of sandy beaches that seem endless. As you get closer to St. Ignace, roadside parks and overlooks offer looks of Lake Michigan and the Mackinac Bridge.

I spent one of my favorite moments on the entire U.S. 2 drive at one of these parks, watching a blazing orange sun slowly set over the still blue waters. Who knows how you'll be rewarded?

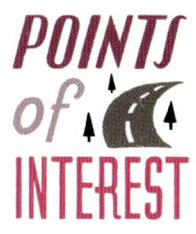

MIDWEST

# POINTS of INTEREST

**LENGTH**
About 300 miles

**SIDE TRIPS**
At Palms Book State Park, at a 40-foot-deep natural spring known as Kitch-iti-kipi (the Indians called it "Mirror of Heaven"), you can board a wooden raft and, using a guide cord, pull yourself across the 200-foot-wide pond. The raft has windows that allow you to look into the depths at trout and limestone-coated fallen trees. The underground aquifer below maintains the water at a constant 45 degrees F.

At nearby Indian Lake State Park, an 8,400-acre body of water was named for the Indians who lived there more than a century ago. Today its pristine beaches attract swimmers and sunbathers, and its whitecapped waters are a lure for anglers.

After rejoining Route 2, head east into Manistique and cross the Siphon Bridge. Designed to float like the hull of a boat, at one time this remarkable road was 4 feet below the surface level of the Manistique River.

▼
*Summer wildflowers bloom on the shore of Lake Michigan.*

▼
*The sun's rays reflect off rocks in Lake Superior near the city of Grand Marais.*

MIDWEST

STORY AND PHOTOS BY
**BOB FIRTH**

# NORTH SHORE SCENIC DRIVE

**DISCOVER THE ALLURE OF MINNESOTA'S WILD SIDE BY CRUISING ALONG THE COAST OF LAKE SUPERIOR.**

**LAKE SUPERIOR'S NORTH SHORE** is full of rugged rock, rivers, inland lakes and beautiful waterfalls. Many people think everything north of the Great Lakes is in Canada, but Minnesota has a nearly 145-mile-long "trail" running along Lake Superior from Duluth to Grand Portage, just miles shy of the border.

Even though it's really Highway 61, I call North Shore Scenic Drive a trail because it makes me feel as if I've gone back in time to the 1600s, when French explorers canoed and hiked here. Much of the land is still wild and unspoiled.

A moody Lake Superior shifts from peaceful sunrises and sunsets to thunderous storms that crash large waves against the rocky shore. In the winter, the lake transforms into an arctic-like landscape of frozen ice sculptures and caves.

People of all abilities can drive, bike, kayak and camp along the coast, explore by motorboat, or hike. The Superior Hiking Trail and Lake Superior State Water Trail draw nature lovers from around the world.

As you start your journey, pay a visit to the Duluth Ship Canal—it's the gateway to Duluth Harbor from Lake Superior for international ships. Standing out on the pier and witnessing

SCENIC DRIVES

MIDWEST

*Split Rock Lighthouse sits on a cliff south of Silver Bay.*

# POINTS of INTEREST

**LENGTH**
About 145 miles

**NOT TO BE MISSED**
The North Shore Fall Color Tour is accessible to anyone who doesn't mind gravel roads. Wind through woodlands of aspen and birch and explore the rolling hills of the Superior National Forest.

**WORDS TO THE WISE**
Since Route 61 is a busy highway, leave plenty of time for your trip.

**NEARBY ATTRACTION**
The Depot, an 1892 landmark train station that houses museums and performing arts organizations, Duluth

these enormous boats pass through the harbor is fascinating, as is watching the historic lift bridge in action.

My children enjoy walking the lichen-covered pathway to the Grand Marais Lighthouse while watching kayakers and bigger seaworthy vessels.

The shoreline offers endless beaches scattered with agates and driftwood. Beachcombing has always been one of my family's favorite pastimes. Several state parks, including Tettegouche, Cascade River and Temperance River, offer access to these natural wonders.

Moving inland, you'll find a multitude of serene lakes, tumbling rivers and endless woodlands. I love to discover hidden waterfalls, and occasionally I encounter loons, moose, black bears and wolves.

Minnesota's North Shore is a place to find your own path and travel at your own pace. The entire trip is truly the destination.

MIDWEST

*The Devil Track River attracts trout anglers, hikers and ice climbers.*

▼ *This maple tree hangs over a horse and buggy on Ohio Route 643.*

MIDWEST

STORY AND PHOTOS BY
**DOYLE YODER**

# OHIO'S AMISH COUNTRY

WANDER THROUGH A TAPESTRY OF CRESTING HILLS, DISTANT FORESTS AND LOVINGLY KEPT AMISH FARMSTEADS.

**I GREW UP IN EASTERN OHIO AMISH COUNTRY,** and I chose to make my life and my living here as a photographer. As far as I'm concerned, the roads that wind through the hills and valleys of Holmes, Coshocton, Tuscarawas and Wayne counties are some of the most inspiring scenic drives in America.

I'd be really hard-pressed to pick one favorite road. State Route 39 from Mansfield to Dover is perhaps the most popular one. It runs through beautiful rolling countryside and classic small towns such as Millersburg, Berlin, Walnut Creek and Sugarcreek, "The Little Switzerland of Ohio."

But to truly appreciate the region's unique blend of scenery and culture, I encourage you to wander off on some of the smaller side roads. State Route 643, for example, runs from the Sugarcreek area southwest toward Coshocton, through the heart of some of the most unforgettable scenes in Amish country.

With birds chirping and a cool morning breeze in my face, life's simple pleasures unfold with each

SCENIC DRIVES  99

MIDWEST

*Colorful quilts dry on the line on a sunny afternoon.*

# POINTS of INTEREST

**NOT TO BE MISSED**
Ohio Swiss Festival, Sugarcreek

**FUN FACT**
With the approach of the bicentennial in 1976, Americans became very interested in their past and in the process discovered the unique art of Amish quilting. Because many of the Amish women spend time gardening and helping with the farming during the warmer months, they spend most of the winter sewing.

**WORDS TO THE WISE**
Beware of slow-moving horse-drawn buggies. Refrain from photographing the Amish.

**NEARBY ATTRACTIONS**
Canton Classic Car Museum and Pro Football Hall of Fame, Canton

passing mile. The view is a constantly changing tapestry of cresting hills, distant forests and lovingly kept Amish farmsteads. Each season brings its unique rewards.

In the spring, teams of magnificent draft horses are out plowing and planting in the fields, while Amish children play joyous games of baseball at recess. In summer, shocks of wheat and oats dry in eye-catching patterns and flowers bloom in well-tended gardens. In the fall, dew glistens off crisp corn shocks while sugar maples along the road burst into awesome color. Winter snows blanket field and forest in pristine white.

People often ask how I create such wonderful pictures. And while I'm always striving to master my trade, I can only reply that the most beautiful pictures I take will never match the beauty God has created here in this blessed little corner of Ohio.

MIDWEST

*A rainbow peeks from the clouds above a farm in Coshocton County.*

*The Sturgeon Bay Ship Canal Pierhead Lighthouse was constructed in 1881.*

MIDWEST

STORY BY
**DARRYL R. BEERS**

# DOOR COUNTY COASTAL BYWAY

**WISCONSIN HIGHWAY 42'S SMORGASBORD INCLUDES VINEYARDS, HARBOR VILLAGES, PARK RETREATS AND STUNNING BAYSIDE SUNSETS.**

**OVER THE COURSE OF SEVERAL DECADES** spent exploring country roads, I find that none is more enjoyable than the 40-mile stretch of Wisconsin State Highway 42 going through northern Door County.

The adventure begins at Bayview Bridge, rising to a height of more than 50 feet above the Sturgeon Bay Ship Canal. The view on a sunny day is stunning—and endless—as the clear blue water stretches toward the waters of Green Bay to the west and Lake Michigan to the east. In any season you may see a massive 1,000-foot Great Lakes freighter sailing into Sturgeon Bay for repairs.

The next 15 miles north is mostly rural, with a sprinkling of markets, vineyards and specialty shops. Take time to stop and search for antiques or to enjoy a cup of gourmet coffee and culinary delights, many of which are unique to Door County.

Countryside suddenly gives way to bayside as Highway 42 veers into quaint Egg Harbor. This is the first of a handful of small, distinctive villages dotting the shoreline of Green Bay. When these lands were first settled, mostly in the mid-1800s, a safe harbor was necessary for survival. Today these harbors serve as a picturesque

SCENIC DRIVES 103

MIDWEST

## POINTS of INTEREST

**LENGTH**
40 miles

**NOT TO BE MISSED**
The Door County "fish boil," an outdoor tradition featured at many restaurants

**WORDS TO THE WISE**
Reservations for lodging are recommended, especially from June to October. Those without reservations may inquire at the 24-hour Destination Door County Welcome Center, located at routes 57 and 42 at the southern edge of Sturgeon Bay.

**NEARBY ATTRACTION**
Green Bay Packers Hall of Fame, Green Bay

*A purple sky sets the scene while sailing at twilight on Green Bay.*

backdrop for swimming, boating, fishing and sightseeing. Each locale offers stunning sunsets that color the bay's long horizon. Village streets are lined with unique shops, art galleries, fine eateries, confectioneries and more.

Cherry and apple orchards border many of the roadways between villages, serving up a visual feast of blossoms in the spring. At both Fish Creek and Ephraim, the highway affords direct access to Peninsula State Park, the crown jewel of Wisconsin's park system. Peninsula State Park encompasses 3,776 acres of forests, meadows, wetlands and towering cliffs, as well as 8 miles of shoreline.

Highway 42's final 1.5 miles zig and zag through a beautiful maple and beech forest, ending at the Northport Ferry dock. Take the half-hour ferry ride to Washington Island or turn around and head back. Either way, I guarantee you'll enjoy the trip.

MIDWEST

*An early morning view of Lake Michigan from Cave Point County Park.*

MIDWEST

STORY AND PHOTOS BY
**BOB FIRTH**

# GREAT RIVER ROAD

CHART A COURSE BESIDE THE UPPER MISSISSIPPI RIVER TO SEE MAJESTIC BLUFFS AND TO VISIT CHARMING TOWNS.

**ALONG A 150-MILE SPAN** of the Upper Mississippi River from Red Wing, Minnesota, to Prairie du Chien, Wisconsin, the Great River Road National Scenic Byway offers beautiful vistas, quaint towns, history and culture, woodland hikes and many other hidden gems.

Without stops or detours, the trip can be completed in a few hours. But I recommend devoting a full day or two and seeing as much as possible.

My favorite tour of river country takes the Great River Road, mainly following U.S. Highway 61 in Minnesota and State Trunk Highway 35 located in Wisconsin. I look for side routes rising from the river's edge through steep woodlands, canyons and ravines. From the upper bluffs, the views of creeks, forests and farms are breathtaking.

Start in Red Wing, fueling up at Hanisch Bakery and Coffee Shop—one of Minnesota's best—and shop at Red Wing Shoe Store & Museum and Red Wing Stoneware & Pottery.

Then head toward Wabasha, Minnesota, to learn about eagles at the National Eagle Center. Cross the Wabasha-Nelson Bridge to see eagles in the wild and some great views of Mississippi River backwaters.

In the small town of Nelson, Wisconsin, grab a tasty bite to eat at J&J Barbecue or the Nelson Cheese Factory. Fountain City, Wisconsin, has a historic downtown, with entertaining stops close by at Elmer's Auto & Toy Museum and the funky Prairie Moon Sculpture Garden and Museum.

Winona, Minnesota, is known for its grand old banks, homes and churches. For super scenery, take some time to hike in Great River Bluffs State Park.

Near La Crosse, Wisconsin, big views of the Mississippi Valley are easily accessible with just a short walk. Check out Goose Island County Park and Grandad Bluff Park.

Farther south, find more stunning vistas at Pikes Peak State Park in McGregor, Iowa, and Wyalusing State Park near Prairie du Chien, Wisconsin.

Let the inspiring sights and sounds of the mighty Mississippi guide you on your way as you explore!

MIDWEST

*Top: Fall foliage frames a red barn in Frontenac, Minnesota. Bottom: A great blue heron fishes on the Mississippi River.*

# POINTS of INTEREST

**LENGTH**
About 150 miles

**NOT TO BE MISSED**
Riverboat excursions from several cities, including La Crosse and Prairie du Chien in Wisconsin, and Dubuque in Iowa

**FUN FACT**
In fall, monarch butterflies and birds flock to Trempealeau National Wildlife Refuge in Wisconsin before they fly south. *fws.gov/refuge/trempealeau*

**NEARBY ATTRACTIONS**
National Mississippi River Musuem & Aquarium, Dubuque, Iowa; *Field of Dreams* baseball diamond, setting for the motion picture, Dyersville, Iowa; Mall of America, the country's largest shopping mall, Bloomington, Minnesota

SCENIC DRIVES  107

MIDWEST

*The golden hues of autumn saturate the Minnesota banks of the Mississippi River.*

MIDWEST

"*In wildness is the preservation of the world.*"

—HENRY DAVID THOREAU

SCENIC DRIVES 109

# Southeast

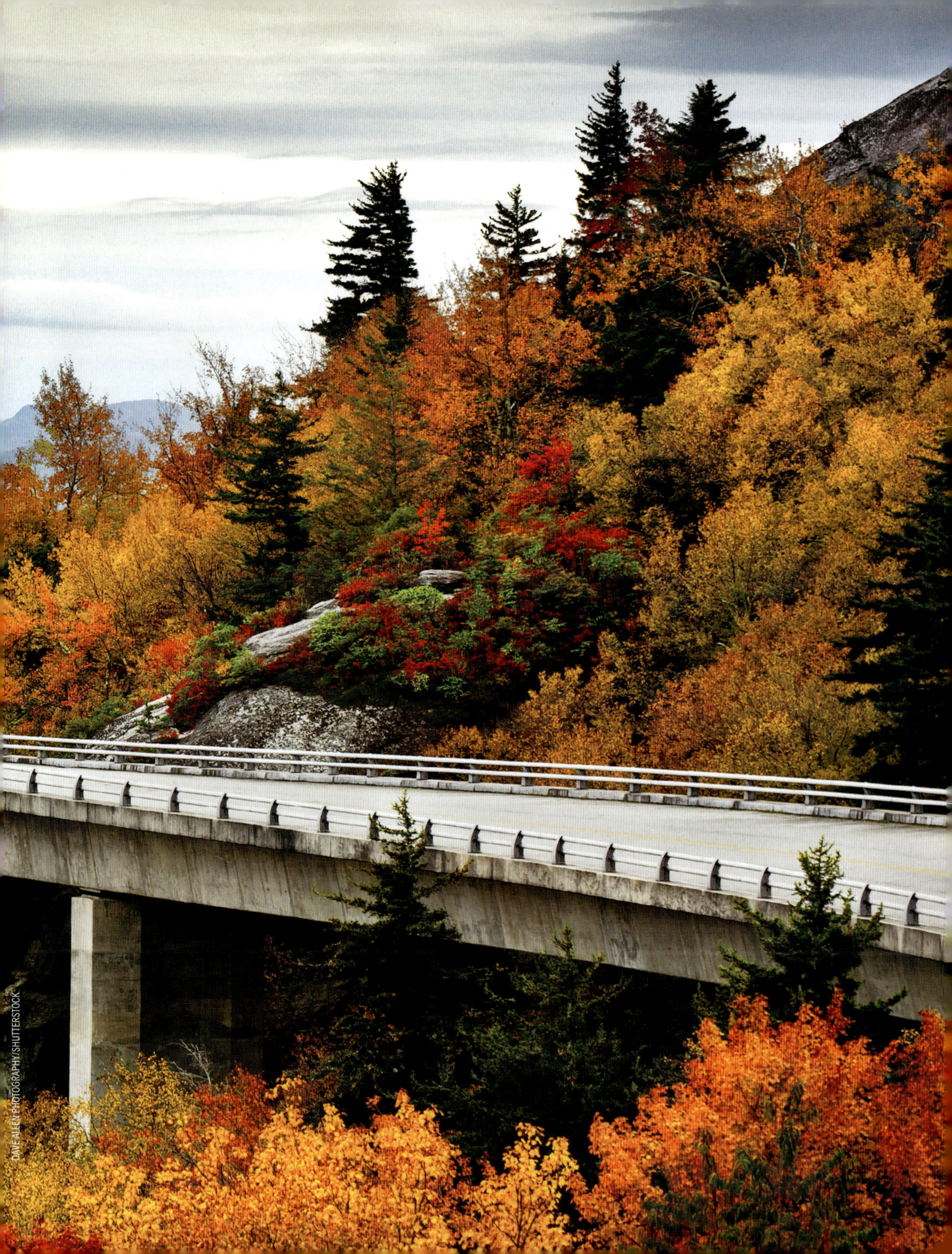
DAVE ALLEN PHOTOGRAPHY/SHUTTERSTOCK

▼ *The setting sun casts a majestic glow over Sam's Throne Recreation Area.*

SOUTHEAST

STORY AND PHOTOS BY
**PAUL CALDWELL**

# SCENIC HIGHWAY 7

ARKANSAS' MOST BEAUTIFUL BYWAY CLIMBS INTO THE OZARK MOUNTAINS, SHOWING OFF BLUFFS, CANYONS AND VALLEYS AROUND EVERY CURVE.

**ARKANSAS HAS MANY WONDERFUL** state highways to explore, but Highway 7 is considered one of the most enthralling drives in America.

There are several places to pull over to enjoy a picturesque view, and plenty of side trips to take. My favorite drive along Highway 7 starts in Russellville and crosses the Arkansas River Valley going north before it climbs up into the Ozark Mountains.

The route stays high on the ridges until its long drop down into the charming mountain town of Jasper, so you can slow down, relax and soak up the scenery.

During the drive, make sure to look for wildlife. It's common to see herds of deer along the road, but if you get an early start, you may see a red fox, bobcat or even a black bear. Also keep your eyes on the power lines to look for the many species of hawks that frequent this part of the state.

Stop along Highway 7 at the scenic Rotary Ann Overlook. It's a treat to look due west at this vast vista and see into the heart of the Ozark Mountains.

About halfway between Russellville and Jasper, you'll encounter Sand Gap, formerly known as Pelsor. From there, you can consider two intriguing short side trips.

Highway 123 leads west to Haw Creek Falls, an impressive waterfall nestled in a mature hardwood forest. Highway 16 takes you east to Pedestal Rocks Scenic Area, a high bluff eroded into huge pedestals in lots of interesting shapes and sizes.

North of here you can make another short side trip to visit Sam's Throne Recreation Area, a long bluff line that wraps around the Big Creek valley. It's an easy hike to another stunning view of autumn colors at their peak. There is a campground here, so you can spend the night and rest up before continuing on your drive.

All along Highway 7, you'll notice lovely old barns and homes. Many of these rustic structures are located on

SCENIC DRIVES 113

SOUTHEAST

## POINTS of INTEREST

**LENGTH**
290 miles

**WORDS TO THE WISE**
Steep grades make some roads off-limits to RVs.

**SIDE TRIPS**
Sam's Throne is a popular rock climbing destination with multiple paths for all experience and ability levels. It also draws hikers and tent campers.

Once you reach Jasper, look for the junction with Highway 74. Turn onto this road to reach the Buffalo National River. Two of the most popular areas to visit along this river are Ponca, home to herds of elk, and the Steel Creek Recreation Area and Campground. If you have extra time, consider renting a canoe for a float trip to view stone bluffs that stand more than 400 feet tall.

**NEARBY ATTRACTIONS**
Little Rock, the state capital; Eureka Springs, a mountainside resort community; Ozark Folk Center State Park, Mountain View

▼
*Haw Creek Falls, near Sand Gap, is majestic in springtime.*

national forest land, and you can pull off the highway to get some great pictures. Also look for antique cars and trucks; sometimes they're all that's left of the old homesites.

One of my favorite vantage points from high on the Ozark Mountain ridges is the view from the western rim of the Arkansas Grand Canyon.

For early risers, it's the perfect place to catch a sunrise. If you wish to explore this area in more depth, reserve a room at the Cliff House Inn, located 6 miles south of Jasper. The hotel offers wonderful views of the canyon, and its delicious morning breakfast menu is an added incentive to stay the night.

Once you're on the road again, look for the junction with Highway 374, just before the road drops into Jasper. This detour descends right into the Arkansas Grand Canyon and offers many intimate views of the area's lesser-seen beauty.

Arkansas' Scenic Highway 7 is an incredible drive through America's heartland in every season. ◆

114  SCENIC DRIVES

SOUTHEAST

*Erosion has left behind impressive formations at Pedestal Rocks.*

SOUTHEAST

STORY AND PHOTO BY
**MARK LAGRANGE**

# BAYOU COUNTRY

THE ROMANCE AND HISTORY OF SOUTHERN LOUISIANA ARE REVEALED ALONG THE SOUTH'S OLD SPANISH TRAIL.

**CHOOSING ASSORTED INGREDIENTS** for a good gumbo is a fine parallel to meandering along the beautiful, uncommon traces of southern Louisiana. A journey through bayou country, which is steeped in Cajun French culture, isn't a traditional road trip. Although Highway 90, once known as the Old Spanish Trail, is the main route, it's the side roads that lead to places with a Southern culture all their own.

As you make your way westward on Highway 90 across southern Louisiana, the influence of the Atchafalaya River Basin on the surrounding landscape becomes evident. It is the largest intact river swamp in the U.S. and holds some of Louisiana's most scenic views. The basin, which stretches into the Gulf of Mexico, is a National Heritage Area.

From Highway 90, take Louisiana 329 to Avery Island, one of five salt domes that have moved the land above them to form "islands" within the marsh. Avery is also known as the birthplace of Tabasco pepper sauce. Take the Tabasco factory tour, and then spend time at the island's Jungle Gardens. The 170-acre preserve is dotted with blooming azaleas and camellias when in season. During warmer months, alligators sometimes sunbathe on the edge of several ponds throughout the gardens. Springtime offers a fabulous view of the thousands of egrets nesting in Bird City, the island's private pond.

Just north of Avery Island, the salt domes push up out of the swamp to form Jefferson Island, where you'll find the Joseph Jefferson Mansion. Built in the 1800s, the mansion boasts elegance and grandeur. The great oaks that surround it have stood for nearly 350 years.

No tour would be complete without a sampling of Louisiana's preserved Cajun French culinary culture. It's worth the time to stop in Breaux Bridge, which the state Legislature proclaimed the crawfish capital of the world. Visit during the famous Crawfish Festival the first weekend of May to savor authentic Cajun and Creole cuisine and enjoy zydeco and Cajun music. Are you ready to dance?

SCENIC DRIVES

SOUTHEAST

# POINTS of INTEREST

### NOT TO BE MISSED
Guided tours of the swamps are available in Kraemer, Houma and other towns. In Henderson, take an airboat deep into the Atchafalaya Basin. *basinlanding.com*

### SIDE TRIP
Louisiana boasts 2.6 million acres of marshland, and you can see a largely unspoiled portion on the 180-mile Creole Nature Trail. Starting at Sulphur (about 80 miles west of Lafayette), take Highway 27 south through the Sabine National Wildlife Refuge. At Holly Beach, continue east along the Gulf Coast on Highways 27/82, amid stands of ancient live oaks on the way to Creole, where the route veers sharply northward on Highway 27, then follows Highway 14 north and west to Lake Charles.

### NEARBY ATTRACTION
The French Quarter, New Orleans

*Stands of cypress trees rise out of the Louisiana swamp.*

SCENIC DRIVES

▼ *At a scenic overlook near Cove Road in Accident, Maryland, bright red barns and rich fall colors are a feast for the eyes.*

SOUTHEAST

STORY AND PHOTOS BY
**PAT AND CHUCK BLACKLEY**

# HISTORIC NATIONAL ROAD

TRAVEL THROUGH TIME ON THE PATH OF STAGECOACHES AND SOLDIERS ALONG AMERICA'S OLDEST INTERSTATE HIGHWAY.

**WHETHER YOU WANT TO ESCAPE** to high elevations to beat the summer heat or take in stunning fall foliage, a drive along the National Road in Maryland is always rewarding. Anyone who is interested in outdoor recreation or early American history will marvel at the hidden treasures in the state's western mountains.

Our 41-mile journey began on Alternate Route 40 in Cumberland, which has served as a departure point for travelers since the mid-1700s. In 1806, Congress authorized construction of a national road to improve the old Cumberland Road route and provide access to the Ohio River Valley. It was the first interstate highway built with federal government money.

Outside the city of Cumberland, The Narrows, a mile-wide valley, or water gap, offers passage through the otherwise impervious Allegheny Mountains. It's fascinating to imagine all the stagecoaches and Conestoga wagons that passed through here as pioneer Americans ventured westward in search of land and opportunity.

We had to smile when we saw the 1830s LaVale Toll Gate House. It's no longer in service, but former toll rates are posted.

In Frostburg, charming shops and restaurants await. We were entertained

SCENIC DRIVES   119

SOUTHEAST

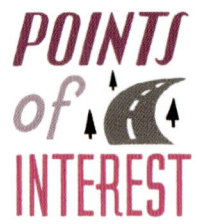

# POINTS of INTEREST

**LENGTH**
41 miles

**NOT TO BE MISSED**
The Great Allegheny Passage, a 150-mile recreational trail between Cumberland, Maryland, and Pittsburgh, Pennsylvania. *thegreatallegheny passage.com*

The Western Maryland Scenic Railroad, from Cumberland to Frostburg and back.

**FUN FACT**
The old National Road is an ancient footpath first forged by Native Americans, then traipsed by explorers and militiamen into the unmapped lands beyond the Appalachians. This historic route was designated a National Scenic Byway in 2003.

**NEARBY ATTRACTION**
Harpers Ferry National Historic Park, Harpers Ferry, West Virginia

▼
*The Youghiogheny Scenic & Wild River lives up to its name.*

by the gigantic turntable in the rail yard near the depot and the about-face it provides to the Western Maryland Scenic Railroad steam engines.

Continue driving through the rural countryside to Grantsville, called Little Crossings in Colonial times. Here we found Spruce Forest Artisan Village, where you can watch artists working in their studios.

All the sightseeing might make you hungry for a meal at the Penn Alps Restaurant and Craft Shop, housed in a former stagecoach stop, the Little Crossings Inn. Later, visit Stanton's Mill, a restored gristmill built in 1797.

West of Grantsville, turn south at the intersection with Highway 219 to visit the small historic town of Accident. A bit farther south, the beauty of Swallow Falls State Park, with trails through old-growth forests that lead to tumbling waterfalls, is the perfect place to end the drive.

SOUTHEAST

▼
*The Drane House, a log cabin built in 1798 in Accident.*

*The Natchez Trace Parkway Bridge is a concrete double arch span in Franklin, Tennessee.*

SOUTHEAST

STORY BY **DONNA B. ULRICH**
PHOTOS BY **LARRY ULRICH**

# NATCHEZ TRACE PARKWAY

THIS TIMEWORN PATH UNVEILS THE SCENIC APPEAL AND FASCINATING HISTORY OF THE OLD SOUTH.

**LIKE ITS EASTERN COUSIN** the Blue Ridge Parkway, the Natchez Trace Parkway winds through centuries of history, taking visitors through countryside and cities, past battlefields and barns. "Trace" is from the French for a line of footprints or animal tracks.

In use since pre-Columbian times, the trail was followed first by Native Americans seeking hunting and trading grounds, and later by early European and American explorers and immigrants. Today the 444-mile parkway runs from just south of Nashville, Tennessee, to the city of Natchez, Mississippi.

Though much of the original trail is now unrecognizable, the parkway awaits modern-day explorers. There are no commercial vehicles allowed, making it a slow, relaxing journey.

Years ago we traveled the Natchez Trace for almost a week, inhaling the sights as well as the fragrance of spring lilacs on dewy mornings. Off the main parkway, side roads provide access to remnants that Native Americans, immigrants and armies left behind. Among the witnesses to America's fascinating past are archaeological sites, sunken roads, Civil War battlefields and memorials, historic

SOUTHEAST

# POINTS of INTEREST

**LENGTH**
444 miles

**WORDS TO THE WISE**
Observe the 50 mph speed limit, which is strictly enforced. When driving, be on the lookout for bicyclists and deer; when hiking, beware of ticks, snakes and poison ivy.

**SIDE TRIP**
The Hermitage, Andrew Jackson's white-columned home and site of his tomb, covers 1,120 acres and includes a 25,000-square-foot visitor center. Inside his residence, visitors will find original artwork, furniture, personal items and more.

**NEARBY ATTRACTIONS**
Vicksburg National Military Park, Vicksburg, Mississippi; Mississippi Petrified Forest, Flora; Country Music Hall of Fame, Nashville, Tennessee; Helen Keller Home, Tuscumbia, Alabama

▼
*Vicksburg National Military Park honors a decisive Civil War battle.*

plantations and Southern towns with lavish antebellum Victorian homes.

On a side road near Natchez, Emerald Mound was built more than two centuries before Columbus landed in America, and is the second-largest ceremonial earthwork in the U.S. This mound, like others in the South and Midwest, is thought to have been a center for religious and social events.

Another excursion took us to Vicksburg, a key Civil War site. We silently toured past rows of cannons. We gazed with respect and awe at the USS *Cairo*, a resurrected ironclad warship at its final resting place as a museum along the Mississippi River.

On the Natchez Trace, you'll discover a fascinating history as old as the dirt under your feet. Along the way, amid exceptional scenery, you may even sense the strength of the settlers who set our country on its zigzag path to the present. ❧

SOUTHEAST

▼ *Lake Lee in Tombigbee State Park, Mississippi, is worth a stop.*

▼ *The Bodie Island Lighthouse at sunset, Cape Hatteras National Seashore.*

SOUTHEAST

STORY BY **PAULETTE ROY**
PHOTOS BY **PAUL REZENDES**

# OUTER BANKS SCENIC BYWAY

NORTH CAROLINA'S ROUTE 12 BOASTS 200 MILES OF COASTAL CHARM AND A RICH PAST.

**THE OUTER BANKS OF NORTH CAROLINA** are a narrow string of barrier islands located a few miles out, with white beaches, shifting dunes, effervescent surf, picturesque fishing piers and five historic lighthouses—a winning formula that keeps us coming back!

We approach traveling east through central North Carolina on Highway 64, driving through Roanoke Island and running right into north-south Route 12, a nearly 200-mile-long road spanning the Outer Banks. We opt to turn south, and for long stretches, the narrow road bordered by sand dunes is the only barrier between the expanse of the Atlantic Ocean and Pamlico Sound. All around us, the interplay of ocean, sand and wind creates an ever-changing landscape.

At Pea Island, a crucial feeding and resting habitat for migratory birds, we see an amazing avian array as we hike the trails. It's a breezy day, so we check the famous windsurfing spot, Canadian Hole between Avon and Buxton.

Our trip isn't complete without sunrise and sunset photos at the Bodie Island and Cape Hatteras lighthouses. At the southern terminus of Route 12,

SCENIC DRIVES  **127**

SOUTHEAST

# POINTS of INTEREST

**LENGTH**
About 200 miles

**FUN FACTS**
Fishing season never ends, so take some time to find your inner angler. This is known as one of the best places to catch a half-ton marlin!

For nearly 150 years, the towering striped lighthouse at Cape Hatteras has warned sailors away from dangerous shoals. Over time, shifting sands and rolling swells came to threaten the 208-foot beacon, the tallest brick lighthouse in the country. In 1999 it was moved about half a mile to protect it from the encroaching sea. Visitors can climb to the top from mid-April through mid-October.

**WORDS TO THE WISE**
Keep your car on the road and on paved pull-offs; if you try to park on the shoulder, you'll almost certainly get stuck in the sand. Swim only where lifeguards are on duty.

▼
*Footprints in the sand at Pea Island National Wildlife Refuge.*

a 40-minute free ferry takes us to Ocracoke Island Lighthouse.

Eventually we head north, past Whalebone Junction, and turn into Jockey's Ridge State Park, the tallest natural sand dune system in the eastern U.S. Families explore dunes and fly kites, while more adventurous folks sandboard and hang glide.

At Nags Head Woods Preserve, a maritime forest, we stroll quietly among the trees and freshwater ponds. Refreshed, we continue north to Kill Devil Hills and the Wright Brothers National Memorial, a must for history buffs and aviation enthusiasts.

Finally, at the northernmost end of Route 12, the 162-foot-tall red brick Currituck Beach Lighthouse beckons. All who climb its 220 steps earn a drink of the gorgeous panoramic view. It's the perfect place to reflect on the overabundance of beauty in North Carolina's Outer Banks.

128  SCENIC DRIVES

SOUTHEAST

*The Roanoke Marshes Lighthouse can be found at the east end of Manteo.*

SOUTHEAST

STORY BY
**LOUIS BUTTINO**

# CHEROKEE FOOTHILLS BYWAY

THE CAROLINA MOUNTAINS AND SURROUNDING WILDERNESS OFFER SUPERB FALL COLOR FOR ROAD TRIPPERS.

**OUR THREE-CAR CARAVAN** hopped on South Carolina Highway 11, known as the Cherokee Foothills National Scenic Byway, north of Spartanburg and headed west. The "Upstate Voyagers" range in age from 56 to 77, with five septuagenarians. We are a no-quit, no-complaints, adventure-loving group of travelers.

Lush orchards lined both sides of the road until we passed Gowensville. We admired the pastoral roadside greenery; rows upon rows of peach trees clung to their leafy cover.

From here, the colors started to change to the yellow, orange and early reds of autumn as we slowly gained altitude. To the north of Highway 11, we could glimpse Hogback Mountain with a patch of sheer vertical granite exposed. All along the byway, we were shadowed by the southernmost peaks of the imposing Blue Ridge Mountains.

Next, we made our much-anticipated stop at the MacGregor Orchard for a delicious supply of fresh apples to snack on during our trip. Back on the road, we passed some of South Carolina's nicest state parks.

Jones Gap, Caesars Head and Table Rock all have different diversions to offer, including trout fishing, hiking trails, a scenic overlook, a swimming hole and waterfalls. Caesars Head is connected to Jones Gap, totaling 13,000 pristine wooded acres in the Mountain Bridge Wilderness Area.

Our caravan crossed over the upper stretch of mountain stream-fed Lake Keowee with its clear water. We headed across the North Carolina state line.

Frequently we have taken fall color trips during the second weekend in October to coincide with local arts and crafts fairs. On this trip, however, we scheduled our travels toward the end of the month to catch the foliage closer to its peak.

This was yet another successful trip for the Upstate Voyagers. I am already thinking about next fall's trip to the Carolina mountains.

SOUTHEAST

## POINTS of INTEREST

**LENGTH**
About 130 miles

**NOT TO BE MISSED**
Victoria Valley Vineyards; waterfalls of the upcountry

**FUN FACT**
Table Rock is one of 16 South Carolina state parks built by the Civilian Conservation Corps. The park's Historic District is listed on the National Register of Historic Places.
*southcarolina parks.com*

**NEARBY ATTRACTIONS**
Kings Mountain State Park, with a re-created homestead, and Kings Mountain National Military Park, an American Revolution battleground, northeast of Gaffney via Route 29; Oconee State Park, north of Walhalla via Route 107

*The sun rises on a misty morning at Table Rock State Park.*

SCENIC DRIVES 131

▼ *A cozy farm dressed in autumn hues on Route 640.*

SOUTHEAST

STORY AND PHOTOS BY
**PAT & CHUCK BLACKLEY**

# BLUE GRASS VALLEY ROAD

**TUCKED AWAY IN THE ALLEGHENIES IS A LITTLE-KNOWN HAVEN WHERE VISTAS NEVER FAIL TO COMFORT AND DELIGHT.**

**FROM OUR HOME** in Virginia's Shenandoah Valley, we enjoy making frequent visits to Highland County, often called Virginia's Little Switzerland for its steep mountains, deep valleys and abundant snowfall.

The drive of less than 50 miles can be a challenging trip of hairpin turns and some white-knuckle moments, but our arrival in this little piece of paradise reminds us why the trip is so worth the effort. Located in the Allegheny Mountains, within what's called the Ridge and Valley province of the Appalachians, Highland County borders West Virginia to the west and the Shenandoah Valley to the east. Named for its lofty altitude, the county has one of the highest average elevations east of the Mississippi.

The region, isolated by mountains, is home to only about six people per square mile. With only a few small towns or hamlets, it is known and loved for its gorgeous scenery and rural charm. While other areas have been overdeveloped, Highland remains much as it was when we were children.

SOUTHEAST

# POINTS of INTEREST

**LENGTH**
About 50 miles

**SIDE TRIPS**
Framed by the Blue Ridge and Allegheny mountains, the Shenandoah Valley is renowned for its magnificent vistas. The history, art and culture of this region are represented at the Museum of the Shenandoah Valley. In addition to the museum, the site includes the 18th-century Glen Burnie Historic House, home to descendants of Col. James Wood, founder of the city of Winchester, and 6 acres of beautifully landscaped gardens.

At Natural Chimneys Park, the chimneys soaring above the surrounding plain are a remnant of a time, centuries ago, when an ocean covered the Shenandoah Valley, leaving behind these rocks etched by nature. A jousting tournament has been held on the plains below the chimneys since 1821. Modern knights on galloping horses try to spear rings suspended over the 75-yard course in a meadow called the National Jousting Hall of Fame.

*Pisgah Church sits quietly among the hills near Hightown.*

There are no four-lane highways, no subdivisions, no fast-food restaurants or shopping malls; you are presented with just miles of peaceful countryside and tightly knit farming communities.

We've traveled countless country roads all around the United States and into Canada, but the quiet, winding drive on Blue Grass Valley Road remains our all-time favorite.

Turning off State Route 220 north of the county seat of Monterey, we are met by the wooded hills and pretty farms of Blue Grass Valley Road. The drive begins as Route 642 goes through the village of Blue Grass, then continues on Route 640 for about 15 miles to the intersection with Route 84, having briefly passed through Hightown.

Meandering through the road's namesake, the beautiful Blue Grass Valley, the route reveals breathtaking wide-open vistas that stretch into the

134  SCENIC DRIVES

SOUTHEAST

*Enjoy bucolic valley farms with bright green pastures.*

SOUTHEAST

*Sheep graze together near Blue Grass, Virginia.*

SOUTHEAST

*An afternoon respite in lush grass.*

mountains beyond, reminding us of scenery we've found in Wyoming and Montana.

The fence-lined road passes barns and neatly kept farmhouses scattered among the rolling hills and broad pastures tucked in among the wooded mountain ridges.

Cattle and sheep graze in lush meadows and drink from the waters of the Potomac and James rivers. The headwaters for both rivers are located here. According to local legend, there's a barn in Hightown where rain from the roof's north side runs off into the Potomac and rain from its south side runs to the James.

Each season is alluring, especially for photographers like us. Winter's snow-covered landscape provides a tranquil beauty that grips our souls. Spring and summer bring wildflowers, baby farm animals and the farmers working their fields.

In March, the Highland County Maple Festival celebrates syrup season with events like sugar camp tours where you can learn more about the area from the people who live and work here. A fiddlers' convention, farmers market and delicious trout dinners bring us back each summer.

Our favorite season, though, has to be autumn, when the sugar maples that produce Highland's famous syrup in spring turn the most glorious shades of red, yellow and orange, painting this magnificent landscape with vibrance.

An unhurried drive along this soothing country road reminds us of the way life used to be in earlier times. Selfishly, we hope it never changes, so we can continue to enjoy its remote and pristine beauty for years to come.

▼ *The Bluff Mountain Tunnel is one of 26 tunnels along the parkway, and the only one located in Virginia.*

SOUTHEAST

STORY AND PHOTOS BY
**PAT & CHUCK BLACKLEY**

# BLUE RIDGE PARKWAY

THE GORGEOUS 469-MILE ROLLER COASTER IS MORE THAN
A SCENIC DRIVE; IT'S THE ADVENTURE OF A LIFETIME!

**WE HAVE TRAVELED THE BLUE RIDGE PARKWAY** hundreds of times, photographing the uncommon loveliness and historical charm that make it such a popular scenic destination.

Stretching 469 miles, the parkway connects two national parks in the southern Appalachian Mountains. From its northern origin at Virginia's Shenandoah National Park, the parkway follows the crests of the Blue Ridge Mountains south through Virginia and North Carolina for the first 355 miles. It then skirts the southern end of the Black Mountains and winds through the Craggies and the Balsam Mountains before reaching Great Smoky Mountains National Park.

With a maximum speed limit of 45 mph and no commercial vehicles allowed, the parkway offers a peaceful and relaxing drive, with plenty of opportunities to get out of the car and enjoy the scenic views of mountain ranges, forests and farmlands from its many overlooks and trails. There are no commercial signs or billboards to distract drivers from the natural wonder around them. In fact, the planners who designed and built the parkway in the 1930s intended the journey to be more important than the destination.

The road roller-coasters between deep valleys and high peaks, dropping to an elevation of 649 feet at the James River in Virginia and climbing to more than 6,000 feet at Richland Balsam in North Carolina. This wide range in elevation spans many different climate zones that support an incredible variety of plant and animal life.

There are more than 1,400 plant species along the parkway from early spring through late fall. In spring and summer, we love the dazzling floral displays of azaleas, mountain laurel and rhododendrons. In autumn, a wide variety of deciduous trees makes for an unparalleled extravaganza of fall color.

Chance encounters with wildlife are always highlights of our trips, and we've been fortunate to enjoy numerous sightings of white-tailed deer and black bears, as well as foxes, raccoons and other small critters.

SOUTHEAST

# POINTS of INTEREST

**LENGTH**
469 miles

**NOT TO BE MISSED**
Mabry Mill is an icon on the parkway. Built more than a century ago, the mill embodies the history and spirit of Appalachia. To this day, neighbors gather there to hear folk and mountain music and to see traditional crafts in action.

**FUN FACT**
Eighty years ago workers cleaned and graded land that would become the first 12½-mile segment of the parkway. Planners envisioned a road that made the journey more important than the destination.

**WORDS TO THE WISE**
Because of snow and ice, some sections of the parkway may be closed in winter.

**SIDE TRIP**
Take a driving break and visit lovely, tree-lined Price Lake in North Carolina to rent a canoe. It's the only lake on the parkway that allows boating.

▼
*A Blue Ridge sunrise dazzles the eyes and nourishes the soul.*

Each year we also look forward to watching the seasonal migration of hawks and other raptors.

When we tire of driving, we hop out of the car and hike one of the parkway's plentiful trails to waterfalls, wildflower meadows or high, rocky summits. One of our favorites is the Tanawha Trail in North Carolina. High atop the trail's Rough Ridge section, a boardwalk crosses the mountain's fragile ecosystem and provides expansive views of the mountains stretched out as far as you can see. In June, this area is spectacular with blooming mountain laurel and rhododendrons, while in October it's ablaze with blueberry heaths that turn a fiery red.

Scotch-Irish, German and English settlers homesteaded this region of the Appalachians. Visitor center exhibits and restored historic structures along the parkway provide opportunities to see how those hearty mountain folk lived and played. You can almost always catch demonstrations of weaving, wood carving and other crafts. And talented musicians with dulcimers, fiddles, banjos and guitars fill the air with lively mountain music during numerous festivals.

On each journey down the parkway, we never fail to experience or glimpse something new. We'll hike a different trail, discover a new waterfall or wildflower meadow, or spot wildlife somewhere we've never seen it before.

And no matter how many sunrises and sunsets we witness from the lofty overlooks, each one is different. It's as if God chooses new shades of reds, pinks, purples and oranges from his infinite color palette to create his daily masterpieces.

For us, the parkway is not just a scenic drive. It's an adventure, a journey back, an exploration of nature. It's an opportunity to escape to the mountains, immerse ourselves in their tranquil beauty, and reflect on nature's magnificent creation.

SOUTHEAST

*The well-photographed Mabry Mill invites visitors to the past.*

SOUTHEAST

▼
*The Blue Ridge Parkway curves through the peaceful meadows of Doughton Park.*

SOUTHEAST

> **"The health of the eye seems to demand a horizon. We are never tired, so long as we can see far enough."**
>
> —RALPH WALDO EMERSON

SCENIC DRIVES 143

# Northeast

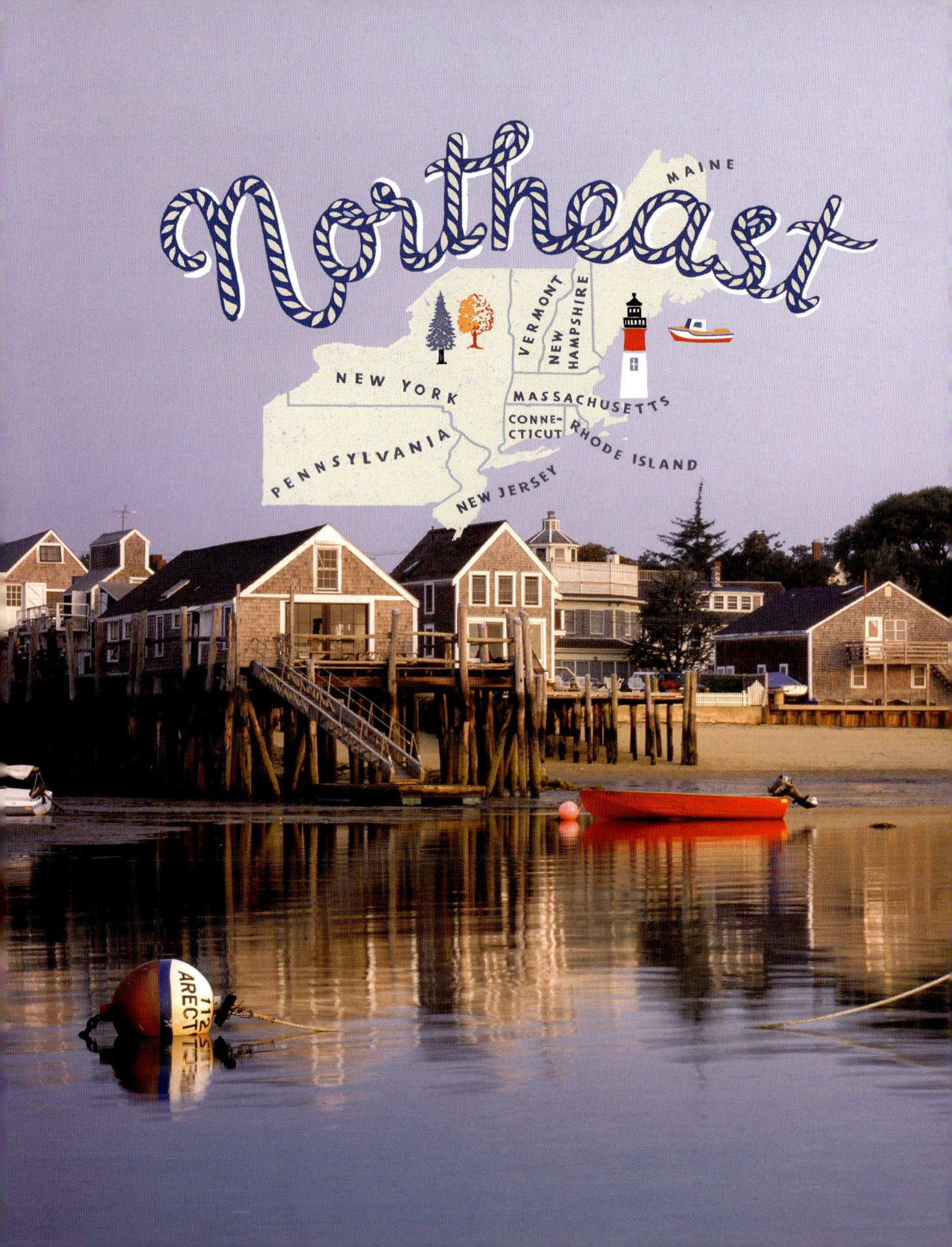

MAINE
VERMONT
NEW HAMPSHIRE
NEW YORK
MASSACHUSETTS
CONNECTICUT
RHODE ISLAND
PENNSYLVANIA
NEW JERSEY

MARY LIZ AUSTIN

▼ *Mount Katahdin stands in the distance as the sun rises above the East Branch Penobscot River near Medway.*

NORTHEAST

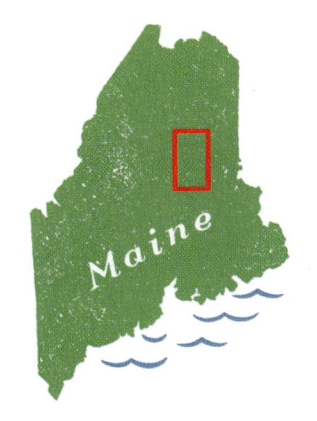

STORY BY **PAULETTE M. ROY**
PHOTOS BY **PAUL REZENDES**

# KATAHDIN WOODS

THE SHOWY FALL FOLIAGE OF NORTH-CENTRAL MAINE IS A MUST-SEE FOR LEAF-PEEPING ENTHUSIASTS.

**VIEW MAINE'S HIGHEST MOUNTAIN,** raft down a mighty river or explore the state's prettiest inland park as you travel the 89-mile Katahdin Woods & Waters Scenic Byway. You can access the route near its middle from either of the towns of Sherman or Millinocket, so you'll need to backtrack a bit in order to travel the entire route, but it's worth it.

We entered near Sherman and made our way north, as that entails the least amount of backtracking. Every bend in the road opened to another camera-worthy wilderness view of warm reds, yellows and oranges of autumn. The mighty Mount Katahdin, which is Maine's tallest peak at 5,268 feet and the northern terminus of the Appalachian Trail, popped in and out of view. There aren't many amenities along this northern stretch of the byway, but deep woods, lovely lakes and streams, curvy roads, and one spectacular overlook at Ash Hill in Patten shouldn't be missed.

Near the northern end of the scenic byway, we took a slight detour into the Katahdin Woods and Waters National Monument on the eastern side of Baxter State Park. Be aware that there is no monument, though the locals are fond of asking tourists if they found it! These northern roads are rough, and flat tires are not uncommon, as we discovered after heading back south.

Once we backtracked to Sherman and headed west and south into new territory, the East Branch of the Penobscot River paralleled the road near Hay Brook, a small village north of Medway. We made a quick stop at Grindstone Falls, a popular spot to picnic, walk along the river or cast a fishing line. There's even a riverfront campground that's ideal for watching the sun set or rise.

After enjoying a nice blue and pink sunrise on the river, we made our way to Millinocket, the "big" city along the route. We stopped briefly to grab a bite to eat and get supplies. Moose watching

NORTHEAST

## POINTS of INTEREST

**LENGTH**
89 miles

**REST STOPS**
From campsites to cottages, Shin Pond Village is a peaceful overnight retreat on the northern end of the scenic byway. shinpond.com

Just miles from the south entrance of Baxter State Park, in the New England Outdoor Center, take advantage of River Driver's Restaurant for casual lakeside dining with views of Mount Katahdin.

**SIDE TRIPS**
Experience the thrill of mild or wild whitewater rafting on the Penobscot River. Penobscot Adventures has tours for all activity levels. penobscotadventures.com

Let Katahdin Air give you a bird's-eye view of the beautiful fall foliage and terrain on one of its scenic plane rides. katahdinair.com

Maine's logging industry comes alive at the Patten Lumbermen's Museum through displays, photos and thrilling tales. lumbermensmuseum.org

▼
*A beautiful bend of the Katahdin Woods & Waters Scenic Byway.*

is by far one of the area's major outdoor activities. Wander the back roads wherever there are wetlands, and your chances of spotting one are good. Just keep your distance.

Traveling northwest out of Millinocket, we followed signs for Baxter State Park as the byway leaves Routes 11 and 157 behind and continues westward on Millinocket Road between Millinocket and Ambajejus lakes. Both of these large lakes are popular spots for recreation, including fishing, boating and swimming.

Though we were determined to complete the entire length of the scenic byway, we took a few side roads along the way, including the well-known Golden Road. This rough dirt road, with washboard bumps in places, parallels the byway; a number of crossover roads provide access. It is worth the adventure, but watch for logging trucks.

NORTHEAST

▼
*More interested in lunch than the view, these grazing cows add to the ambiance of the Ash Hill scenic overlook.*

NORTHEAST

▼
*Take a selfie at the iconic Pockwockamus Rock near the southern entrance to Baxter State Park.*

NORTHEAST

*Brilliant color decorates the banks of the East Branch Penobscot River.*

As we headed west, we came to Compass Pond, a favorite moose habitat that boasts Mount Katahdin as a backdrop. An even more spectacular view of the mountain awaited at Abol Bridge over the West Branch of the Penobscot River. Just a few miles down the road is Nesowadnehunk Falls, an often-roaring waterfall on the West Branch of the Penobscot.

Back on the byway and nearing its end, we entered deep woods with brilliant fall foliage arching over the road. Every now and then we would glimpse Mount Katahdin in the distance, looming above all else, although there are other mountains in the park worthy of attention.

When Pockwockamus Rock, the iconic boulder with the words "Keep Maine Beautiful" painted on it, appeared on the right side of the road, we knew we were getting close. There's a small area for safe parking—it seems no tourist is able to pass by without taking at least one selfie with the rock.

A few miles beyond, we reached the end of the byway at the Togue Pond Gate entrance to Baxter State Park. The road continues past the gate (there is an entrance fee to the park), where more adventures and photo opportunities await. If you have time, spend a day visiting the park and hike up one of the smaller mountains. Photographers will want to stroll to Sandy Stream and Stump ponds to capture stunning foliage and wildlife. Plus, every pondside park campground rents canoes and kayaks for you to take a relaxing paddle along a colorful shoreline. It's a splendid way to end a trip. However you end your journey, it will be a trip worth remembering.

SCENIC DRIVES  151

▼ *Reds, golds and oranges reach as far as the eye can see near Dallas Plantation, Maine.*

NORTHEAST

STORY BY **PAULETTE M. ROY**
PHOTOS BY **PAUL REZENDES**

# RANGELEY LAKES SCENIC BYWAY

FOR FALL COLOR WITHOUT THE CROWDS, DISCOVER THE MAJESTIC PEAKS AND DENSE FORESTS OF MAINE.

**THE RANGELEY LAKES REGION** of Maine offers leaf peepers the perfect alternative to view spectacular foliage and avoid the crowds in the White Mountains across the border in New Hampshire.

Six major lakes comprise the Rangeley Lakes region, plus hundreds of smaller bodies of water and thousands of acres of forests. In the eastern part of the region, the Bigelow Range and Sugarloaf Mountain form a grand backdrop to the lakes.

Our scenic drive begins at Stratton, on the southern end of Flagstaff Lake. Traveling south and west along state Route 16, we pass wetlands.

The first highlight comes with a detour up Quill Hill via Oddy Road for a 360-degree view of the lakes and mountains. To drive up and see the view will cost a small fee of $10 per car.

Though the vista is popular and it's often windy at the top, my husband, Paul, and I once managed to be there alone on a still morning, with the valleys shrouded in fog and the sun bursting through the clouds.

After heading back down the road, we continue on to Rangeley—a rustic resort town on the lake of the same name—to get gas, supplies and lunch. Then we head westward on routes 16 and 4, along the Rangeley Lakes National Scenic Byway to the village of Oquossoc, where we pay a quick visit to the historic 1916 Union Log

SCENIC DRIVES 153

NORTHEAST

# POINTS of INTEREST

**LENGTH**
About 35 miles

**SIDE TRIPS**
Once a bustling gold mining site, Coos Canyon gives visitors a chance to try their luck panning for glittery nuggets. *cooscanyonrockandgift.com*

Every August for more than 60 years, Harbor Park in Rockland, a historic harbor town along Maine's midcoast, attracts thousands of people to its Lobster Festival for five days of feasting and fun. Here visitors will find 20,000 pounds of fresh lobster, dozens of artisans and vendors, cooking contests, road races, a parade, carnival rides and U.S. Navy ship tours, just to name a few of the exciting events. *mainelobsterfestival.com*

**NEARBY ATTRACTIONS**
Washburn-Norlands Living History Center, Livermore; Thorncrag Nature Sanctuary, Lewiston

▼
*The Lovejoy Bridge in South Andover was built in 1868.*

Church before turning south onto state Route 17.

There are a number of overlooks along the byway worth checking out, but a must-stop is the Height of Land atop Spruce Mountain, near where the Appalachian Trail crosses the road. At Height of Land, there are views of the mountains in western Maine and of Mooselookmeguntic Lake, a tongue-twisting name derived from a native Abenaki word meaning "portage to moose-feeding place."

From here we continue south along Route 17 to Beaver Pond in Franklin, enjoying the stillness of lily pads at the water's edge.

We end our drive at the 500-yard gorge and waterfall at Coos Canyon, on the Swift River in Byron. It's a top spot for picnics and swimming in summer, but on this cool fall day, the brilliant foliage keeps us warm.

NORTHEAST

*Mooselookmeguntic Lake looks both refreshing and calm on a fall day.*

▼ *A red barn in Charlemont almost upstages the fall foliage behind it.*

NORTHEAST

STORY BY **PAULETTE M. ROY**
PHOTOS BY **PAUL REZENDES**

# BERKSHIRE BYWAYS

**SPECTACULAR HILLSIDES ABLAZE IN AUTUMN DAZZLE TRAVELERS ON THE ROADS IN WESTERN MASSACHUSETTS.**

**AS LIFELONG NEW ENGLANDERS,** we've had ample opportunity to photograph foliage throughout the years. Although we travel far and wide, we often find some of the best fall foliage within a couple of hours' drive from home. A terrific area is the Berkshire Mountains of western Massachusetts.

From our home in north-central Massachusetts, we head west along Route 2, the famous Mohawk Trail, which is another prime scenic byway for fall foliage. We continue west, cross the Connecticut River at French King Bridge, and begin our slow, gradual ascent of the rounded-top mountains of the Berkshire Plateau. No craggy, sharp-peaked mountaintops here, but on a clear day, three-state vistas treat us to spectacular hillsides of red, gold, orange, yellow and russet leaves.

After a thrilling descent through the hairpin curve that lies just beyond the western summit of the Hoosac Range, we go through North Adams and head south on Notch Road toward Mount Greylock State Reservation, which was the state's first wilderness park. We pass by old-growth forests on our way to the summit of the 3,491 foot Mount Greylock, the highest peak in Massachusetts. We soak up the 360-degree view of other distant mountains and numerous river valleys below, all ablaze in autumn colors. Since we're on a photo mission, we travel on, but there are many hiking trails on the mountain, including a portion of the Appalachian National Scenic Trail.

Once off the mountain, we take Route 7 south to Pittsfield, where a side trip west via Route 20 brings us to Hancock Shaker Village, a historic village with museum exhibits, a farm and family activities.

After this detour, we continue on Route 7 to the picturesque towns of Lenox, Lee and Stockbridge. Truly the cultural center of western Massachusetts, the trio is host to many theater, dance and music venues, including world-renowned Tanglewood, the summer home of the Boston Symphony Orchestra. In season, you can picnic on the expansive

SCENIC DRIVES 157

NORTHEAST

# POINTS of INTEREST

**SIDE TRIPS**

See the world's largest collection of original art by Norman Rockwell at the Norman Rockwell Museum in Stockbridge. nrm.org

In a place like the Berkshires, many country roads lead to gorgeous scenery and New England charm. Take time to explore the Mohawk Trail, which runs from east to west through the northern Berkshires. *mohawktrail.com*

In Mohawk Trail State Forest you'll find a wild terrain of gorges, tumbling brooks, sudden ridges and rocky outcrops, all in a densely mixed forest. Hikers can sample gentle to moderately ambitious trails. Anglers can try their luck for trout. And wildlife watchers will find the woods are alive with wonders.

**NEARBY ATTRACTIONS**

Historic Deerfield, featuring well-preserved 18th- and 19th-century homes; Natural Bridge State Park, a 550-million-year-old marble formation, North Adams; The Clark Art Institute, Williamstown

*The First Congregational Church in Dalton is nestled in ivy.*

lawn there and listen to some of the world's greatest musicians perform.

The trio of towns has a bit of literary history, too. Author Edith Wharton's summer home, The Mount, is located in Lenox and is open to the public. Nathaniel Hawthorne wrote *The House of the Seven Gables* while living in a little red cottage in Stockbridge.

A few miles outside of Stockbridge, we come to one of our favorite overlooks: Monument Mountain. This view does require a hike, and although it's less than a mile if you take the shortest and steepest ascent, we usually plan to spend at least two hours to truly enjoy the adventure.

Once back in the van, we continue south along Route 7 through Great Barrington, following the valley's farmlands through Sheffield, where we make a quick visit to Lime Kiln Farm Wildlife Sanctuary. There's a magnificent view of Mount Everett from the walking trails that amble through the sanctuary's old fields and pastures. The farm is home to more than 500 plant species. The hayfields, limestone ridge and conifer forest attract more than 50 species of butterflies and several birds, including pileated woodpeckers and alder flycatchers.

Our final road trip destination is Bartholomew's Cobble, a rare gem of twin rocky knolls created by geologic upheaval. The cobbles are made of quartzite and marble. The bedrock is 100 feet high and is especially known for a large number of fern species. It has such amazing biological diversity that it has been designated a National Natural Landmark. Worthy of a day visit in itself, the property has 5 miles of hiking trails to explore as well as marshes, beaver ponds, small caves, the Housatonic River and Hurlburt's Hill.

At 1,000 feet, Hurlburt's Hill is the highest point in the park and offers a panoramic view of the Massachusetts-Connecticut border and Housatonic River Valley.

Our good times in the Berkshires have only just begun!

NORTHEAST

*The Bissell Covered Bridge spans Mill Brook in Charlemont.*

▼ *The Cape Cod Highland Lighthouse in Truro, Massachusetts, creates the perfect New England scene.*

NORTHEAST

STORY AND PHOTOS BY
**PAUL REZENDES**

# CAPE COD'S ROUTE 6

SAND DUNES, HIDDEN FORESTS AND OCEAN VIEWS ABOUND ON THIS DRIVE THROUGH THE CAPE.

**THERE'S A 25-MILE STRETCH** of U.S. Route 6 from the elbow to the tip of Cape Cod that I love. It's difficult to get far on this road, which runs through the Massachusetts towns of Eastham, Wellfleet, Truro and Provincetown, because there's so much beauty to explore—and, for me, to photograph.

On either side of Route 6, you'll find sandy beaches, marshes, dunes, maritime forests and a simply exquisite national seashore, not to mention quaint villages, historic lighthouses and picturesque harbors.

The peninsula narrows to a mere 1.14 miles across at one point and is not more than 5 miles wide along the entire distance. One of my favorite things to do is park just off the highway in Provincetown—P'town, as the locals call it—and hike into the sand dunes. They are quite vast; as popular as the cape is in summer, I've spent hours there without meeting another person.

There's lots of soft white sand, covered in some places with beach grasses. Within the dunes stand beautiful forests of pitch pine, some so dense they're impassable, while other spots are open and inviting, with a lush carpet of pine needles. Another delightful discovery is that amid all the sand and trees there are small oases of wild blueberry and huckleberry bushes, plus wild cranberry bogs, providing visitors delicious fruit for a quick snack along the way.

I like to visit the dunes in fall, when the leaves of the fruit bushes and cranberry bogs turn a brilliant ruby red. They make a stark contrast to the dark trees and white sands, creating vivid scenes for the photographer and painter willing to hike to them.

SCENIC DRIVES

NORTHEAST

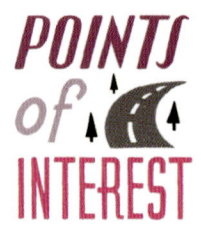

# POINTS of INTEREST

**LENGTH**
25 miles

**NOT TO BE MISSED**
Whale-watching excursions depart from Barnstable Harbor and Provincetown.

**FUN FACT**
The Cape Cod Baseball League provides the opportunity to enjoy some of the best collegiate talent in the country. Games are free and played daily, from June to mid-August, in nearly every town on the Cape. Many Major League players got their start here.

**WORDS TO THE WISE**
On summer weekends, expect bumper-to-bumper traffic at Sagamore Bridge. To avoid crowds, visit before July 4 or after Labor Day.

**NEARBY ATTRACTIONS**
Cape Cod Museum of Natural History, Brewster; Plimoth Plantation, Plymouth; Martha's Vineyard and Nantucket Island

*An old fire road at Cape Cod National Seashore.*

Most people go to the cape in summer to enjoy the spectacular beaches, many miles of which are protected by the National Park Service. Along with pristine sands, some beaches on the ocean side have sand cliffs that rise close to five stories high. I tend to like quieter, more secluded spots, so I escape from the hubbub of the season at several small, crystal-clear ponds in the pine forests near Truro and Wellfleet.

The phenomenal sunrises over the Atlantic Ocean make it worth the effort to rise early. In the evenings, I head to Cape Cod Bay for the sunsets. Here it's quite a different scene, with miles of salt marshes and tidal flats that seem to go on forever.

I try to get out to the cape in different seasons, but no matter how many times I travel Route 6 from Eastham to Provincetown, I never run out of places to visit and pictures to take.

162   SCENIC DRIVES

NORTHEAST

*Cahoon Hollow Beach in Cape Cod National Seashore basks in the sun's glory.*

▼ *Albany Bridge was built in 1858 to replace a bridge that was destroyed in a storm.*

NORTHEAST

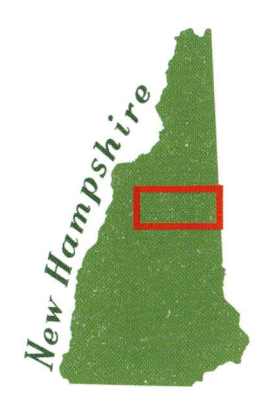

STORY AND PHOTOS BY
**PAT & CHUCK BLACKLEY**

# KANCAMAGUS SCENIC BYWAY

**LEAVE THE HUSTLE AND BUSTLE BEHIND AND HEAD OUT TO ONE OF NEW ENGLAND'S MOST STRIKING FALL DRIVES.**

**AUTUMN AND NEW ENGLAND** seem to go together like Thanksgiving and turkey, so we often head north when we're making plans for autumn. And the Kancamagus Scenic Byway in the White Mountains of New Hampshire is one of our favorite destinations.

The Kanc, as it's known locally, winds through the White Mountain National Forest alongside the pristine Swift River. It's a beautiful drive any time of year, but the Kanc is absolutely fabulous in the fall.

The mixed deciduous trees—maple, white birch, beech, black cherry and poplar—with their vivid shades of red, yellow and orange, contrast dramatically with the dark greens of spruce and hemlock. You also stand a good chance of spotting black bears, deer and the ever-popular moose. The best fall color usually begins during the second week of September at the higher elevations and peaks during the first two weeks of October.

The area's rich history also played a large role in earning the Kanc its designation as an American Scenic Byway. The highway and surrounding mountains are named after some of the area's most famous Native Americans. In the 1600s, Chief Passaconaway united 17 regional tribes to form the Pennacook Confederacy. His grandson, Kancamagus, meaning "the fearless one," was the third and final ruler of this confederacy.

The byway itself began simply as disconnected mountain roads to the small towns of Passaconaway and

SCENIC DRIVES **165**

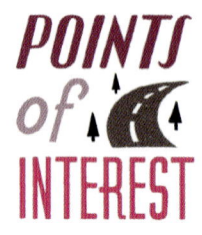

NORTHEAST

*Swift River at Rocky Gorge is a terrific spot to stop and take a photo.*

## POINTS of INTEREST

**LENGTH**
34.5 miles

**FUN FACTS**
Named for a Pennacook chief, "The Kanc," as locals call it, rises to an elevation of 2,900 feet, making it one of the highest roadways in the Northeast.

**WORDS TO THE WISE**
When making the drive on "The Kanc," you'll find no gas stations, no restaurants and no hotels or other businesses. Also, be on the lookout for moose while driving—especially after dusk, when they often cross the road.

**NEARBY ATTRACTIONS**
The Frost Place, featuring a nature trail and memorabilia of the celebrated poet Robert Frost, near Franconia

Lincoln. The road to Passaconaway was completed in 1837, but the two roads weren't connected between Conway and Lincoln until 1937. The highway, a 34.5-mile section of Route 112 that climbs to nearly 3,000 feet as it crosses the flank of Mount Kancamagus, was completed and opened to through traffic in 1959.

Along the way, it passes a number of interesting historic sites, including the Albany Covered Bridge and the Russell-Colbrath Homestead. This humble Cape Cod-style farmhouse was built in the early 1830s by Thomas Russell and his son Amzi. The U.S. Forest Service purchased it in 1961 to preserve the historic location and show what it might have been like to earn a living in these mountains 200 years ago. A post and beam barn built in 2003 serves as an interpretive center.

While there's nothing wrong with admiring the scenery from the comfort

NORTHEAST

▼
*The White Mountains and Lily Pond, a popular place to go moose-watching.*

NORTHEAST

▼
*New Hampshire's state Highway 112 winds through the unforgettable White Mountains.*

# NORTHEAST

*One of the highway's many awesome lookout points.*

of your car, the highway abounds with enticing opportunities to get out and explore. Several scenic overlooks offer stunning vistas, and there are plenty of picnic areas.

You can also discover a variety of hiking trails—ranging from short and easy to long and strenuous—that lead to beautiful waterfalls, ponds or mountain summits. One of our favorites, Sabbaday Falls Trail, is just a short hike that rewards you with a series of picturesque cascades flowing through a narrow rock flume. We love to seek out secluded spots by the river to sit and drink in the beauty of autumn foliage reflected in the water.

Or we head to Rocky Gorge Scenic Area, where the Swift River plunges through a chasm carved through the rock by runoff from a mile-high glacier in the last ice age. The area features a large parking lot and a short paved path that leads to a footbridge with an outstanding view up the gorge. Across the bridge the path leads to a mile-long loop around idyllic Falls Pond, which is also a popular fishing area.

While there are no restaurants, motels, gas stations or stores on this truly pristine byway, it does offer six national forest campgrounds. And noncampers will find plenty of lodging and restaurant options in both Conway and Lincoln—along with interesting gift shops and many locally crafted treasures such as wood carvings and copper cupolas.

Autumn in New Hampshire's White Mountains is an experience not to be missed, and the Kancamagus Highway transports us into the heart of that grandeur while leaving intrusions from the modern world behind.

NORTHEAST

STORY AND PHOTOS BY
**PAT & CHUCK BLACKLEY**

# OLD MINE ROAD

DRIVE THIS HISTORIC ROUTE THROUGH THE DELAWARE WATER GAP TO DISCOVER NEW JERSEY'S SCENIC SIDE.

**MAJESTIC VIEWS. HISTORIC SITES.** Hiking trails, swimming and fishing. Old Mine Road on the New Jersey side of the Delaware Water Gap National Recreation Area beckons you.

The 1,000-foot-deep Delaware Water Gap is the key passageway through the Appalachian Mountain range between Pennsylvania and New Jersey. Each year about 5 million visitors enjoy the Gap's 70,000-acre national recreation area, the largest in the eastern United States.

The 104-mile Old Mine Road connects incredible fall scenery and recreation that includes hiking a section of the famous Appalachian Trail and boating, picnicking or viewing waterfalls along the Delaware River.

Begin your journey at the Kittatinny Point Visitor Center at the southern end of River Road (which soon becomes Old Mine Road going north). Drive north to Millbrook Village, a re-created farm community from the mid-1800s. With a wagon shop, general store, hotel and church, the village has plenty for visitors to see.

Continue north to take in the view from Kittatinny Mountain via Route 624 and Skyline Drive, a spectacular mountain vista. On a crisp day, fall colors paint a sea of trees as far as the horizon. It's a welcome place to stop and stretch your legs on part of the Appalachian Trail.

Back on Old Mine Road, stop for a picnic and a swim in the river or explore more historic structures. To view additional fall color, detour from that drive and linger in Walpack Center, a small 1800s village that's listed on the National Register of Historic Places. Then it's time to link back up to Old Mine Road again for more adventure.

NORTHEAST

# POINTS of INTEREST

**LENGTH**
104 miles

**REST STOPS**
Jam to jazz and sleep late at charming Deer Head Inn on the Pennsylvania side of the Gap, northwest of the Kittatinny Point Visitor Center. *deerheadinn.com*

Stop at the rustic Walpack Inn, established in 1949, to indulge in a lovely meal served with its famous brown bread and set against the stunning views of Walpack Valley. *thewalpackinn.com*

**SIDE TRIPS**
Coppermine Trail, a moderate to difficult 2-mile, one-way trail through the forest along streams and cascades, is part of more than 100 miles of hiking trails in the Delaware Water Gap National Recreation Area. *nps.gov/dewa*

Browse through the handmade items created by artists in the gallery and shop at the Peters Valley School of Craft. Or sign up for a one-day workshop to try blacksmithing, basketry, woodworking, ceramics and more. *petersvalley.org*

*Top: Historic Millbrook Village's Methodist Episcopal Church takes visitors back in time. Bottom: Spend a peaceful day surrounded by fall's glory at Crater Lake on Mount Kittatinny.*

SCENIC DRIVES **171**

▼

*A visitor admires the view from an observation deck at Moss Lake.*

NORTHEAST

STORY AND PHOTOS BY
**PAT & CHUCK BLACKLEY**

# CENTRAL ADIRONDACK TRAIL

**FOLLOW SCENIC ROUTE 28 FOR SPARKLING LAKES AND CHARMING MOUNTAIN VILLAGES.**

**THE ADIRONDACK PARK** encompasses the largest area of publicly protected land in the Lower 48 states. Idyllic country roads abound, and you'd be hard-pressed to find an area that isn't scenic.

The state of New York created the park in 1892 out of concern that this magnificent area—with its abundant forests, majestic mountain peaks, and shimmering lakes and rivers—was in danger of being exploited. Two years later, the Adirondack Forest Preserve was established, which made the park a Forever Wild area. This designation means the land is protected under the constitution of New York to preserve it.

Almost half of the park's total 6 million acres is state property, preserved for the public's enjoyment of pursuits such as camping, hiking, biking, swimming, skiing, boating and fishing. The remainder of the land is privately owned and includes farms, businesses and more than 100 small towns and villages. This is ideal for travelers who relish a wilderness experience, but still appreciate the comforts found in nearby towns.

On one recent fall visit we drove along a 50-mile stretch of state Route 28/28N. This is part of the 150-mile-long Central Adirondack Trail, which is an Adirondack Scenic Byway.

We began at the intersection of Routes 28N and 30 in Long Lake and traveled southwest along a chain of lakes that ends at Old Forge. The trees were magnificent, with their vibrant colors of red, orange and yellow reflecting in the clear lake waters.

The community of Long Lake, one of the oldest in the region, is nestled on the shores of a 14-mile-long lake of the same name. If you wish to stop and soak up the scenery, boat and seaplane tours offer a different perspective.

SCENIC DRIVES

NORTHEAST

*Seaplanes offer aerial tours of Long Lake.*

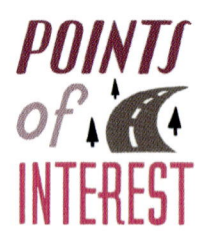

## POINTS of INTEREST

**LENGTH**
150 miles

**WORDS TO THE WISE**
Black flies and other insect pests can be numerous, especially in early summer.

**SIDE TRIP**
The Museum on Blue Mountain Lake tells the history of the Adirondacks region and its people. *theadkx.org*

**NEARBY ATTRACTION**
Lake George Beach State Park, with swimming and picnicking, east of Fort William Henry

We continued south along Routes 28N/30 to Blue Mountain Lake, one of the most beautiful of the approximately 3,000 Adirondack lakes. Set against the backdrop of 3,759-foot Blue Mountain, the scenery is gorgeous. The hamlet of Blue Mountain Lake is home to the Adirondack Lakes Center for the Arts, which hosts concerts, plays and classes. The Blue Mountain Lake Boat Livery offers lake tours and rents all types of vessels, from fishing boats to canoes and paddleboats.

We stayed at the Prospect Point Cottages, one of many lodging choices in the area. It's right on the lake, and the private beach has spectacular views of the water and mountains. Plus, our hosts served a brunch buffet that kept us going until supper!

After visiting Lake Durant, just to the east, we resumed our trip along Route 28 west, past Eagle Lake and Utowana Lake and onward to Raquette Lake. As the largest natural body of water within the park, Raquette Lake is renowned for nearly 100 miles of primarily state-owned shoreline.

In the late 1800s, this area attracted Gilded Age millionaires like Vanderbilt, Carnegie and Morgan who built large summer homes they referred to as camps. One of the grandest, Great Camp Sagamore, is down the road from the hamlet of Raquette Lake.

Route 28 runs along a long chain of eight lakes, called the Fulton Chain, which are known only by number, First through Eighth. We made frequent stops at pullouts and public beaches to admire and photograph the picturesque lakes. We also explored small villages and towns such as Eagle Bay and Inlet before ending our drive in Old Forge.

Like the other lake communities, Old Forge offers plenty of choices for outdoor enthusiasts, plus boat tours and even a scenic chairlift ride for viewing fall color at the McCauley Mountain Ski Resort.

Another popular activity is the fall foliage tour aboard the Adirondack Scenic Railroad.

A drive along Route 28 would be delightful any time of the year, but we found it especially enjoyable in fall.

174 SCENIC DRIVES

NORTHEAST

▼
*Blue Mountain Lake is a splendid place to watch the sunset.*

NORTHEAST

STORY AND PHOTO BY
**CINDY RUGGIERI**

# HIGH PEAKS BYWAY

**MAP OUT A COURSE FOR ADVENTURE WITH AN AUTUMN BACKDROP IN THE ADIRONDACKS.**

**NO MATTER WHAT OUTDOOR ACTIVITY** you're into—mountain biking, canoeing, camping, fishing or snow skiing—"forever wild" Adirondack Park has it all.

Each season in the Adirondacks has its own recreational appeal, but for me, autumn hiking is awe-inspiring! The park's forest preserve offers more than 6 million acres of breathtaking scenery.

My favorite drive is in the High Peaks region. Jump off Interstate 87 to Route 73 and drive about 40 miles northwest to pretty Saranac Lake. Give yourself plenty of time for stops along the way.

Route 73 winds and curves through a hiker's paradise, with plenty of trailheads along the roadside. Of the 46 mountain peaks in the Adirondacks, all but four are located in this area. Serious hikers who set a goal to hike all of them can be recognized as members of the Adirondack 46ers club.

I always make my first stop at Chapel Pond for a peaceful walk along the shore. The slabs opposite the road are popular spots for rock climbers, with some 700 feet of smooth climbing surface. From here, follow the road north to Keene and make a quick pit stop at the Cedar Run Bakery & Market for baked goods and sandwiches.

On one of our visits my husband and I turned onto Owl's Head Lane, a few miles west of Keene, to take the half-mile hike to the Owl's Head peak. It may have been a short hike, but it was a lot of work going up, climbing over tree roots and rocks.

The payoff was worth the effort—the vistas were spectacular. With only a slight breeze to break up the peace and quiet, we stood in wonder at the mountains around us, bursting with bold autumn colors.

With that memory to treasure, we hiked back down to the road and continued on 73. The road winds along Upper and Lower Cascade Lakes. Pull into the parking area between the lakes for sightseeing, fishing, hiking and paddling on the water.

Whether you end your trip in beautiful Lake Placid or follow Route 86 on to Saranac Lake, this drive is always worth the trip.

NORTHEAST

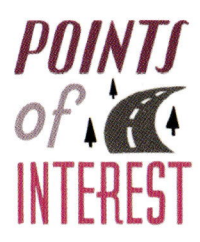

# POINTS of INTEREST

**LENGTH**
30 miles

**WORDS TO THE WISE**
Black flies and other insect pests can be numerous, especially in early summer.

**SIDE TRIPS**
Lake Placid hosted the 1980 Winter Olympics. This winter, take a bobsled ride at the Olympic Sports Complex. *lakeplacid.com*

After dipping into a broad valley, the drive heads into the town of Keene. A side detour from there diverts to the west to the High Peaks Wilderness, where travelers can park and then head out on foot to sample some of the scenery afforded by the 238 miles of hiking trails that lace the area.

**NEARBY ATTRACTION**
Six Nations Indian Museum, with displays of native crafts, Onchiota, 14 miles north of Saranac Lake

*Owl's Head peak is a nice spot for repose.*

SCENIC DRIVES 177

▼ *Women of the Nebraska Amish group travel the back roads amid fall elegance.*

NORTHEAST

STORY AND PHOTOS BY
**DOYLE YODER**

# PENNSYLVANIA ROUTE 655

THE BIG VALLEY LIVES UP TO ITS NAME ON THIS JOURNEY THROUGH AMISH COUNTRY.

**CENTRAL PENNSYLVANIA** is a land of rural valleys tucked away in the Appalachian Mountains. Probably the most amazing of them all is the Kishacoquillas Valley, or as the Amish call it, the Big Valley.

For an afternoon drive through this idyllic country, start on U.S. Route 22 and turn onto Pennsylvania Route 655 at Mill Creek. You'll wind through a cut in the mountains for a few miles and then you'll come to the opening of the valley.

At 30 miles long and 5 miles wide, the Big Valley is surrounded by mountains, including Stone, Front, Jacks and Back. It's also home to three Amish groups—the Byler, Peachey (or Renno) and Nebraska. Each group is known by the color of their buggy tops: yellow, black and white respectively.

As you proceed north on 655, you will pass some of the tidiest Amish farms to be found anywhere. With so many farms along the roads, you can imagine that this is what the area must have looked like in the 1800s.

Fall is a fantastic time to visit. The Amish are out in the fields with their draft horses, gathering the corn into shocks. Mountains stand along either side of the valley ablaze in fall color, and the road runs parallel to all this country beauty.

As you drive along 655, you are sure to find a farm stand with fresh produce or an artisan's workshop. The first town on this route is Allensville, with small shops catering to the locals as well as tourists. In Allensville, stop by the Kishacoquillas Valley Historical Society for an overview of Big Valley history. The two-story building is a relic—it was built in 1838. The museum preserves 150 years of Amish history. Tour an 1830 Pennsylvania bank barn

NORTHEAST

# POINTS of INTEREST

### NOT TO BE MISSED
The toil of summer and fall deserve a festive nod. In the Big Valley, the fun takes place during Harvestfest on the first Friday and Saturday in October. Festivities include carriage rides, a quilt raffle and more. visitbigvalley.com

### FUN FACT
In the 1700s, the Big Valley was home to several Native American tribes. The legacy of Chief Kishacoquillas of the Shawnee lives on throughout the area. In fact, the valley between Jacks Mountain and Stone Mountain was named for him.

### WORDS TO THE WISE
Bring a cooler to store foods purchased at roadside stands, but note that most of them are closed on Sunday for observance of the Sabbath.

### SIDE TRIP
Poe Valley State Park offers 3 miles of beautiful fall trails that connect to Bald Eagle State Forest. dcnr.state.pa.us/stateparks

*An Amish man and his son sell produce at the market in Belleville.*

filled with wagons, sleds and other farm tools used by the Amish.

The next town is Belleville, which is the biggest in the valley. If you make your trip on Wednesday be sure to stop at the Belleville Livestock Auction, which is on the northeast side of town. This farmers market is a busy place and the hub of this rural community.

As you pull into the parking lot you'll see yellow-, white- and black-topped buggies mixed in with cars. From March through November local vendors sell their wares, including produce, eggs, flowers and whoopie pies (also known as moon pies). My advice to you: Take a quick tour of the market before buying. Who knows what treasures you'll find at the next booth?

If you'd like to see the valley from a mountain's point of view, take a drive on East Back Mountain Road, which travels through Barrville; or Front Mountain Road, which can be accessed from Route 655 north of Airydale, near the southern tip of the valley. One of my favorite routes is Jacks Mountain/Wills Road, which leads to a summit overlooking the valley. There you'll see a patchwork of quaint farms in the shadow of the surrounding mountains.

Escape to Pennsylvania's Big Valley, where simple is better, and neighborly folks greet you like an old friend.

180 SCENIC DRIVES

NORTHEAST

*Tidy farms and autumn's flare make this drive enchanting.*

▼ *Vermont's country roads reveal a bounty of picture-perfect moments like this.*

NORTHEAST

STORY AND PHOTOS BY
**PAT & CHUCK BLACKLEY**

# SCENIC ROUTE 100 BYWAY

FALL IN LOVE WITH THE COLOR, CHARACTER AND ALLURE OF THE GREEN MOUNTAIN STATE.

**WE WILL ADMIT TO HAVING A LOVE AFFAIR** with Vermont. Over the years, we've explored nearly every highway and rural road in the state. But we often find ourselves returning to one particular road, because it includes most everything we adore about this New England gem.

Much of this journey follows the Scenic Route 100 Byway, which runs through the center of Vermont along the full length of the Green Mountain range. All of the scenic sites you picture—quaint villages, country stores, covered bridges and neat farms—can be found on this road, with a few side trips.

You could do our 160-mile drive in a few hours. But with so much to see, try devoting at least two days.

Every season is beautiful here, but you'll see excellent scenery in autumn. With its abundant sugar maple trees, Vermont has the most vibrant fall foliage imaginable, plus many homes and storefronts are decorated with cheerful harvest displays.

Begin the journey in Manchester. Besides its charming town center that boasts lovely 19th century architecture, Manchester also has a number of lodging and dining options, making it an enjoyable place to explore and stay overnight.

The next morning, hop on Route 11, head east over the mountains for 16 miles and admire the views of the Green Mountain National Forest. Stay on Route 11 for a side trip when you reach the intersection with Route 100 at Londonderry.

After 14 miles, stop in the cute town of Chester to check out the interesting shops and buildings surrounding its village green. Then take Route 35 south for 7 miles to reach the tiny hamlet of

NORTHEAST

# POINTS of INTEREST

**LENGTH**
160 miles

**NOT TO BE MISSED**
Honora Winery, Jacksonville; Jamaica State Park; Warren Covered Bridge

**WORDS TO THE WISE**
Book reservations early for fall foliage tours and accommodations. Mountain roads may be closed in winter. Some attractions are seasonal.

**SIDE TRIPS**
Billings Farm & Museum, a working dairy in Woodstock, offers tours and demonstrations that depict 19th century rural life. *billingsfarm.org*

Back roads in the Mad River Valley offer rustic covered bridges, stonewalls, pretty farms and mountain vistas. The tiny town of Warren has a country store with a great deli, and Waitsfield has many cozy inns. *madrivervalley.com*

During autumn, visit Jenne Farm near Reading, considered the most photogenic spot in Vermont. Take Route 106 south out of Woodstock to Jenne Road.

▼
*Horses soak up the sun in a picturesque pasture near Waitsfield.*

Grafton. In an effort to preserve the rural Vermont way of life, a nonprofit foundation bought and restored many of the buildings in this 19th century town, including the historic Grafton Inn. The handsome buildings along Main Street house shops, galleries and museums.

Return to Londonderry and head north on Route 100. Soon you'll arrive in Weston, a town with a tree-lined green, museums, galleries and plenty of shops, including the iconic Vermont Country Store.

Continuing north through the village of Ludlow, splendid views abound along the Okemo Valley. After passing a series of mountain lakes, bear right onto Route 100A to visit the President Calvin Coolidge State Historic Site, his boyhood home and birthplace, in Plymouth Notch.

Follow Route 100A for 6 miles, and then turn right onto Route 4 and travel 8 miles farther to Woodstock, one of the prettiest villages in New England. Elegant homes, little white churches and a bustling shopping area surround the village green.

While you're in Woodstock stop by Vermont's only national park, the Marsh-Billings-Rockefeller National

NORTHEAST

*Reflections of autumn shimmer on a mill pond in the village of Weston.*

NORTHEAST

▼ *The sun sets on a cool autumn day at Jenne Farm, one of the most photographed farms in Vermont.*

NORTHEAST

*An eye-catching Baptist church in Ludlow graces the town green.*

Historical Park. Visit the mansion there that was once home to George Perkins Marsh, father of the American conservation movement, and later Frederick Billings, who advocated for the establishment of Yosemite National Park. An 1895 carriage barn houses the visitor center, and the formal gardens and more than 20 miles of wooded trails are a pleasure to walk through.

Driving around Woodstock will reward you with pristine country scenery. This is where we saw our first Vermont moose!

Return to Route 100 via Route 4 and climb into the mountains to reach Killington, the state's largest ski area. Take a gondola ride for panoramic views. Farther down the road, Gifford Woods State Park holds one of Vermont's few remaining stands of old-growth hardwood trees.

Descending the mountains, the route travels through the bucolic White River Valley, dotted with red barns, dairy farms and peaceful small towns like Rochester.

The valley ends north of Granville, and here the road narrows as it winds 6 miles through the Granville Gulf Reservation, a densely forested wilderness. Make sure you stop and view Moss Glen Falls as it tumbles down 80 feet.

A drive through rural Vermont is like traveling back to yesteryear, and in fall it's magical. The weather is cool and crisp with a hint of woodsmoke in the air, and foliage glows. Cornstalks and pumpkins adorn porches, and shops are filled with friendly folks sipping apple cider. Life doesn't get much better than this.

SCENIC DRIVES 187

▼ *Grist Mill Covered Bridge spans Brewster River in the village of Jeffersonville.*

NORTHEAST

STORY BY **PAULETTE M. ROY**
PHOTOS BY **PAUL REZENDES**

# VERMONT ROUTE 108

FIND MOUNTAIN VIEWS AND STUNNING HUES ALONG THIS ROAD WITH A STORIED PAST.

**WE TEND TO ROAM,** mostly away from crowds if we can manage it, and that's how we came upon a 17.3-mile portion of Route 108 in Vermont that travels from Stowe to Jeffersonville through a narrow mountain pass known as Smugglers' Notch.

Considered by many to be Vermont's most dramatic road, Route 108 travels through Mount Mansfield State Forest and over Mount Mansfield. At 4,393 feet, the peak is the highest in Vermont. This drive winds around boulders that jut into the country road beneath 1,000-foot cliffs, narrowing to one lane in sections. It is definitely not for the faint of heart, and beeping your horn is essential around the curves. It is so steep (an intense 18% grade) that the road is not plowable, and therefore it's closed in late fall and winter.

The name Smugglers' Notch comes from the road's infamous history. Smugglers used it to bring embargoed goods into Canada during the War of 1812. Later, fugitive slaves crossed this deep, narrow mountain pass to find freedom in the North. The path graduated to a carriage road in 1894, and the present paved route dates from around 1910. During Prohibition, bootleggers used it to move contraband liquor into the United States.

Most travelers begin their journey on the scenic byway at Stowe. You'll find shops, restaurants, lodging, museums, historic sites and art centers along the first several miles. There is much to see and do along the way, so plan to spend several hours.

Consider a jaunt down the Stowe Recreation Path, which parallels the road and has several access points where you can stretch your legs by strolling through cornfields, green meadows, and along the West Branch of Little River.

Perhaps the most popular side trip is the 4-mile Auto Toll Road at Stowe Mountain Resort. You can drive to the summit of Mount Mansfield for sweeping views of the Adirondacks. Many people opt to take a gondola ride up the mountain for a bird's-eye view.

SCENIC DRIVES **189**

NORTHEAST

# POINTS of INTEREST

**LENGTH**
17.3 miles

**NOT TO BE MISSED**
Vermont Ski and Snowboard Museum, Stowe

**FUN FACT**
Stowe's alpine cachet was helped by the arrival, more than half a century ago, of an Austrian family named Von Trapp—the real-life inspiration behind the popular musical *The Sound of Music*. Just a few miles north and west of the village, off Route 108, the Trapp Family Lodge commands a view of meadows and mountains that might have been imported from the Tyrol, along with the familiar strains of music.

**SIDE TRIPS**
A quieter, more peaceful and contemplative exploration of fields, forests, ponds, rivers and farmlands awaits the adventurous traveler who is willing to take the not-so-beaten path through the surrounding communities of Cambridge, Fletcher, Bakersfield and Enosburg. These storied towns are home to many historic sites.

▼
*Wagons and old barns on the route are part of the fall scenery.*

Across from the entrance to Stowe Mountain Resort, you'll find the Barnes Civilian Conservation Corps building now repurposed as the Smugglers' Notch Visitor Center. Linger over the exhibits and the educational programs or ramble along a boardwalk through wetlands. There's also a trailhead for the Long Trail, one of the oldest long-distance hiking trails in the U.S.

Once back on Route 108, you enter the deep woods of Mount Mansfield State Forest and begin the climb up the mountain, arriving at the entrance to Smugglers' Notch State Park. Wild and rugged, it makes a great base camp for exploring the area, and there are several camping options.

From the entrance, the road continues its winding, steep ascent to its namesake, Smugglers' Notch. We stopped at Big Spring, which has a picnic area and leads to rocks with names like Elephant's Head.

From this point begins the sharp descent along breathtaking curves edged with boulders and cliffs through colorful forests. About 3 miles from Elephant's Head, Smugglers' Notch Resort is a popular family destination with year-round activities.

Route 108 eventually levels out in the village of Jeffersonville along the Lamoille River, for a totally different experience from Stowe. Before entering the village, we stopped to photograph the Grist Mill Covered Bridge spanning the Brewster River on Canyon Road. Built in the 19th century, it was added to the National Register of Historic Places in 1974.

The drive continues north to the Canadian border, but from here we usually take advantage of several country roads off Route 108 to view beautiful farm landscapes with Mount Mansfield as a backdrop. As thrilling as it is to drive along the highway (and it's worth going in both directions at least once), the contrast between the mountain's alpine grandeur and the pastoral scenes of the Lamoille Valley never ceases to take our breath away.

We never know which bend in the road will reward us with a spectacular view. We've had some great surprises!

NORTHEAST

*Camel's Hump, the bumpy peak in the background, is part of the Green Mountain range.*

NORTHEAST

"*Beauty, spiced with wonder, is the greatest lure to travel.*"

—CONFUCIUS

▼
*Farms awaken at the foot of Mount Mansfield in Vermont.*